Revised 2nd Edition

RETIRE RICH WITH YOUR SELF-DIRECTED IRA

What Your Broker & Banker Don't Want
You to Know About Managing Your
Own Retirement Investments

Nora Peterson AND
Alexander L. Kaplan, Esq.

Retire Rich With Your Self-Directed IRA: What Your Broker & Banker Don't Want You to Know About Managing Your Own Retirement Investments Revised 2nd Edition

Copyright © 2016 by Atlantic Publishing Group, Inc.

1405 SW 6th Ave. • Ocala, Florida 34471 • 800-814-1132 • 352-622-1875–Fax

Web site: www.atlantic-pub.com • E-mail: sales@atlantic-pub.com

SAN Number: 268-1250

Library of Congress Cataloging-in-Publication Data

Peterson, Nora, 1948-
Retire rich with your self-directed IRA : what your broker & banker don't want you to know about managing your own retirement investments / Nora Peterson and Alexander L. Kaplan, Esq. -- Revised 2nd edition.
pages cm
Includes bibliographical references and index.
ISBN 978-1-60138-943-5 (alk. paper) -- ISBN 1-60138-943-4 (alk. paper) 1. Individual retirement accounts--United States. 2. Retirement income--United States. 3. Investments--United States. I. Title.
HG1660.U5P48 2015
332.024'01450973--dc23
2014033744

DISCLAIMER: The material in this book is provided for informational purposes and as a general guide to starting your self-directed IRA. Basic definitions of laws are provided according to the status of the laws at the time of printing; be sure to check for a change or update in laws. This book should not substitute professional and legal counsel for the development of any business decisions or anything related to your self-directed IRA.

TRADEMARK: All trademarks, trade names, or logos mentioned or used are the property of their respective owners and are used only to directly describe the products being provided. Every effort has been made to properly capitalize, punctuate, identify and attribute trademarks and trade names to their respective owners, including the use of ® and ™ wherever possible and practical. Atlantic Publishing Group, Inc. is not a partner, affiliate, or licensee with the holders of said trademarks.

Printed in the United States
BOOK PRODUCTION DESIGN: T.L. Price • design@tlpricefreelance.com

Reduce. Reuse.
RECYCLE.

A decade ago, Atlantic Publishing signed the Green Press Initiative. These guidelines promote environmentally friendly practices, such as using recycled stock and vegetable-based inks, avoiding waste, choosing energy-efficient resources, and promoting a no-pulping policy. We now use 100-percent recycled stock on all our books. The results: in one year, switching to post-consumer recycled stock saved 24 mature trees, 5,000 gallons of water, the equivalent of the total energy used for one home in a year, and the equivalent of the greenhouse gases from one car driven for a year.

Over the years, we have adopted a number of dogs from rescues and shelters. First there was Bear and after he passed, Ginger and Scout. Now, we have Kira, another rescue. They have brought immense joy and love not just into our lives, but into the lives of all who met them.

We want you to know a portion of the profits of this book will be donated in Bear, Ginger and Scout's memory to local animal shelters, parks, conservation organizations, and other individuals and nonprofit organizations in need of assistance.

*– **Douglas & Sherri Brown**,*
President & Vice-President of Atlantic Publishing

Table of Contents

Chapter 10. Buying Options: The Ultimate In and Out Transaction 193

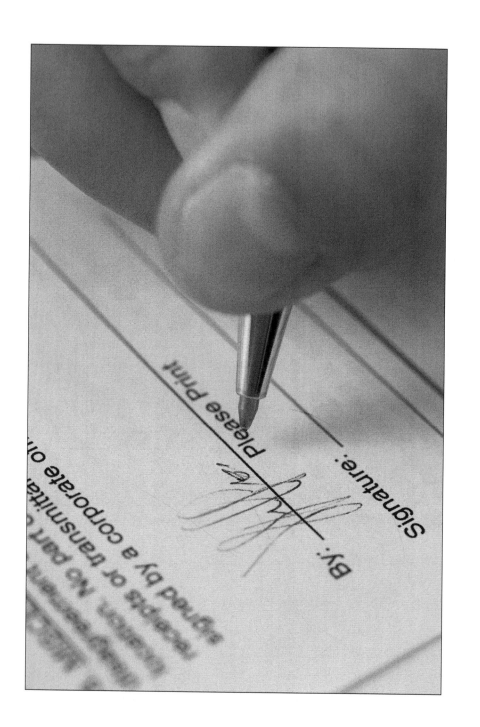

Recognizing Opportunity

At the outset, let it be stated that this book is not a textbook on economics or investment advice; nor is it "IRAs for Idiots". If we have taken a light-hearted approach to very complex legal and economic issues, so be it. After all, we don't want to lose the reader only after a few pages. It is the authors' intent to provide a person with average intelligence and experience a starting point from which to secure and take control of his or her financial future and retirement without being bored to death.

No one chooses to retire poor, or even with just enough money to get by (at least not consciously). Yet, day in and day out, millions of Americans pass up the opportunity to change the course of their financial futures. Perhaps they don't recognize opportunity when it brushes shoulders with them as it passes by "disguised as hard work," as Herbert V. Prochnow observed.

By opening the cover of this book (even if you only peek inside to see what this "retire rich" business is all about), you're at least willing to look for the opportunity—and perhaps do a little work to get there. That's only the start of the good news. Bear with us for a moment, and you'll see exactly what we mean.

The next time you're at the gym, making small talk at a cocktail party, or refilling your mug at the coffee station at work—any place where two or three people are standing around talking—ask any one of them if they've ever heard of a self-directed IRA. Then watch the expressions on their faces go from a puzzled look to confused frown to eyes glazed over. While you're watching, count the seconds it takes before someone changes the subject or suddenly remembers a phone call that needs to be made. Any conversation that includes words such as *taxes, IRA (individual retirement account),* or *investments* will typically provoke that kind of response. It's like a money version of the flight-or-fight response. Sure, you might get lucky and get a sentence or two of polite conversation first, but odds are that before long, you'll be standing there keeping yourself company. That's when you're going to whip out this book and learn what everyone concerned about their financial security needs to know.

To be sure, your broker and banker would rather you didn't know about it. But, if you're willing to ask questions, ponder answers, locate a qualified IRA advisor, and put your newfound knowledge to work, then you can join the ranks of people who have turned their money into a workhorse. The only real question is, *"Why wouldn't everyone be willing to make that commitment?"*

Forty years after Congress established the IRA, U.S. taxpayers hold assets totaling in trillions of dollars in various types of IRA accounts. Some of that wealth was built a teaspoon at a time, by depositing the annual maximum contributions of $1,500, $2,000, or even $5,000, depending on the year in which they were made. More was built by dumping great big buckets of money from company and government retirement plans into personal IRA accounts.

Getting money into an IRA account is only the first step to building retirement wealth. How it's managed and invested afterward is equally important. Consider this: Mutual fund holdings accounted for roughly $5.3 trillion, or about 30 percent of IRA assets in 2012. On the surface, that may sound like a good thing. After all, it means seasoned investment professionals tend to almost half of all IRA holdings.

This type of assurance shouldn't make the owners of those assets sleep better at night. The sad truth is that, as of 2012, 84 percent of all mutual funds have underperformed the stock market when earnings are adjusted to account for hefty fees charged by actively managed mutual funds. For the small percentage of investors who turn out to be both astute and lucky enough to enjoy better-than-average growth in their investments, the IRS waits on the horizon to collect its fair (rather unfair) share right off the top.

The challenge to retiring rich, then, is twofold: first, to make money and second, to keep as much of it for yourself as the law will allow.

That may seem like a pretty tall order. Tax law only works for the benefit of the rich, right? Those who can afford to hire high-priced lawyers and tax professionals to find the loopholes in the law doesn't apply to the average Joe. Not so.

We won't lie and say it's easy; very few things of value ever are. But, believe it or not, the IRS has provided the tools to make it possible. The only thing standing between you and retiring rich is your willingness to use them.

If you're part of the vast majority of IRA holders with money sitting in traditional investments like stocks, mutual funds, and annuities, don't hold your breath waiting for your broker or banker to clue you in on the possibilities.

Don't get us wrong. It's not that they don't want you to get rich. They do. After all, the more money you have, the more of their products you can buy. It's what biologists call a symbiotic relationship. Both parties benefit from their mutual success. And therein lies the rub.

Your broker and banker have a product or set of products to sell, and their formula for measuring your success does not include a yardstick for determining whether or not those products are the *best* choice for your individual situation. That job belongs to you alone.

Think about all those invitations you get in the mail to receive a "free" meal from an expensive restaurant if only you'll sit through a sales presentation. The sponsor is selling a product, which they will try to convince you to buy, whether or not it fits in your investment strategy and plan. That's how they make *their* money, by selling a product.

Isn't depending on your current IRA custodian to educate you on all your options akin to going into a bicycle shop to look at a slick, new touring cycle and expecting the salesclerk to point out that the hot, little sports car at the car dealership next door might be more to your liking? Like the bike shop owner, your broker or banker has no vested interest in steering you toward alternatives.

Don't expect the IRS to map out the universe of investment options open to you, either. IRS Publication 590, which documents the rules and regulations pertaining to IRAs, was 114 pages long in 2013 and, for the most part, does not tell you what you can do with your IRA. It does tell you with some consistency, however, what you cannot do and spells out, with surprising regularity, what the financial penalties are for getting the two confused. Learning to understand the difference is left to you, which probably goes a long way toward explaining why most Americans have not even taken the vital, but simple, step of opening an IRA account—and the vast majority of individuals who fail to contribute to it regularly or make their money work as hard as it could.

That leaves you with the ominous task of discovering these things for yourself. That's where this book comes in. In the following chapters, you're going to learn from the experiences of my fictional friend, Joanne Moneymaker. The authors created Jo to put the sometimes confusing, and often intimidating, IRS rules into a real-world context. She's generously agreed to let us tag along with her as she discovers what she's been doing wrong, devises a plan to reach her retirement goals, and then puts that plan into action.

To do that, this book was divided into four sections. In Part One, you'll examine the barriers that most people face to acquire wealth they need for a comfortable and secure retirement. Once you understand the challenges, you'll look at strategies for overcoming those barriers. To be sure that Jo doesn't run afoul of the IRS, she'll learn the differences between IRA plans and 401(k)-type plans, limits on contributions, disallowed investments, the basic rules governing distributions, and how to safely move the money between tax-sheltered accounts. Of course, this book will also discuss the tax implications and penalties that come into play when the rules are broken.

By the time you get to Part Two, Jo will be ready to attend to the preliminary work of transforming her wealth-building strategy into an action plan. Jo will decide what she's looking for in a plan administrator and will choose one. But, before she can actually get to the fun part—investing in her self-directed IRA— she'll need to fund the account, consider her investment options, and assemble a backup team of professionals she can call on when needed. Then she'll need to stop, take a deep breath, and give some serious thought to how she's going to manage the risk that is inherent with every investment.

About the time Jo is starting to think that she's never going to reach the point where she can start putting her self-directed IRA to work, the day finally arrives. In Part Three, she'll learn the ins and outs of real estate and real estate-related investments, as well as how to buy a business or precious metals using her IRA. Like everyone else, Jo knows about buying real estate through a broker or from a private party. Sometimes, taking the road less traveled can yield larger returns though. So, before you move on, you'll investigate nontraditional places to locate investment opportunities and how to leverage investment dollars with limited liability companies and other structures that allow Jo to pool her assets with others to buy investments that she might not be able to afford on her own.

Breaking IRS distribution rules can be as costly as sloppy investing. In Part Four, the authors will discuss how a single careless misstep at the end of the process can wipe out years of hard work and good planning. You'll learn when the IRS allows penalty-free withdrawals and when it requires distributions. Using those rules, this book will discuss ways to design a compliant distribution plan that will keep Jo's taxes as low as possible, let her live out her retirement dreams, and still preserve much of her wealth for the benefit of her heirs.

Finally, once Jo has her own future secured, it will be time to think about what happens after she's gone. As with every other step in the process, Jo has choices to make. If she makes them well, her heirs will have the opportunity to continue along the same path of principal preservation and tax reduction that Jo followed throughout her life. So, before you part with Jo, you'll tag along on one last lesson—gaining a general understanding of IRA beneficiary distribution rules and how Jo can preserve the most options for her heirs.

You'll be happy to know that we're going to do all that without pages of legalese and financial mumbo jumbo. Because we make no assumptions about how much or how little you already know about any of these subjects, we've included both an IRA primer and a glossary for easy reference. Wherever we thought that an immediate clarification of the terminology used would be helpful to you, we've inserted a definition box to keep you moving forward.

Before you get started, you need to establish a few ground rules and take care of a bit of legal housekeeping.

Assumptions

No doubt, you've read books and articles on finance and investment in which the author paints a fairy-tale picture of mind-boggling returns on various investments—usually ones the author has a vested interest in promoting. The book's goal in providing the examples that follow is to explain your options for structuring your retirement plan, not to sell you on a certain investment vehicle. To do this, there are calculations and projections that assume a typical investment portfolio will return an average of roughly 8 percent over time. Additionally, the authors' assumptions do not distinguish between the returns from differing investment classes. In real life, some investments yield higher returns than others. The same is true with investors. Two investors can buy and sell the same product and have entirely different results. We've dealt with that disparity by choosing a relatively conservative number that we hope will not distract from the real points being presented.

There are many references available that can help you with the arduous task of figuring out how much money you will need to fund your own retirement. This is not one of them. Therefore, we have intentionally not included factors like inflation in my calculations. We strongly recommend that once you have explored the investment opportunities available to you through your self-directed IRA, you proceed to that type of detailed planning as part of your overall strategy.

To avoid getting bogged down in endless variations, we've also restricted my tax computations in the examples to the taxes paid to the federal government. When you do your own planning, you will be well advised to remember that state and local taxes can have a sizable impact on your returns. Be sure to include them.

Terminology

The terms *IRA administrator, custodian,* and *trustee* are sometimes bandied about as if they all mean the same thing: the person or organization with which IRA accounts are established and maintained. The truth is, the law recognizes significant differences between the three entities that provide IRA services. You'll examine those differences in greater detail when you get to Chapter 4, but you should note here that the distinctions boil down to licensing, regulation, and authority.

- A *custodian* is licensed to hold your assets for you.

- A *trustee* is permitted a certain degree of authority to act on your behalf.

- An *administrator* tends to the administrative details of your account and acts as an interface between you and your custodian, trustee, or both.

For the purposes of this book, the authors have chosen to use the term administrator because, regardless of which custodian holds your IRA assets or with which trustee you establish the account, a plan administrator or facilitator will more than likely serve as your point of contact.

You'll also notice that the authors have generously used the word "generally" throughout because every rule has an exception. While the vast majority of people reading this book will likely fit into the "general" application of IRS law, your personal situation has the potential to fit within the range of the numerous exceptions included in the fine print of the IRS Code. That is why you need to consult with a qualified IRA advisor, tax accountant and lawyer when you get down to the serious business of putting together your own plan to retire rich with a self-directed IRA. And once you put your plan into operation, it is imperative that you consult with qualified professionals on a continuing basis to keep abreast of future changes that may impact your plan considerably.

Since this book was originally written, the market has changed, which may directly affect your choices of investments. Fortunately, while always in a state of flux and subject to tinkering by Congress, the basic laws and statutes have not changed all that much. This revised edition has attempted to call your attention to these "land mines" so you can avoid stepping on them. As authors, we also will repeatedly emphasize that you must do your "due diligence" and try to protect yourself and your money as best as you can…this means consulting the professionals as needed to assist you in avoiding those "land mines". We have also commented and modified our original thoughts where appropriate about some of the traditional choices for investments you have so that you are aware of hidden dangers in light of current economic conditions.

In the past six to seven years, we have witnessed a substantial meltdown in the securities and real estate markets; we have been through a period of economic recession from which we are only slowly recovering, and it has been clearly demonstrated to one and all that world market conditions and current events can have a direct impact on local investments and your retirement funds. Can you say "global economy"? Every day, more and more, people are coming to the awareness that we no longer live in a localized economy…everything, anywhere in the world, can have a financial impact on the U.S. economy and your investments.

For these reasons it becomes even more imperative than ever before for anyone who has a self-directed IRA to invest carefully and understand the risks involved and the land mines to watch out for. While it may be impossible to avoid the risks entirely and still make some money, you must "choose wisely" as best as you can. After all, if it all goes bad, you can blame no one but yourself.

Now, if you're ready, it's time to go find Jo.

PART ONE

Choosing to Retire Rich

"There are two primary choices in life: to accept conditions as they exist, or accept the responsibility for changing them."

—DENIS WAITLEY

CHAPTER ONE

Extreme Makeover — Retirement Style

I am opposed to millionaires, but it would be dangerous to offer me the position.

–MARK TWAIN

Meet Joanne Moneymaker—Jo, for short. Jo is not much different from you. She might be a little older, or she might be a little younger. She might earn a little bit more than you, or she might earn a little less. Still, her goals for retirement are very similar to your own. She wants to accumulate sufficient assets to secure a comfortable and worry-free retirement.

For the past 12 years, Jo worked as a budget analyst for a Fortune 1000 homebuilder that specializes in developing resort-style retirement communities. That is, until she lost her job when the company reorganized and downsized.

Jo was lucky. She landed on her feet with a better job. Her new position with a start-up construction business pays more and offers her a better career path than the old company. The only problem in her life right now is the $200,000 question—what should she do with the funds in her former employer's retirement plan? It doesn't sound like a terribly difficult decision on the surface, but the laws governing retirement savings are complex, and there are very few do-overs where the IRS is concerned, so Jo wants to consider her options carefully.

When Opportunity Knocks . . .

Sometimes life's blessings come disguised as a kick in the pants. So it was with Jo. She was having a hard time recognizing it, as she sat at her desk reading and re-reading the small mountain of paperwork she had been handed, along with that ugly little pink slip that thanked her for her service and wished her well in her future endeavors. Each sheet of paper seemed to demand one more decision from her, and the one outlining what she had to with her 401(k) had her completely stumped.

Several friends had told her to roll it into the 401(k) with her new employer. Another told her to roll it into her Roth IRA. None could explain why one recommendation was better than the other. One thing she knew for sure was that her clock was ticking.

The company's policy gave her a deadline for submitting rollover paperwork, or they would write her a check for the balance in her account. With only a month to go before her deadline, Jo had pretty much decided that rolling one 401(k) into another 401(k) seemed like the simplest and most logical answer.

As luck would have it, a telephone call from an old college buddy saved her from making that mistake. After laying out her dilemma yet one more time, the friend gave her the name of a certified financial planner. Two days later, Jo was sitting across a conference table from Bill Cash. Going to see Bill may turn out to be the smartest financial move she will ever make.

A House Made of Straw

Until Jo met Bill Cash, she operated under the mistaken belief that she had her financial house in tip-top shape. Through her work, she'd had ample opportunity to see that some people retire well and others not so well. As a result, Jo decided early on that, when her turn to retire comes along, she would be counted among the former.

Jo has given serious thought to how much money she will need to have put aside when she retires. Even though her goals are modest, she figures she'll still need a sizable nest egg to ensure that she can, at the very least, maintain her current lifestyle. With a little good fortune, she might even have enough money to do some of the things that people promise they'll do when a job is no longer the centerpiece of their daily lives. Her plan was basic, but aggressive.

Save Early and Often

Jo understands the power of compound growth. It was a lesson her parents taught her when she was eight years old. At that time, she received a $10 weekly allowance. They required that she save 20 percent of it. Each week, she put $2 into a cookie tin. At the end of each month, she counted it out with her father, and he paid her 10 percent compound interest on the balance. The first interest payment of seven cents failed to generate much excitement on her part, but the next month her father paid the interest in nickels and dimes. Within a few months, he was paying her the interest in quarters and then in dollar bills. The longer she left her money in the cookie tin, the faster the balance grew. The experience made a believer out of her. Before long, she voluntarily started dropping $3 a week into the box and, as her father periodically increased her allowance, she voluntarily increased the portion she saved.

It worked then and it has worked for the 12 years since Jo landed her first job and opened an IRA account. From the beginning, she has contributed the maximum the IRS allowed, which means that her early contributions amounted to $2,000 a year and increased to $3,000 in 2004 and then to $4,000 in 2005. During the same period of time, Jo also maxed out her contributions to her company's 401(k) plan. Her employer's savings- incentive policy, which matched her contributions dollar for dollar, combined with the returns on her investments, has kept her balance steadily growing, and Jo is optimistic about her financial future.

Timing Is Everything

Jo does one more thing to give her IRA balance an extra boost. She makes it a January 1 ritual to write the check for her IRA, instead of waiting until the end of the year like her brother, Ted, typically does. Even though they started their accounts in the same year and have contributed exactly the same amounts to them, Jo's account has earned hundreds of dollars more than Ted's. Part of that difference can be attributed to her investment choices, but even if we assume that she and Ted earned the same 8 percent return on their IRA accounts, Table 1 clearly shows that a small decision about timing can yield a big bonus on a year-after-year basis. In 2015 alone, Jo's $4,000 New Year's contribution earned her $332 by the time her brother got around to making his own IRA contribution.

Table 1. ONE-YEAR COMPARISON OF JO'S AND TED'S IRA GROWTH

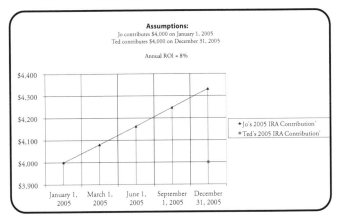

The difference in their earnings is even more dramatic if we look at what happens to their balances over the course of 20 years. If Jo and Ted continue their contribution patterns for the next two decades, Jo will earn a full $18,644 more than her brother, just by choosing to make her deposit at the beginning of each year instead of at the end of it. The difference would be even greater if Ted waited until the following April 15, as the IRS allows.

Table 2. 20-YEAR COMPARISON OF JO AND TED'S IRA GROWTH

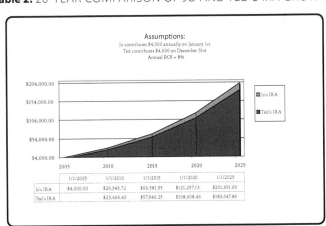

Diversify Holdings

To Jo, investing all of your money in one stock or class of stocks would be as foolish as jumping out of a perfectly good airplane. She's not that kind of risk taker. At the same time, she recognizes that without risk, there is little reward. She balances that risk-reward relationship by using an asset-allocation strategy that makes certain her investments are as diversified as the administrators of her 401(k) and IRA accounts permit, which basically means that she primarily owns stock, index funds and mutual funds in her retirement accounts. She limits her holdings in her employer's stock to no more than 10 percent of her total 401(k) portfolio, so that if the company hits on hard times, she won't lose both her income and her future security.

Outside her retirement accounts, Jo has been busy building assets. She owns her own home, a handful of stocks and index funds, some gold coins and a few other small investments. Until recently, she'd owned a rental property, but sold it when her tenants made her an offer she couldn't refuse. The cash, less capital gains taxes, is sitting in treasury notes until she finds another property to buy.

Capital gain: The net profit realized from the sale of a capital asset (stocks or real estate, for example). Taxes on capital gains are paid at a different rate than on regular income, depending on how long the asset was owned.

On the surface, Jo appears to be doing everything right. She started early, saves aggressively in tax-sheltered accounts, and invests her money wisely. So you can imagine her surprise at finding out that the financial house she'd so carefully constructed was a house of straw, waiting for the big wind of the IRS to blow through.

Bill's Extreme Makeover Plan

Jo arrived at Bill's office with what she thought was a basic multiple-choice question.

What should she do with her 401(k) account?

>   a. Roll it over to her new 401(k) plan.
>
>   b. Roll it over to a Roth IRA.

Bill gave her a quick and straightforward answer: none of the above.

He then went on to explain that option "a" was nothing short of a bad idea, and option "b" was against IRA rules. Pursuing either would cost her thousands of dollars in unnecessary taxes and penalties. There was a better way: a self-directed IRA.

The Dark Side of 401(k) Plans

Over the course of the next hour, Jo had an eye-opening conversation with Bill about retirement plans. Like most people Jo knows, she viewed a 401(k) plan as the single most important component of her long-term financial security because of the speed with which the funds can grow, compared to an IRA. Bill concurred with the basic premise. With higher contribution limits and employer matching funds, 401(k) plans give plan participants a leg up over a basic IRA. At the same time, the sacrosanct 401(k) plan also has a dark side that few people know or talk about.

The Tax Time Bomb

It is true that 401(k) plans are a valuable tool for acquiring and building tax-deferred savings. Who wouldn't like the idea of being able to take a slice of your income right off the top and sock it away for retirement? Income that doesn't even show up on your W-2 form at tax time. No deductions. No tax credits. No fuss. No muss. It's like it doesn't even exist, except in the balance of the monthly statement from the plan administrator.

As if that isn't great enough, employer-matching funds amount to a monthly income bonus—except that, like the deferred income contributions from your own salary, the employer contributions only show up in your rapidly growing balance.

There's only one problem with this scenario. No income escapes the grasp of Uncle Sam forever and, depending on the plan's distribution policy, the deferred income part can trigger an income tax time bomb. Some companies, like Jo's former employer, require retirees to take a lump-sum distribution when they leave the company. They do this because administering the accounts cost the company money—money they can save if the account is moved out of the program. The problem for Jo and other retirees is that a lump-sum distribution of deferred income—income on which not a penny of tax was ever paid—can generate a staggering tax bill when it comes due at retirement.

The Potato Sack Race to the Finish Line

Remember at the company picnic when they passed around burlap sacks? You stepped inside, grasped the open edge tightly and started hopping for all you were worth toward the finish line. You could see where you wanted to go and you knew that if you and your competitors could just drop the sack and hit the ground running, you could beat the entire pack. Instead, you hopped. You stumbled. You fell. And you finished... Well, you did finish, didn't you?

Given the limited investment options available within most 401(k) plans, trying to build wealth can feel about as constricting as the potato sack. Plan offerings typically include a handful of managed funds and perhaps even some index funds. Company stock is always an option, and the most progressive plans even allow participants to buy and sell listed investments like individual stocks. All this would be perfect if it weren't for the larger universe of investment options that can sometimes offer better returns and may even serve to balance out risk by diversifying your holdings.

CLASSIFIED CASE STUDY

Company: Equity Institutional
(Formerly Known As Sterling Trust Company)
Location: Equity Institutional is located in Westlake, OH.
Phone: (800) 955-3434

Services: Accounts at Equity Institutional are truly self-directed, meaning you and your financial advisor make the decisions to invest in the investment products you choose. Our goal is to assist you in consolidating your entire retirement portfolio on one statement with one online account access login. This company can be reached at www.equityinstitutional.com or by phone at 800-955-3433.

Advice from Equity Institutional:

One of the biggest mistakes we see in this business is when an individual leaves his/her job and decides not to rollover their 401K or other qualified retirement funds to an IRA. The lure of "money now" rather than saving it for retirement certainly has appeal, but by not rolling it into an IRA, you lose out on the power of compounding.

Or, when an IRA owner under 59 ½ decides to withdraw funds from their IRA (for purchasing a new car, etc.) and has to pay a 10 percent premature penalty on top of paying income taxes.

Starting Over With Block

Knowing that Jo is in the construction business, Bill summed up his assessment of her existing retirement savings plan by comparing it to a cookie-cutter tract home built with a mix of both quality and inferior materials. It was possible that parts of it would stand the test of time, but weakness in a few critical components could put the entire structure at risk. He then laid out an alternative strategy for turning her straw house into solid block construction.

Earlier, this book discussed the dual goals of acquiring wealth and saving taxes. Bill's strategy was designed to do exactly that. Under each goal, he listed steps Jo could take to reach them. As he reviewed the plan with Jo, he noted the things Jo was doing right, areas where she needed to improve, and the areas she'd completely overlooked. Clearly, she had a long way to go. A self-directed IRA would help her get there.

BILL'S EXTREME MAKEOVER PLAN	JO'S SCORE
Step 1: Build Wealth	
Capitalize on compound growth	
• Start early	10
• Save the max	10
• Roll over 401(k) to an IRA whenever possible	TBD
• Redistribute assets between accounts as needed	TBD
• Stretch distributions over the longest period possible	TBD
Choose the right investments	
• Stocks, bonds, financial instruments	10
• Real estate	5
• Real estate-backed notes	0
• Business ownership	0
• Precious metals	2

BILL'S EXTREME MAKEOVER PLAN	JO'S SCORE
Manage risk	
• Planning	10
• Due diligence	10
• Structure	TBD
Step 2: Keep What's Yours	
Reduce taxes	
• Pay taxes up front for high-yield investments (Roth IRA)	7
• Defer taxes for low-yield investments (traditional IRA)	7
Use 401(k) rollover to best advantage	
• Boost IRA balance	TBD
• Capture stretch opportunities on more of your savings	TBD
Avoid extra taxes and penalties	
• Avoid early withdrawal penalties	TBD
• Take required distributions on time	TBD
• Use a Roth IRA to avoid required distributions (a technique called a stretch)	TBD

Her greatest deficiencies centered on a missed opportunity—that universe of investments that until now were reserved for her taxable investments. By rolling her 401(k) into a self-directed IRA, she immediately boosted the most versatile and manageable tool at her disposal. Used properly, it would provide her with bigger and better opportunities for compound growth, while taking some of the teeth out of the tax bite she will eventually face.

You may have noticed by now that "trust me" is not in Jo's vocabulary. While Jo found Bill's presentation interesting, maybe even a bit intriguing, she wanted evidence, and Bill was prepared to provide it.

Bill handed Jo a printout containing the following example that shows how, given enough time, compounding can do much of the hard work of building her retirement assets.

Power of Compounding

Two friends, Dick and Jane, each came into a sizable cash windfall. Each invested their money on the day they received it and earned an 8 percent annual after-tax return on investment (ROI). Although Jane started out with twice as much as Dick, his savings quickly overtake hers, thanks to the power of compound growth. Ultimately, Dick's money earns just a little bit more than Jane's.

Table 3. EFFECT OF TIME ON COMPOUND GROWTH

	BALANCE IN 2000	BALANCE IN 2015	NET GAIN
Dick's windfall	$1,165,239	$1,612,814	$444,575
Jane's windfall	$1,079,462	$1,494,094	$414,632

A Tax Penny Saved Is Way More Than a Penny Earned

Everyone knows that saving taxes beats paying them any day. It's more money in your pocket. It's also dollars that go straight to the bottom line, where compounding works its miracles. To drive the point home, Bill gave Jo two more printouts. The first one demonstrated exactly that. It showed that over the course of 20 years, Dick's money grew more in a tax-sheltered account than it would have in a taxable savings account.

Table 4. EARNINGS ON TAXABLE SAVINGS VERSUS TAX-ADVANTAGED SAVINGS

	BALANCE IN 2000	BALANCE IN 2015	NET GAIN
Dick's windfall invested in a tax-deferred savings account	$ 1,165,239	$ 1,612,814	$ 444,575
Dick's windfall invested in a taxable savings account	$ 801,784	$ 1,109,754	$ 307,970
Dick's increased earnings on tax-advantaged versus taxable savings			$ 136,605

Tax-advantaged account: A savings account, such as a 401(k) or IRA, which receives favorable tax treatment by the IRS.

The Hidden Cost of Spending

The impact of starting to save early in a tax-advantaged account like an IRA on overall earnings growth can hardly be overstated. But it's only the beginning. Assuming the funds are invested well (and you'll cover that subject shortly), there's also the inevitable question of how and when to use the wealth you've amassed over the years.

To see exactly how critical those decisions are, Bill showed Jo what might happen with Dick and Jane if they both retire at age 65, each with a million dollars in an IRA. For this example, it doesn't matter if it's a Roth IRA or a traditional IRA because the purpose of it is only to demonstrate how fast the accounts continue to grow once they begin to take distributions from them.

For this example, assume that Jane begins to take an annual distribution when she retires at age 65, but Dick does not. In fact, let's further assume that Dick is fortunate enough not to need to withdraw any of the assets in this IRA account.

Although Jane only withdraws a total of $1,040,000 over the next 25 years, she actually earns $2,924,238 less than Dick. How did that happen? They started with exactly the same amount of money and the same 8 percent return on their investments. But every dollar withdrawn from the account is one less dollar working for her. In the end, that million dollars or so that she withdrew cost her almost $3 million more. This principle is the cornerstone of what has come to be called the *stretch IRA*.

Table 5. EFFECT OF DISTRIBUTIONS ON IRA GROWTH

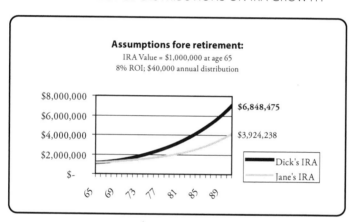

Once more, Bill turned to his computer: out came another printout. This time, he showed Jo, not how Dick or Jane might fare over time, but how a stretch IRA could make her money last almost forever by delaying distributions and stretching them out as long as possible. Again, he presented two different scenarios. With both, he began with the current combined balances of her IRA and 401(k) accounts. Then, assuming an average annual ROI of 8 percent, he estimated that Jo would have accrued $1,060,000 by the time she reaches 60.

In the first example, Jo begins taking a $20,000 voluntary annual distribution right away. You'll notice in Table 6 that even with the withdrawal of $200,000 ($20,000 a year for 10 years), her balance continues to grow. By the time she reaches age 70½, the year in which the IRS says she must begin taking distributions from a traditional IRA, she has grown her retirement savings to $2,076,479.

In the second scenario, Jo delays tapping her IRA assets until age 70½. Without the steady drain of the $20,000 annual distributions, her account has grown to a whopping $2,433,074. That's a full $356,595 more than in the first example and $156,595 over and above the $200,000 she withdrew over the course of 10 years.

This example is not to suggest that Jo should be afraid to use her assets at any time she needs them. But it does demonstrate once again the benefit of stretching out the distributions so that compounding can do the heavy lifting.

Table 6. EFFECT OF STRETCHING OUT DISTRIBUTIONS

JO'S AGE	JO'S UNIFORM LIFE EXPECTANCY	JO'S VOLUNTARY & MINIMUM DISTRIBUTION	BALANCE	JO'S AGE	JO'S UNIFORM LIFE EXPECTANCY	JO'S REQUIRED MINIMUM DISTRIBUTION	BALANCE
JO TAKES VOLUNTARY DISTRIBUTIONS BEGINNING AT AGE 60				**JO DELAYS TAKING DISTRIBUTIONS UNTIL AGE 70½ (WHEN REQUIRED)**			
60	36.8	$20,000	$1,060,000	70	27.4	$85,096	$2,433,074
61	35.8	$20,000	$1,124,800	71	26.5	$91,814	$2,535,906
62	34.9	$20,000	$1,221,784	72	25.6	$99,059	$2,639,719
63	33.9	$20,000	$1,299,527	73	24.7	$106,871	$2,744,026
64	33.0	$20,000	$1,383,489	74	23.8	$115,295	$2,848,252
65	32.0	$20,000	$1,474,168	75	22.9	$124,378	$2,951,735
66	31.1	$20,000	$1,572,101	76	22.0	$134,170	$3,053,704
67	30.2	$20,000	$1,677,869	77	21.2	$144,043	$3,153,957
68	29.2	$20,000	$1,792,099	78	20.3	$155,367	$3,250,907
69	28.3	$20,000	$1,915,467	79	19.5	$166,713	$3,344,266
70	27.4	$78,793	$1,989,911	80	18.7	$178,838	$3,432,970
70.5	27.4	$72,624	$2,076,479	81	17.9	$191,786	$3,515,821
71	26.5	$78,358	$2,164,240	82	17.1	$205,604	$3,591,483
72	25.6	$84,541	$2,252,839	83	16.3	$220,336	$3,658,466
73	24.7	$91,208	$2,341,858	84	15.5	$236,030	$3,715,113
74	23.8	$98,397	$2,430,809	85	14.8	$251,021	$3,761,301
75	22.9	$106,149	$2,519,125	86	14.1	$266,759	$3,795,446
76	22.0	$114,506	$2,606,149	87	13.4	$283,242	$3,815,839
77	21.2	$122,932	$2,691,709	88	12.7	$300,460	$3,820,647
78	20.3	$132,597	$2,774,450	89	12	$318,387	$3,807,911
79	19.5	$142,279	$2,854,126	90	11.4	$334,027	$3,778,517
80	18.7	$152,627	$2,929,829	91	10.8	$349,863	$3,730,935
81	17.9	$163,678	$3,000,538	92	10.2	$365,778	$3,663,632
82	17.1	$175,470	$3,065,111	93	9.6	$381,628	$3,575,094
83	16.3	$188,044	$3,122,276	94	9.1	$392,868	$3,468,234
84	15.5	$201,437	$3,170,621	95	8.6	$403,283	$3,342,410
85	14.8	$214,231	$3,210,040	96	8.1	$412,643	$3,197,160
86	14.1	$227,662	$3,239,180	97	7.6	$420,679	$3,032,254
87	13.4	$241,730	$3,256,585	98	7.1	$427,078	$2,847,756
88	12.7	$256,424	$3,260,688	99	6.7	$425,038	$2,650,538

JO'S AGE	JO'S UNIFORM LIFE EXPECTANCY	JO'S VOLUNTARY & MINIMUM DISTRIBUTION	BALANCE
JO TAKES VOLUNTARY DISTRIBUTIONS BEGINNING AT AGE 60			
89	12.0	$271,724	$3,249,819
90	11.4	$285,072	$3,224,732
91	10.8	$298,586	$3,184,125
92	10.2	$312,169	$3,126,686
93	9.6	$325,696	$3,051,124
94	9.1	$335,288	$2,959,926
95	8.6	$344,177	$2,852,542
96	8.1	$352,166	$2,728,580
97	7.6	$359,024	$2,587,843
98	7.1	$364,485	$2,430,385
99	6.7	$362,744	$2,262,072
100	6.3	$359,059	$2,083,979

JO'S AGE	JO'S UNIFORM LIFE EXPECTANCY	JO'S REQUIRED MINIMUM DISTRIBUTION	BALANCE
JO DELAYS TAKING DISTRIBUTIONS UNTIL AGE 70½ (WHEN REQUIRED)			
100	6.3	$420,720	$2,441,861

Comparing the two distribution plans, it becomes clear that the slower Jo withdraws money from her IRA, the greater her chances of turning a small personal fortune into a family fortune that has the potential to continue for generations.

Choose a Self-Directed IRA

Before moving on, Bill and Jo spent a few minutes reviewing her investment holdings both inside and outside her retirement accounts. She told him that she's always believed that stocks and bonds have their place in her portfolio, but she has a special

fondness for real estate. In the past, she's earned excellent returns on it, and she plans on buying another income property when she settles this 401(k) dilemma and can devote time to the task.

Then Bill showed her how choosing a self-directed IRA would make it more possible for her to accomplish almost every other item on the list. He started by asking her to think about how much she paid in capital gains over the past few years and, if she had it to do over again, would she rather pay that amount to the IRS or keep it in her retirement account where it can continue compounding? When he had her attention, he rattled off the types of investments available to her within a self-directed IRA account and how each one might work for her. The taxes in each instance could be managed, and potentially reduced, by matching the investments to the appropriate IRA account.

Becoming a Landlord: Investing in Income Property

Buying income property is one of the simplest nontraditional investments available for Jo's self-directed IRA. The idea, of course, is that she would purchase a parcel of real estate and rent it out for some period of time. The income from the rental would pay the mortgage and maintenance. Excess revenue would then be held within the IRA where it would remain available until needed for another investment.

While Jo can certainly buy real estate through a real estate broker or private party for her IRA, she can also acquire investment property through foreclosures, REOs, and tax liens. She is not limited to purchasing single-family residential property either. Condos, apartment buildings—even entire apartment complexes—and commercial property are options, too.

Owning a Business

If Jo someday decides that she wants to own her own business, she has the option of doing so within her self-directed IRA. The IRS dictates whom she can choose as a partner for such a purchase, but as long as she follows the rules, there's no reason why she can't use her IRA to make her dream a reality.

Real Estate-Backed Promissory Notes

An investor does not have to actually take title to a piece of property to profit from a real estate transaction. You probably recall that when you bought your home, you signed both a mortgage and a note promising to pay the mortgage. Perhaps a few months later, you received a letter in the mail informing you that your mortgage company had sold the note to a New York bank. This type of transaction is commonplace among financial institutions. Jo can use her IRA to buy existing mortgage notes in the same manner.

Excluded (or prohibited) transactions: IRA investments and business transactions specifically prohibited by the IRS.

Excluded individuals: Parties with whom your IRA is specifically prohibited from transacting business.

Becoming a Lender

In addition to using her self-directed IRA to buy existing real estate-backed notes, Jo can also use it to underwrite a new loan, just like she did last year for her cousin Shirley. She is not limited to originating notes for friends and family, of course. In fact, loaning money to certain family members is an excluded transaction for IRAs and carries stiff penalties.

Tax Sale Certificates and Tax Deeds

When a property owner falls behind on taxes, he or she risks losing his or her property to the IRS—or more accurately, to an investor like Jo, who might be interested in purchasing the property for sometimes pennies on the dollar. Buying *tax sale certificates* and *tax deeds*, which are instruments that permit the buyer to acquire these properties, is yet one more way that Jo can use her self-directed IRA to dabble in the real estate market.

Real Estate Options

One could argue that buying options on real estate is a form of speculation—with a twist. If Jo were to purchase an option, the seller would grant her the exclusive right to buy the property for a specific price and on a specific date. If she fails to buy the property on the agreed-upon date, the option expires, she loses the money she paid to secure the option, and the seller is free to sell the property to another buyer.

If Jo finds a piece of real estate for sale that is priced sufficiently below market value and believes that she can find a buyer willing to pay more than the option price plus her expense for the same property, she has the potential to turn a very quick profit on the deal.

Owning Precious Metals

Due to recent changes in IRS rules, Jo can now own certain precious metals in her self-directed IRA. As with all IRA assets, she won't be able to take possession of her gold, silver, or platinum holdings, but her administrator will arrange to have them stored in a secure repository.

Redistribute Assets, as Needed

Years ago, when Jo opened her IRA and 401(k) accounts, she'd assumed that all she needed to do to reach her retirement goals was to add to them regularly and invest them well. In 20 to 30 years, she'd be able to retire and start drawing the money out to fund a rosy retirement. Along about the time that Bill was explaining to her that most people change jobs three to five times during their careers, she was getting the picture that this would not be a one-time exercise.

In fact, as Bill pointed out, changing jobs has the potential to boost her retirement savings, because each time she does, she will have the opportunity to again roll over her company retirement plan into her self-directed IRA. What could be better? How about being able to choose the right kind of self-directed IRA too?

In the next couple of chapters, this book will discuss in greater detail the differences between traditional IRAs and Roth IRAs. You'll also cover how to go about moving assets between them—a process known by several different names, depending on where they originate, where they end up, and sometimes depending on the steps followed to accomplish the move. For the purposes of making Bill's point, however, it is only necessary to understand that the unique tax treatment of each type of IRA account can be used to reduce her tax obligations and boost her after-tax ROI.

In general, contributions to traditional IRAs are tax-free going into the account and taxed coming out (along with any earnings, of course). Roth IRAs, on the other hand, are always taxed going in and are generally tax-free coming out. This is an important distinction, because it allows you to choose which investments belong in each type of account.

Higher-yielding investments, for example, are often most appropriate for a Roth account, provided, of course, that they will have sufficient time to grow enough to earn back the advance tax bite and then some before you need to begin using the money.

By contrast, you certainly don't want to pay up-front taxes on slower-growing investments or those that stand a chance of not yielding any profit at all. And, since you'll likely be in a lower income tax bracket when you begin taking distributions than when you made the contribution, you'll want to employ those investment vehicles in your traditional IRA.

Highly speculative investments deserve a separate mention. One could justifiably argue that high-risk investments have no place in an IRA account. Your opportunities to contribute to an IRA are limited, and money lost on risky investments (or any investment for that matter) cannot be replaced by just writing another check to the account at will. If you're the type who tests the ice by driving your car over it, however, you might be inclined to do it anyway. Whether you choose to make the investment in your Roth IRA or traditional IRA should be carefully considered in light of each account's tax treatment.

Pay Only Your Fair Share of Taxes

Assuming that Jo does everything else right, she still needs to look out for the inevitable tax hit that her distributions, and ultimately her estate, will face. In Chapter Three, you will explore strategies to take the teeth out of Uncle Sam's bite, but right now, you need to make note of how he manages to get a grip on our money in the first place.

U.S. tax law is designed around something called a *taxable event*. Taxable events can happen any time that money changes hands. For example, let's say that Jo pays tax on her income (after taking every legal deduction and exemption, of course). She uses a portion of her after-tax income to buy a new washing machine from an appliance store. The appliance store declares the purchase as income, subtracts every possible deduction and exemption, and pays taxes on the remainder. The salesclerk at the appliance store receives a commission from his or her employer, which is declared as income, and so on.

The rules about when those taxes become due are rigid and mostly unforgiving. The key to avoid paying anything more than her fair share, then, is for Jo to control when and how her money transfers into and out of her retirement accounts.

Even if Jo succeeds in getting her money into her IRA account without triggering an unintentional taxable event, she still has to be mindful of how the assets are used, because the IRS has a built-in "gotcha." If Jo violates any of the IRS taboos that we'll go over in Chapter Three, the IRS can disallow the tax-sheltered status of her entire account. In effect, she could end up taking an immediate lump-sum distribution. If that happens, Jo may owe an early withdrawal penalty and taxes on the entire amount in the account.

Fortunately for Jo, following the rules is not a complicated matter, although it does require a bit of diligence and strict adherence to the guidance from her IRA administrator.

At the end of her meeting with Bill, Jo went home to do a little homework. As enticing as Bill's recommendations sounded, Jo has learned not to blindly follow other people's advice. She figured it was time to beef up her knowledge about IRAs.

CHAPTER TWO

An IRA Primer

*People who complain about taxes can be divided
into two classes: men and women.*

–UNKNOWN

As Jo set about the task of learning everything about IRAs she never thought she needed to know, the term *self-directed IRA* gnawed at her. *Aren't all IRAs self-directed*, she wondered? She quickly learned that the answer to her question is about as exact as every other answer she's been handed since her 401(k) odyssey began: "Yes, but . . ."

Many people mistakenly believe that IRA stands for *individual retirement account*. The Employee Retirement Income Security Act of 1974 (ERISA), which established IRAs, gave each of us the freedom to make our own *individual retirement arrangement*, 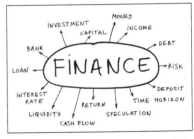 or IRA. This watershed legislation meant that workers were no longer solely dependent on employer pension plans for retirement security.

Certainly, many individuals already diligently saved every spare penny for a rainy day, as well as for retirement. Those who did watched their balances crawl painfully, slowly upward after handing over a percentage of their interest, dividends, and capital gains to the IRS every April 15. Others saved at a slower rate, or not at all. Either way, it was clear that something had to be done to help workers prepare for retirement. The ERISA legislation was one in a long series of steps in the right direction.

ERISA established tax incentives for retirement savings. Although the annual limits wouldn't put IRA owners on par with company-sponsored retirement plans, ERISA did something that company plans couldn't do. It put us in the driver's seat with at least a small portion of our investments. It took a decade or more before approaching retirees started figuring out the real power of the IRA, however.

In addition to providing tax-advantaged savings, ERISA also gave us the freedom to choose where and with whom we wanted to open an IRA account and, most importantly, control over how our savings were invested. For most people, that meant a bank, savings and loan, credit union, or stockbroker. Jo was no different. With Jo's new understanding of self-directed IRAs, however, she figures it means that she's been appointed the general contractor of the most important construction job of her life—designing and building her personal retirement security. So, in a manner of speaking, her IRA has been self-directed from the get-go. Talking with Bill made her realize that what she had been missing was the understanding that it also gave her the freedom to choose the building materials, tools, and industry professionals that are right for her.

Jo is a great believer in investment diversity (or asset allocation, as it is often called) for managing risk. That is why her non-IRA investment holdings have long included everything from stocks to income-producing real estate to gold. Yet, it had never occurred to her to ask if she could buy those same types of investment in her IRA. It turns out that, with few exceptions, it is choosing the wrong IRA administrator that imposes restrictions on what she can and cannot invest in within her account—not the IRS.

CLASSIFIED CASE STUDY

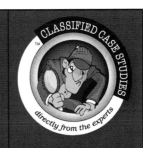

Company: Guidant Financial Group, Inc.

Location: Bellevue, WA

Services: Guidant Financial Group, Inc. is a non-traditional financial services company focused on delivering unique solutions to the self-directed investing market.

Guidant has helped thousands of clients in all 50 states to learn the benefits of using self-directed retirement plans and maintains preferred relationships with custodians, banks and record keepers that help to administer these self-directed accounts. The company's clients have complete control over their investments and can truly diversify the industry that holds those funds. Clients receive world-class customer service and even time with an outside attorney who specializes in tax and ERISA issues. More information can be found at http://www.guidantfinancial.com or by phone at 888-472-4455.

Tips from Guidant Financial:

The Employee Retirement Income Security Act of 1974 (otherwise known as ERISA) essentially passed the responsibility of retirement saving from the employer to the employee. As part of this act, IRAs were created to provide individuals the ability to direct how their retirement funds were invested. These IRAs were initially marketed to consumers by banks and brokerages that specialized in stock & mutual fund transactions.

Due to the overwhelming growth of the stock market during the next 25 years, most individuals were content to hold all of their retirement funds in what are perceived as traditional investments. This has led to a large misconception that stocks, bonds and mutual funds are the only legal investments for your IRA. That is simply not true.

Banks and brokerage houses have a vested interest in promoting this theory because that is how they create company revenue – they don't make money if you buy real estate, businesses and other non-traditional investments.

Don't let personal interests, or lack of knowledge by your financial advisor, limit your ability to maximize the investment potential of your retirement accounts.

A Brief History of Pension Plans

Pensions have been around for hundreds of years. Colonial churches first offered them for the benefit of the widows and orphans of their clergy.[1] Then the newly formed United States government came onboard by paying pensions to Revolutionary War veterans. It took almost 150 years, though, for capitalism to jump on the bandwagon.

Railroad freight company American Express was the first private-sector business to offer a pension. That was way back in 1875.[2] The Pennsylvania Railroad followed suit in 1900.[3] About 30 years later, the federal government took over the Railroad Pension and shortly afterwards, the New Deal created social security. Over the next three decades, workers covered by collective bargaining agreements began earning pensions—the golden eggs that would keep employees happily on the job with their gaze firmly fixed on the retirement horizon and the financial security promised by a company pension.

Generally available only to employees of large firms with the resources to offer comprehensive benefits packages to entice the cream of the employee crop (or to workers covered by collective bargaining agreements), company pensions helped to attract and retain good workers. At the same time, millions of others were

1   Pensions History, The Gale Group Inc., http://www.families.com.
2   Pensions History, The Gale Group Inc., http://www.families.com.
3   Steven A. Sass, The Promise of Private Pensions: The First Hundred Years.

left to rely on personal savings and earnings from investments like equities, mutual funds, bonds, and real estate to fund their own retirements. Social security remained available as a safety net, in case their plans didn't work out quite as well as intended.

This was all well and good until you consider, as you did in Chapter One, the negative impact of taxes on the growth rates of the savings people were putting aside for retirement. Eventually, it became increasingly clear to lawmakers on Capitol Hill that something more needed to be done. That something was the IRA.

The IRA provided anyone with earned income (compensation) the ability to make his or her own personal retirement arrangements. Depending on a few variables, like income levels, the contributions enjoyed favorable tax treatment, giving workers the first tax break ever for the accounts in which they could stash a little extra cash for their retirement.

Table 7. HOW THE IRS DEFINES EARNED INCOME

EARNED INCOME	UNEARNED INCOME
• Wages	• Deferred compensation
• Salaries	• Rental income and other earnings and profits from property
• Self-employment income	
• Commissions	• Income from a partnership in which you do not provide material income-producing services
• Alimony	
• Separate maintenance payments	
• Interest	• Amounts you exclude from your income, such as foreign earned income and housing costs
• Dividends	
• Pensions	
• Annuity income	

The thinking behind offering tax deferrals on IRA contributions was twofold. First, it is generally assumed that when you retire, you will earn less than when you were working and, therefore, will be in a lower tax bracket. Thus, deferring taxes on your contributions until they are distributed during retirement will mean that you pay less in tax overall. The other bonus the IRA offered showed up in the effect of compounding on monies that weren't being sapped by taxes every April 15. Like the contributions that fund the account, the investment earnings within an IRA are tax-sheltered until they are withdrawn—a major advantage when compared to personal savings accounts outside an IRA.

The IRA did more than provide a tax-advantaged savings plan for those workers who were not covered by a company retirement plan. It also offered workers a portable retirement plan (e.g., one that could move from job to job with them) through a process called a *rollover*.

Compared to 401(k) plans, IRAs have dismally low contribution limits. But, compared to self-directed IRAs, 401(k) plans typically have equally arcane investment choices. Rolling the bigger 401(k) balance over to the more versatile self-directed IRA combines the best of both worlds.

Over the next three decades, Congress continued to modify and expand the IRA program. Today's family of IRA products covers more than 40 percent of American households and provides the most flexibility of any retirement plan in history, as well as the only means of preserving tax-sheltered retirement funds for future generations. To appreciate how, you need at least a general understanding of how each plan works.

The Plans

Traditional IRA

Definition

The traditional IRA is the original personal retirement plan established in 1974 for the purpose of giving individuals with earned income an opportunity to fund their retirements with tax-sheltered savings. It also included a means for employees to roll the holdings of their employer-sponsored pension plans into individual accounts when they change jobs.

The underlying principle on which the traditional IRA is based is that by deferring your tax obligation, you'll end up paying less. With a traditional IRA, you contribute pretax dollars to your account while you are working and withdraw the taxable principal and investment earnings during retirement, when it is assumed that your reduced income will place you in a lower tax bracket than you were at the time of the contributions.

Over the years, Congress has increased the number and types of IRAs, but there are still only three basic classifications. Regardless of any other designation, the IRS considers any IRA that is not a Roth IRA or a SIMPLE IRA to be a traditional IRA.

Be sure to consult the current IRS Publication 590, Individual Retirement Arrangements (IRAs) for the most up-to-date numbers and information.

Who can contribute?	Anyone under the age of 70 ½ with earned income can make contributions to a traditional IRA.

Traditional IRA

When can contributions be made?	You are free to make contributions as soon as the traditional IRA is set up. Your contributions for a given year must be made by the filing date for that year. For example, your 2016 traditional IRA contributions must be made by April 15, 2016, the filing deadline for your 2015 taxes.

What are the contribution limits?	**Annual Traditional IRA Contribution Limits**		
	Year	Annual Limit Age < 50	Annual Limit Age > 50
	2015 (In future years these numbers may be changed by Congress.)	$ 5,500	$ 6,500

Exceptions to the contribution limits:	If you file a joint return and you earn *less than your spouse*, your contribution for that year will be limited to the smaller of:
	
	 1. $ 5,500 ($ 6,500 if the spouse with the lower compensation is age 50 or older), or
	
	 2. The combined total compensation for you and your spouse, reduced by both of the following amounts:
	
	     • Your spouse's traditional IRA contribution for the year,
	
	     AND
	
	 • Your spouse's Roth IRA contribution for the year,
	
	     AND
	
	 • Any designated nondeductible contribution for the year made on behalf of your spouse.

How much of the contribution can be deducted?	Generally speaking, you can deduct the amount that is the lesser of: 1. The amount of your traditional IRA contribution for the year. *OR* 2. 100 percent of your compensation.

Traditional IRA

Deduction Exceptions:	If you or your spouse is covered by an employer retirement plan, your traditional IRA deduction will be determined by your modified adjusted gross income (MAGI) and your filing status. In general, as your MAGI increases, your deduction will decrease and then be eliminated altogether when your MAGI reaches a certain threshold.
	
	• If you or your spouse earns more than the other and you file a joint return, the contribution deduction for the spouse with the lower income will be limited to the lesser of:
	
	  1) The standard contribution limit, as listed above.
	
	  2) The total includable compensation of your combined gross income for the year, reduced by all of the three following amounts for the year in question:
	
	    • The IRA deduction for the spouse with the higher compensation.
	
	    • Any designated nondeductible contribution on behalf of the spouse with the higher compensation.
	
	    • Any Roth IRA contributions on behalf of the spouse with the greater compensation.

When can the funds in a traditional IRA be withdrawn or taken as a distribution?	• Withdrawals taken prior to age 59½ are subject to a 10 percent penalty. • A withdrawal from one traditional IRA can be rolled over into another traditional IRA without penalty and without incurring a tax obligation if the rollover is completed within 60 days from the date of withdrawal. • A one-year waiting period applies after a rollover is completed before another one may be initiated without penalty. • Assets can be transferred directly from one traditional IRA account to another without penalty. This is called a *direct trustee-to-trustee transfer.* • Required minimum distributions must begin at age 70½ and are based on the IRS life expectancy tables.

Traditional IRA

What are the tax benefits of a traditional IRA?	• Contributions may be fully or partially tax-deductible, so they can be used to reduce your taxable income in the year of the contribution.[1] • Distributions are taxed as ordinary income in the year they are withdrawn, presumably when you will be in a lower tax bracket.

Modified adjusted gross income (MAGI): MAGI is calculated by adding back in certain deductions, such as foreign income, student loans, and IRA that were subtracted to establish the adjusted gross income (AGI). MAGI is used to determine eligibility for IRA deductions and Roth IRA participation.

ACCOUNTING TIP: For the purposes of the IRS, regardless of the number and types of IRA accounts you hold, you are considered to have only one IRA account. This is an important distinction when it comes to adding up your contributions and calculating your distributions.

Contributions

The combined totals of your contributions during a given year may not exceed the annual limit. For example, if you have three IRAs (one traditional IRA and two Roth IRAs), your 2015 combined contribution limit cannot exceed $4,000, although you may divide that up any way you choose between the three accounts.

Required Minimum Distributions (RMD)

The RMD for each account is calculated individually, and the amounts for each account are totaled. The required distribution can be withdrawn from one account or split up between traditional IRA accounts, as long as the total withdrawn equals at least the RMD.

Roth IRAs do not have a mandated RMD, so they would not be included in the calculation.

ROTH IRA

Definition

The Roth IRA, which was introduced as part of the Taxpayer Act of 1997, offered workers one more way to save for retirement. Unlike your tax-deferred contributions to a traditional IRA, Roth contributions are taxed as regular income in the year they are deposited. Your qualified distributions of the principal and earnings accrued in the account can generally be withdrawn tax-free later, provided that certain requirements are met.

Two other ways in which the Roth IRA differs from the traditional IRA have to do with when contributions can be made and when distributions must be taken. As a Roth IRA account holder, you can continue to make contributions, regardless of age, as long as you earn a salary or other compensation, as defined by the IRS for IRA purposes. And last, but certainly not least, the Roth IRA does not include a mandate for required minimum distributions. In fact, you are free to hold assets in your Roth IRA for your entire lifetime, without any distribution if you choose—a difference that makes the Roth IRA an important estate-planning tool as well.

Who can contribute?	• Generally, anyone with taxable compensation and whose modified AGI falls within the following limits is qualified to contribute to a Roth IRA. **Filing Status Modified AGI is less than:** 　• $ 160,000 if you are married and filing jointly or are a qualifying widow(er). 　• $ 10,000 if you are married and filing separately and you lived with your spouse at any time during the year. 　• $ 110,000 if you are a single head of household or if you are married and filing separately *and* you did not live with your spouse at any time during the year. • You can make Roth IRA contributions on behalf of your spouse, provided the contributions do not exceed the spousal IRA limits described under Traditional IRAs, and your modified AGI is less than $ 160,000.
When can contributions be made?	• Contributions can be made as soon as the Roth IRA is set up. Your contributions for a given year must be made by the filing date for that year. For example, your 2015 Roth IRA contributions must be made by April 15, 2016, the filing deadline for your 2015 taxes. You may continue to contribute to a Roth IRA for as long as you have earned income, even after reaching the age of 70½.

ROTH IRA

What are the contribution limits?	• If you contribute to both a traditional IRA and a Roth IRA in the same year, the limit for your total Roth IRA contributions is reduced by the combined amount of all contributions to all IRAs (other than employer contributions under a SEP or SIMPLE IRA plan). In other words, if you contribute $1,000 to your traditional IRA in 2015, you may only contribute $3,000 to your Roth IRA, because the combined total is $4,000 for the year. • A 6 percent excise tax applies to all excess contributions over and above the annual limit.

Annual Roth IRA Contribution Limits

Year	Annual Limit Age < 50	Annual Limit Age > 50	
		Catch-up	Overall
2015	$4,000	$500	$4,500
2016	$4,000	$1,000	$5,000
2017	$4,000	$1,000	$5,000
2018	$5,000	$1,000	$6,000
After 2018	$5,000 (plus a maximum annual inflation adjustment increase of $500)	$-0-	$5,000 (plus a maximum annual inflation adjustment increase of $500)

How much of the contribution can be deducted?	Roth contributions are not deductible from your taxable income, but qualified distributions are generally tax-free.

ROTH IRA

When can the funds be withdrawn or taken as a distribution?	• You can withdraw the principal at any time and for any purpose; however, if you withdraw funds within the first five years, the distribution will be taxed as regular income. • After you have owned a Roth IRA for five years, you can withdraw funds for certain qualified purposes, such as buying a first home, without penalty. • Qualified distributions from a Roth IRA are not subject to Federal Income Tax. (See page 145 for more information on qualified distributions.) • Unlike the traditional IRA, the Roth IRA does not impose a minimum required distribution schedule.
What are the tax benefits of a Roth IRA?	Because Roth IRA contributions are made with after-tax dollars, the principal and interest are typically withdrawn tax-free. Consequently, if your contributions will have sufficient time to earn back the prepaid taxes before you need to use them, the Roth IRA usually provides a greater tax advantage than a traditional IRA.

Adjusted gross income (AGI): The amount of your income that determines when and if IRA contributions can be deducted. It is calculated by taking your AGI from Form 1040A or Form 1040 and adding back certain items, such as foreign earned income, housing deductions, or both; student-loan interest; tuition and fees; excluded qualified savings bond interest; and exclusion of employer-provided adoption benefits.

TIP: If your IRA contributions for a given year are less than the limit, you may not make up the difference by contributing more after the due date of your tax return.

Required beginning date: The age at which required minimum distributions must begin, typically 70½, although it can vary in the case of an inherited IRA.

Coverdell Education Savings Account (ESA)

Definition

Originally called the Education IRA, the ESA is a type of IRA established to help parents and students build up savings to cover education expenses. The funds can be used for elementary and secondary education expenses, as well as for higher education and home schooling.

Who can have an ESA?	Anyone who is under the age of 18 or has special needs is eligible to have an ESA.
What is the annual contribution limit for an ESA?	A maximum of $2,000 can be contributed each year on behalf of the beneficiary, regardless of how many ESA accounts have been established on his or her behalf.
Who can contribute to an ESA?	• Contributions are not limited to parents and other family members. Generally, anyone (including the beneficiary) can make contributions to a Coverdell ESA on behalf of the beneficiary, as long as the individual's MAGI income is less than $110,000 ($220,000 if the individual is filing a joint return) and the beneficiary is still under the age of 18 or is a special-needs individual. • The $2,000 maximum contribution per beneficiary is gradually reduced if the contributor's MAGI is between $95,000 and $110,000 ($190,000 and $220,000 if the contributor is filing a joint return). • Contributions to an ESA do not need to be made from earned income.
Are contributions to an ESA tax-deductible?	No. Contributions to an ESA are fully taxable in the year of the contribution, but the distributions are tax-free to the beneficiary, provided certain restrictions are met.

Coverdell Education Savings Account (ESA)

When can distributions be taken without penalty?	Tax-free distributions can be taken at any time, provided they are used for qualified education expenses, such as tuition, books, fees, and so on, at an eligible educational institution.
	If the distribution exceeds the actual amount of the qualified education expenses, a portion will be taxable to the beneficiary. An additional 10 percent tax will also apply, except in the case of the death or disability of the beneficiary or if the beneficiary receives a qualified scholarship.
	When the beneficiary reaches the age of 30, the balance in the account must be distributed within 30 days. Because the principal was taxed at the time the contribution was made, only the portion of the distribution representing earnings will be taxed in this case, although the additional 10 percent tax will apply to the entire amount. Taxes and penalties can be avoided if the beneficiary rolls over the full balance to a Coverdell ESA on behalf of another family member.

Special-needs beneficiary: Any individual who needs additional time to complete his or her education or requires ongoing special care due to a physical, mental, or emotional condition.

Simplified Employee Pension (SEP)

Definition

SEPs are a type of traditional IRA for self-employed individuals and small-business owners. They are flexible, easily established, and administered plans, in which contributions on behalf of the employee are fully funded by the employer. The employer remains free to increase or decrease or even skip contributions for a given year.

What are the tax benefits of a SEP?	Employees are not taxed on the contribution, but all withdrawals are fully taxable.

Savings Incentive Match Plans for Employees (SIMPLE IRA)

Definition

A SIMPLE IRA is a tax-favored retirement plan for certain small businesses and small-business owners that is similar in structure to a 401(k) plan. The basic structure of a SIMPLE IRA is a written agreement between the employer and employee laying out the terms of the contributions.

Contributions to a SIMPLE plan have two components, both of which are paid by the employer on behalf of the employee:

- A reduction in salary by a percentage elected by the employer, but not to exceed the maximum allowable.

- Either a matching contribution or a non-elective contribution paid by the employer.

What are the tax benefits of a SIMPLE IRA?	• Salary reductions and matching contributions are treated as deferred income. As such, they are not taxed at the time of the contribution. Instead, the contributions and any investment earnings are fully taxable at the time of withdrawal.

401(k) Plans

Definition	A 401(k) plan is a tax-qualified deferred compensation plan. This means that, as a plan participant, you can elect to defer a portion of your income, which is deposited into a tax-qualified retirement savings account and is administered by the employer (or a company hired by the employer on your behalf). Often the employer will match employee contributions by a defined ratio, sometimes as much as 1:1. Historically, one of the benefits larger companies, charitable organizations and government agencies offered their employees was the option of enrolling in company- sponsored retirement plans. The oldest of those plans is the defined-benefit plan, in which the company promises that if you stay on the job for a defined period of time (often 20 years), you will be rewarded with a specified retirement income. Today, fewer and fewer companies are offering defined-benefit plans, because they are carried on the employer's balance sheet as a debt obligation. Not only do these debts eventually become due and payable, in the interim they can affect a company's credit rating and attractiveness to would-be investors. As an alternative, many larger employers are turning to voluntary savings incentive match plan like the 401(k) or 403(b). Generally speaking, participation in one of these programs does not preclude you from also contributing to an IRA, but your income level could affect whether or not you qualify for the income tax deduction on the contribution.
What are the tax benefits of a 401(k) plan?	Because contributions to a 401(k) account are deferred income, they are not subject to income tax in the year of the contribution. Instead, the principal and any investment income it generates are taxed as ordinary income at the time they are withdrawn. Plans requiring a lump-sum distribution at the time of retirement can subject the account holder to substantial income tax obligations.

403(b) Plans

Definition

Public schools, colleges, universities, churches, public hospitals, and charitable entities may offer their employees a tax-advantaged retirement savings plan called a 403(b).

This plan is very similar to the 401(k), in that as a plan participant, you can opt to defer some of your salary, which is deposited into a tax-qualified retirement savings account.

What are the tax benefits of a 403(b) plan?	Deposits to a 403(b) account are not subject to income tax in the year of the contribution. Instead, the contributions and any investment income they generate are fully taxable at the time they are withdrawn. Like the 401(k) plans, the deferred income tax treatment of 403(b) plans can result in hefty income tax obligations if distributions are taken in a lump sum.

Rollovers and Transfers

While rollovers, transfers, conversions, and re-characterizations all accomplish the same thing (basically, moving assets from one account or type of account to another), the IRS distinguishes between them, and each is accomplished by a slightly different
method. The explanations below describe the mechanics and implications of the different types of transfers and rollovers for traditional 401(k)s, IRAs, and Roth IRAs. It does not address inherited IRAs, which we will discuss separately when we get to estate planning.

Let's take conversions and re-characterizations first. In 2006, Jo decided to move the funds she had in her traditional IRA into the newly introduced Roth IRA. Expecting an arduous process, she was relieved to find out that all she had to do was to call up her IRA administrator and tell her what she wanted to do. The next day she received a Roth conversion form in the mail, which she filled out and returned to her administrator. The transfer then took place behind the scenes without any further involvement from Jo. The change was reflected in her 2006 tax return, which generated a one-time tax obligation for the amount of the conversion.

If Jo decides at some point that she wants to move her Roth IRA holdings back into a traditional IRA, the IRS will call it a *re-characterization*, even though she will follow virtually the same procedure as she did with the Roth conversion.

Moving funds from an IRA account with one administrator to an IRA account with a second administrator is a slightly different process. The safest, least-expensive, and easiest way to accomplish a transfer of this sort is to do a *trustee-to-trustee transfer*. Like the conversion and re-characterization, a trustee-to-trustee transfer is executed by signing a form in which you provide the transfer instructions. Upon receipt of your written instructions, the first administrator will transfer the funds directly to the second plan administrator. You'll see why this is safer and less expensive when we look at the indirect rollover.

If you instruct your plan administrator to do so, he or she will write you a check for the balance in the account. This is called a *lump-sum distribution*, even if you intend to deposit it into another qualifying account. Once you receive your check, the IRS will give you 60 days in which to deposit it into another tax-qualified savings account, like an IRA or another 401(k), or your distribution will become permanent and generate a tax obligation on the full amount. Early withdrawal penalties may also apply.

If you make your deadline and deposit the funds into a qualified savings account, you can exhale the breath you've been holding for 60 days, because the IRS will now consider it an *indirect rollover*, instead of a lump-sum distribution.

Employing an indirect rollover involves one more wrinkle too. Because neither the plan administrator nor the IRS has any assurance that you will meet the 60-day deadline, your administrator will be required to withhold 20 percent for taxes before writing the check. You are free to deposit an amount equal to 100 percent of the original account balance, but here's the rub. Because 20 percent of it will be tied up until after you file your next tax return, you'll have to come up with the difference from some other source. The money can come from anywhere—from your non-IRA savings, from a home-equity loan (not generally a good idea), or borrowing it from a friend or relative. But, if you can't come up with the cash within that narrow 60-day window of opportunity, you're sunk. You cannot deposit it the following week or the following year. That's why we will caution you again and again to avoid indirect rollovers. Your opportunities to contribute or roll over funds to your IRA are limited. Don't waste a single one of them.

If your new employer accepts funds from a previous employer, you have the option of doing a *direct rollover.** This is accomplished by simply instructing the old plan administrator to transfer the balance in your account directly to the new plan administrator.*

When you change jobs, you also have the option of instructing your plan administrator to do a *direct rollover to a traditional IRA*. Like the trustee-to-trustee transfer between IRA accounts and the direct rollover between two 401(k) accounts, this method will take place as a transaction between the account administrators.* The receiving account will be characterized as a rollover IRA and will hold only the funds rolled over from employer retirement accounts.

Rollover IRA: A traditional or Roth IRA that holds assets that originated from an employer-sponsored retirement plan.

The IRS requires that rollovers from an employer plan go directly into another employer plan or into a traditional IRA. From a traditional IRA, they can later be converted to a Roth IRA. By keeping these funds separate from your other IRA assets, you reserve the option of later rolling them into another employer-sponsored plan. But once they are co-mingled with your other IRAs, you lose that flexibility.

TIP: Using a direct rollover your money retains its tax-sheltered status you avoid the 20 percent withholding, and you avoid any chance of being charged the 10 percent early withdrawal penalty.

CHAPTER THREE

Keeping What's Yours

Anyone may so arrange his affairs that his taxes shall be as low as possible; he is not bound to choose that pattern which will best pay the Treasury; there is not even a patriotic duty to increase one's taxes.

–JUSTICE LEARNED HAND

There are almost as many theories about how much money it will take to fund a comfortable retirement, as there are ways to make that money. Not only do theories vary, but individual circumstances vary also, as do definitions of exactly what defines "retiring rich."

Jo Moneymaker's goal started out relatively modestly. When she went to visit her financial planner, Bill, security was her primary consideration. At the very least, she wanted to be able to maintain her standard of living and to feel confident that she had enough money socked away to allow for inflation and unexpected expenses and to cover her medical expenses. Anything she managed to save beyond that amount would be the icing on her retirement party cake, so to speak.

Bill had promptly labeled that vision as little more than a plan for a cookie-cutter, tract-home retirement and recommended an extreme makeover of her entire strategy. Without realizing it, Jo is already starting to think of the project in those terms; she's doing more than getting her financial house in order—she's custom-designing the comfort and security for the second half of her life.

Once Bill pointed out the mathematical possibilities and showed her how she could keep a bigger after-tax share of that cake, she's been allowing herself a new vision—a vision that includes world travel and year-round golf—maybe even a second retirement home in the Sunbelt or starting her own business. That kind of retirement vision comes with a hefty price tag, and she's seen firsthand that too many people reach retirement without enough money set aside to cover that price tag. She also knows the reason is because making money is hard work, and keeping what you earn is even harder. Not as hard as she'd imagined, however, now that Bill has shown her how.

The Big Stick of the IRS

The U.S. tax code is based on the principle of levying taxes on money any time it switches hands. The conditions under which monetary transfers are exempt from taxation are complex, rigid, and backed by the big stick of the IRS. That means that even if she is successful in accumulating a degree of wealth, taxes could undo all of her hard work in the time it takes to write *Joanne Moneymaker* on the wrong form at the wrong time.

The other principle she has learned in talking with Bill is that most tax professionals, whether they are of the legal sort or the bean-counter sort, have been trained to keep you from getting on the wrong side of the IRS. As a result, more times than not, their advice will guide you right back into that little cookie-cutter retirement plan that keeps you from building wealth and then offers up sacrificial tax dollars to keep the tax monster at bay.

When Jo changed jobs, she was given a grace period in which she could decide what she wanted to do with the funds in her 401(k) account. At any time before the end of the grace period, she can instruct the plan administrator to issue a check to her for the balance in the account. Once the check is issued, she will have 60 days to deposit it in another qualified account without incurring any taxes or penalties.

But what happens if Jo misses that 60-day deadline? We already talked briefly about how money changing hands can trigger a taxable event and that if Jo fails to roll the funds from her 401(k) to another qualified plan within the allotted time period, the IRS will treat it as a lump-sum distribution. For Jo, that would have several implications.

- Her lump-sum distribution will be subject to a 10 percent early withdrawal penalty. Because Jo is more than two decades shy of the 59½-year age requirement for penalty-free distributions, if she fails to roll her 401(k) into another qualified account the IRS will help itself to $20,000 of her retirement savings, right off the top.

- Jo will lose a sizable portion of the $200,000 to taxes. Contributions to a 401(k) are treated as tax-deferred income, and those contributions, any employer matching funds and all investment income earned within the 401(k) are then taxed as ordinary income in the year they are withdrawn.

Jo's current salary and non-tax-sheltered investment income give her a taxable income of $71,000 a year and place her near the upper limit of $71,950 for the 25 percent tax bracket. (See Table 8.) An increase in her taxable income of just $951 will move her to the next higher tax bracket, which means that she will be paying taxes on more income, and she will be paying a higher tax rate on the additional income. (See Table 9.) For Jo, that means her tax will increase by $62,014 ($76,429 less $14,415) and that she will lose 38 percent of her $200,000 to taxes by taking a lump-sum distribution. Even the 10 percent penalty is included as taxable income.

Losing that $20,000 in penalties and $62,014 to taxes is bad enough. To make matters worse, she would also lose the income-earning potential of more than 40 percent of her 401(k) money.

- Once the funds in her 401(k) have been taken as a lump-sum distribution, they lose their tax-sheltered status—forever. That's right. Lump-sum distributions operate like a one-way door. Funds can leave tax-sheltered status, but the door only swings in one direction. Once removed, Jo will never again have an opportunity to move those funds into either her new employer's 401(k) plan or into an IRA or other tax-qualified retirement plan. From that day forward, everything she earns on the investments made with those funds will be fully taxable as either ordinary income or capital gains.

Table 8. INTERNAL REVENUE TAX TABLE

TAXABLE INCOME IS OVER	BUT NOT OVER	THE TAX IS	PLUS	OF THE AMOUNT OVER
$-	$7,300	$-	10%	$-
$7,300	$29,700	$730	15%	$7,300
$29,700	$71,950	$4,090	25%	$29,700
$71,950	$150,150	$14,653	28%	$71,950
$150,150	$326,450	$36,549	33%	$150,150
$326,450	$-	$94,728	35%	$326,450

Table 9. JO'S TAX ON LUMP-SUM DISTRIBUTION

JO'S 2015 TAXABLE SALARY AND NON-SHELTERED INVESTMENT INCOME	JO'S 401(K) LUMP-SUM DISTRIBUTION	JO'S 2015 TOTAL TAXABLE INCOME	JO'S 2015 BASE TAX IS	PLUS	JO'S 2015 TOTAL FEDERAL TAX
$71,000	$-	$71,000	$4,090	$10,325	$14,415
$71,000	$200,000	$271,000	$36,549	$39,881	$76,429

Clearly, Jo has very strong motivation to make every effort to ensure that she does not miss her rollover deadline. Based on what she learned from her meeting with Bill, she has decided to move her 401(k) into a self-directed traditional IRA. Rolling it into a Roth IRA is not an option at this point. IRS rules stipulate that only assets held in a traditional IRA can be transferred to a Roth IRA, and there will be a one-year waiting period before she can do a Roth conversion on any of those funds. Even if IRS rules permitted rolling her 401(k) assets into a Roth IRA at this time, there is another good reason not to do it— at least not yet. Taxes.

Between the 401(k) plan, traditional IRA, and Roth IRAs, only Roth contributions are taxed up front. It follows, then, that Roth distributions are also the only ones that are typically tax-exempt. Traditional IRAs and 401(k) s are exactly the opposite, which suits Jo just fine. She likes the idea of simply continuing the tax-deferred status of her 401(k) for the time being. If she later decides to transfer some of it to a Roth, she can do so in a time frame that makes sense in the total scheme of things.

Transferring Her Existing Roth IRA

Jo has the option of transferring her existing Roth IRA to a self-directed account, also. For now, she's leaning toward splitting up the move. If she moves at least a portion of it to a self-directed account, she'll gain additional flexibility with a larger percentage of her IRA savings. If she ultimately chooses an administrator that offers brokerage services as well as non-traditional IRA investment services, she might decide to move the rest of it, too. Again, she doesn't have to make every decision at once.

When she is ready to make the move, she can follow any of the procedures for a rollover or transfer laid out in Chapter Two. It bears, though, repeating that a direct trustee-to-trustee transfer is always the safest method of transferring assets between IRAs because it avoids any possibility that an unforeseen event might cause the rollover deadline to be missed.

What About Future Rollovers?

Over the course of her career, Jo could end up changing jobs a number of times. Her future employers might offer 401(k) plans, 403(b) plans, or any one of the family of IRA plans designed for smaller employers. With each job change, she will likely have the option of rolling her company retirement plan over to her self-directed IRA, giving the balance a nice boost each time. In short, she will likely encounter various situations in which she needs to transfer or roll over retirement funds from one account to another. To keep the funds out of the reach of the IRS, she needs to remember a few basic rules:

- Generally speaking, you can do a rollover from any qualified retirement account to a traditional IRA.

- There is no dollar limit on the amount that you can roll over from a qualified retirement plan to a traditional IRA.

- Your rollover transaction does not count against your annual IRA contribution limit.

- Getting 401(k) funds into a Roth account is a two-step process. They must be rolled into a traditional IRA and from there can be rolled into a Roth IRA.

- All indirect rollovers must culminate with the deposit of the funds within 60 days of the distribution date.

- Assets you roll over from an employer retirement plan must remain segregated from your other IRAs to avoid tainting them. Tainted IRA assets retain their tax-free or tax-deferred status, but generally can't be rolled back into another or the same employer-sponsored account later.

- Your Roth IRA contributions (including conversions) are taxed as ordinary income at the time they are made, so you need to have money available to pay the taxes at the time of the transfer or deposit.

Table 10. IRA TRANSFER AND ROLLOVER TAX IMPLICATIONS

IF YOUR ROLLOVER/ TRANSFER STARTS HERE...	... AND ENDS HERE	YOUR ROLLOVER/ TRANSFER IS TAX-FREE	YOUR TRANSFER IS TAXABLE
Traditional IRA	ROTH IRA		X
Roth IRA	Traditional IRA (called a re-characterization)	X	
SEP IRA	Traditional IRA	X	
SIMPLE IRA	Traditional IRA	X	
401(k)	Traditional IRA	X	

Pay Now or Pay Later?

No matter what she decides to do in the long term, Jo first needs to get her 401(k) assets into a traditional IRA. Next year she can decide if converting some of it to a Roth IRA makes sense. In the meantime, she has plenty of time to do her planning.

Benjamin Franklin said, "In this world, nothing is certain but death and taxes." If he's right, then Jo's challenge—and yours and mine too—is to determine when best to pay those taxes to keep them as low as possible. It's the age-old question of whether it will cost less to pay now or to pay later and whether or not she has the available non-IRA cash to pay those taxes, of course. So let's look at Jo's numbers and a few assumptions.

At Bill's recommendation, Jo has compiled a complete inventory of her assets. That means everything from cash to stocks to real estate to life insurance to the red sports car sitting in her garage. Everything. As she compiled her list, she designated each item as liquid or non-liquid. A liquid asset is one that is easily converted to cash. Stocks are considered a liquid asset. Real estate is not, because it can take time to find a buyer and close the sale. You'll see soon why this matters. Table 11 shows Jo's list.

Table 11. JO'S LIQUID AND NONLIQUID ASSETS

JO'S NON-IRA HOLDINGS	MARKET VALUE	LIABILITIES	NON-LIQUID ASSETS	LIQUID ASSETS
Primary residence	$ 350,000	$ 120,000	$ 230,000	
Cash in a money market savings account	$ 5,000			$ 5,000
Treasury notes	$ 155,000			$ 155,000
Gold coins	$ 10,000			$ 10,000
$ 500,000 term life insurance	No cash value			
Promissory note from her cousin Shirley, due in 24 months	$ 10,000		$ 10,000	
Car	$ 23,000	$ 20,000	$ 3,000	
Personal property (personal items and household furnishings)	$ 50,000		$ 50,000	
Total assets	$ 628,000	$ 140,000	$ 293,000	$ 170,000

Table 12. JO'S 401(K) AND IRA NET ASSETS AFTER TAXES AND PENALTIES

ACCOUNT	CURRENT VALUE	NET VALUE AFTER 10% PENALTY FOR EARLY WITHDRAWAL AND TAXES
Total 401(k) holdings	$ 200,000	$ 117,986
Total IRA holdings	$ 140,000	$ 80,786

While the funds in both her 401(k) and Roth IRA accounts are technically liquid, touching them would be worse than foolish. Not only would it cut their value by more than half after taxes and penalties, it would set her back years in her plans for a secure and enjoyable retirement. In Jo's mind, that puts them in the non-liquid column.

Thanks to the sale of her rental property, Jo is sitting with $155,000 in treasury notes at the moment. Her intention has been to use the money to buy another rental unit. With a total of $170,000 in liquid assets, she has the option to reserve some of it to pay the taxes on next year's Roth conversion and use the balance to buy her next rental unit. While she doesn't like the idea of forking over a sizable chunk of it to taxes, she does like the idea that distributions from high-yielding investments within the Roth account would come out tax-free. Fortunately, she has the financial flexibility to take whichever route the analysis leads her.

A Sound Business Objective

Investing is serious business, and every good business decision starts with a justifiable financial basis. So, even though Jo has the option of moving her assets from one IRA account to another, she needs to have a good reason to do it. In short, will it bring her closer to her stated goal of retiring rich? To answer this question, Jo will have to look at the anticipated ROI for a given investment.

Paying the up-front taxes might make sense if Jo expects the return on an investment to exceed the tax obligation generated by moving the cash. On the other hand, if the return is less certain, she might be better off leaving it in the traditional IRA and paying the taxes on both the principal and earnings as she withdraws them as distributions later.

Another consideration is Jo's age. A Roth IRA requires that the funds remain in the account for five years before distribution to avoid penalties. If Jo may need this money, moving it could be counterproductive.

At this point, Jo has developed a tentative plan to move as much as $50,000 into the Roth IRA when her one-year waiting period is up. That's how much she thinks it will take to bring her balance up to the threshold where she can afford to buy a rental property within her account and get it ready for occupancy. At her age, she doesn't have to worry about the five-year rule, but to validate her plan, she needs to figure out what sort of a return she expects the investment to yield and whether it would be sufficient to make up for the taxes generated by the Roth conversion.

The transfer will generate approximately $14,000 in additional tax obligations in the year that she makes the transfer, but if she can pull $7,000 a year in net profit out of the investment, she will earn the tax expense back in short order. The real payback will come when she sells the property, provided the value of the property increases between the time she buys it and the time she sells it, of course. And because the property will be held within a Roth IRA, she will not have to pay capital gains tax on the profits, meaning that her earnings on the new property will be tax-free even when she withdraws them as part of her retirement distributions.

These are conservative estimates, but Jo is aware that circumstances could change. When it comes time to actually execute the plan, reality could end up looking considerably different from her present-day vision, making the payment of the up-front taxes a bit of a gamble against her profit expectations. This is why Jo has chosen to keep the bulk of her assets in the traditional IRA for the foreseeable future and move only a portion into the Roth account. She can always adjust her plan as time goes on, as long as she waits one year between transfers.

Part and parcel of this decision is the fact that Jo is still in her mid-30s. She has at least 20 years and perhaps 30 or more years before she will need to use the money in her IRAs. During the course of those 20 or 30 years, any assets in her traditional IRA that have been converted to a Roth will likely be turned over numerous times in a long string of investments. So recouping her prepaid taxes for the conversion does not have to be considered in terms of one single investment. It is Jo's choice, however, to apply this type of analysis as a reality check and to make sure that she is proceeding with a specific goal in mind.

Undoing Good Planning

In Chapter One, you looked at examples that demonstrated the power of compound earnings on Jo's self-directed IRAs. In fact, compounded growth over the maximum period of time is the very foundation of her retirement wealth-building strategy. It is the flexibility and tax-favored treatment of IRAs that makes it possible. That's why Jo's overriding objective will be to manage her investments in complete accordance with the rules that govern IRA accounts. The alternatives get ugly.

Even if Jo succeeds in getting her money into her IRA account without triggering an unintentional taxable event, she still has to be mindful of how the assets are used. Remember when we referred to the built-in gotcha of the IRS? It works like this.

The ERISA rules that established IRAs basically returned control over your financial future to you, where it belongs. Some ERISA rules, however, work to ensure that neither your IRA, nor the taxes the IRS waives or defers for the benefit of your retirement savings, ends up being abused. Those rules establish parameters for the way you manage your IRA, rather like an electronic fence that keeps the cattle where the rancher wants them. You're free to move about with your investments anywhere within the defined perimeter. But touch the fence and you get zapped.

And how do you suppose the IRS zaps you? By taking away the tax-favored status of the account. That's right. The penalty can be levied not only on the funds used for that particular investment, but on all the funds in the account. So if Jo violates IRS excluded transaction rules, the IRS can treat the transaction as a lump-sum distribution of the entire account—immediately and forever. No do-overs allowed. By now, we shouldn't have to tell you what that means in terms of taxes and early withdrawal penalties.

CLASSIFIED CASE STUDY

Guidant Financial

Advice from Guidant Financial:

The legal consequences of prohibited transactions are bad news. Even in an IRA – a prohibited transaction is an automatic, self-executing disqualification of the entire IRA.

With a 401K or a qualified plan, if you have a prohibited transaction with a qualified plan there is an elaborate "get right with God" program, in which you can confess your sins and receive absolution. It's gong to cost you some dough, but you're going to eventually get this thing squared away and go on with life and never have to see it again. Not so with an IRA.

With an IRA, it's over. The disqualification is retroactive to January 1 of that year, and the entire IRA is disqualified. So if you have a prohibited transaction for $100, and you have a $1 million IRA, you've disqualified the entire IRA. So if you step on the pooch on December 31 for $100, you've disqualified a $1 million IRA back to January 1. Not good. The disqualification is an immediate taxable event. The tax is on the entire amount. Plus if you're under the age of 59.5, there's an excise tax, early distribution penalty... So it's just as bad as that gets.

Prohibited Transactions

You already know that those rules permit Jo to own real estate within her self-directed IRA and that the IRS has specific restrictions on how that property can be used—and by whom. The basis for those rules is tied to the objectives on which IRA accounts were initially established: namely, for the sole purpose of benefiting individual retirement security. By extension, you can see that if Jo personally occupies a home or business property that is held in the IRA, she gains benefit now and deprives the account of the chance to earn the money it would bring in if it were collecting rental income.

So rule number one is that Jo cannot use any property held within her IRA as her primary or part-time residence. Likewise, she cannot rent it out to any of her direct descendants or ancestors. In short, Jo cannot rent it out to her parents or grandparents or to her children or grandchildren. If she marries, her spouse cannot occupy it; nor can his children, grandchildren, parents, or grandparents. The same restrictions apply to anyone involved in the administration of Jo's account. So who does that leave—besides strangers, of course? Plenty of people. Here's a quick and easy cheat sheet for speedy reference.

Table 13. WHO CAN USE/OCCUPY A PROPERTY OWNED BY JO'S IRA?

YES	NO
Jo's... ❑ Aunts, uncles, cousins ❑ Brothers, sisters ❑ In-laws (parents-in-law, brothers/sisters-in-law) ❑ Stepparents, step-grandparents, stepchildren (but not adopted children)	**Jo's...** ❑ Spouse ❑ Ancestors (parents, grandparents, great-grandparents) ❑ Lineal descendants (children, adopted children, grandchildren) ❑ Spouses of lineal descendants (sons- and daughters-in-law)
Jo's IRA administrator's... ❑ Aunts, uncles, cousins ❑ Brothers, sisters ❑ In-laws (parents-in-law, brothers/sisters-in-law) ❑ Stepparents, step-grandparents, stepchildren (but not adopted children)	**Jo's IRA administrator and her administrator's...** ❑ Spouse ❑ Ancestors (parents, grandparents, great- grandparents) ❑ Lineal descendants (children, adopted children, grandchildren) ❑ Spouses of lineal descendants (sons- and daughters-in-law)

The basis for the restrictions is an assumption that in a transaction with close family members, Jo might be motivated more by charity for her family than a desire to build her retirement account and make money. So, to avoid any potential conflict of interest, the IRA prohibits transactions with these individuals. This does not mean that she can't rent it out to her sister or brother or uncle, however.

Similar restrictions apply to business property also. IRS rules say that a business in which Jo holds greater than a 49 percent ownership cannot occupy property held in her IRA. To do so would be considered self-dealing, and self-dealing is strictly forbidden.

Let's look at a scenario in which Jo and her cousin Shirley form a business partnership. We'll assume for this example that Jo and Shirley will each hold a 50 percent interest in the business. We'll also assume that Jo has already purchased a condo as an IRA investment, and it is currently vacant. She and Shirley are thinking that, since they are going to be recruiting a number of new employees, the company could lease the condo from her IRA and use it for housing employment candidates when they come to town for interviews and house-hunting trips. They agree that the company will pay fair market value for the lease and will even cover a portion of the cost of the homeowners' association fee, since their guests will be using the recreational facilities while they are staying at the condo. It sounds like a win-win arrangement for all concerned, right? Wrong.

True, the company would be paying fair market value for the use of the property. It would also be paying some of the homeowners' association fees, which would increase Jo's annual return by over a thousand dollars. But, the IRS rules explicitly say that because Jo owns more than 49 percent of the business, the arrangement would taint her entire IRA, and all the assets in it would lose their tax-advantaged treatment. Ouch!

There is a simple solution, however. Certainly, the company could lease a different property. Or Jo and Shirley could renegotiate their partnership. If Jo limits her ownership interest to *49 percent or less*, then the company would be operating completely within IRS rules when it leases the condo from Jo's IRA.

Given the hefty penalties for violations, Jo might be tempted to merely walk away from a number of fruitful transactions for fear of running afoul of IRS rules. Unfortunately, that would have the effect of shuffling her right back into the narrow box her bank and stockbroker have had her in for years. A better solution is to seek good advice from qualified advisors and use diligence on her part to follow that advice. That's where her lawyer, CPA, and perhaps most of all, her account administrator come into play.

PART TWO

Laying a Solid Foundation

"The beginning is the most important part of the work."

—PLATO

CHAPTER FOUR

Choosing an Administrator

The first 9 pages of the Internal Revenue Code define income; the remaining 1,100 pages spin the web of exceptions and preferences.

–WARREN G. MAGNUSON

When Jo went looking for an administrator for her very first IRA, she got in the car and drove straight to her bank. The personal services representative there helped her to open an IRA account and place her first contribution into a high-interest certificate of deposit until Jo had a chance to decide what else she might do with the money. A year later, she moved her funds to a new IRA account with a stockbroker, whom she picked because of the online services and deep-discount commission offered. This is not the approach she will want to follow this time around.

Of course, Jo will want to choose a self-directed IRA administrator that offers the services she wants at a price that won't eat up her profits. But first and foremost, she absolutely must find one that she can trust to give her accurate information about what is and is not allowed with regard to her account. The risks are too great to settle for anything less.

Custodians, Trustees, and Administrators: What's the Difference?

A general understanding of what constitutes an administrator was enough for Jo during her preliminary investigations, but now that she's about to go in search of one, it's time to get down to specifics. From a distance, the lines of demarcation between a custodian, a trustee, and an administrator may seem blurry. Up close, the picture becomes more distinct.

Most people are familiar with the concept of a trust, wherein assets are owned by the trust on behalf of the beneficiary. The trust has limited fiduciary authority over the trust assets, but is obligated by law to act in the best interest of the beneficiary. An IRA trustee arrangement is very similar.

> **Fiduciary:** A person or institution with a special relationship of financial trust or responsibility to others.

In contrast, a custodian serves as a repository for the assets. A custodian holds the assets on behalf of, and exercises the instructions of, the account holder. Other than following those instructions and acting prudently regarding the manner in which the assets are held, a custodian has no fiduciary obligations to the account holder. Because a custodian actually holds the assets on behalf of the account holder, additional federal and state licensing and certifications may be required. Furthermore, custodians are required to remain neutral in regard to guiding a client's investment decisions, limiting their role to the conveyance of IRS regulations and their own company policies. In other words, Jo's custodian won't give her investment advice, but will tell her if the investment she wants to pursue complies with IRS rules.

IRS Code sets out very specific requirements for who can serve as a trustee or custodian of an IRA account. Federal law says that a trustee or custodian may only be a bank, savings and loan association, or credit union, as defined under 408(n), *except that other individuals and institutions may qualify to serve as custodians, provided they have obtained approval by the IRS to do so.*

By contrast, an IRA administrator neither holds assets nor has any fiduciary authority over the assets within the account. An administrator does the paperwork. "But so do trustees and custodians," you say. Of course they do. So let's look at how an administrator differs from a trustee or custodian by considering the rose.

A rose is a flower. All roses are flowers, but not all flowers are roses. Likewise, all trustees and custodians can administer, but not all administrators are legally permitted to be custodians or trustees.

Table 14. IRA ADMINISTRATOR'S DUTIES

An administrator will typically handle the paperwork on behalf of the account holder and trustee/custodian, for the following activities:
❏ Administering the process of opening and closing the IRA account.
❏ Receiving and accurately applying contributions to the IRA account.
❏ Executing transfers, rollovers, and distributions.
❏ Acting as a conduit for the account holder's transaction instructions.
An administrator is not permitted to hold account assets.

More often than not, companies offering self-directed IRA administration are structured in such a way that they have an administrator positioned up front to act as the interface for day-to-day routine activities. Behind the scenes, they work closely with the trustee and custodian, which hold the assets, tend to the IRS reporting activities, and approve or disapprove transactions based on IRS rules.

Compare it to an IRA with a stockbroker. When you opened the IRA, the account was established with your broker, but the paperwork designated a separate company to act as your trustee/custodian.

When you call your broker's office with an instruction to buy or sell a particular stock or fund, you speak to a licensed broker who passes your order on through the system where the trustee ultimately records it. To be sure that you don't violate IRS rules or company policies, the broker is thoroughly trained on what types of instructions he or she can and cannot accept from you.

If you instruct your broker to buy land in Idaho with the funds in your account, you will be turned down flat, because he or she knows that the trustee is not set up to handle land sales. If your broker is unsure of the rules, however, he or she will find out what the rules are regarding land purchases within your IRA account.

Now consider how it will work if Jo has an account established with an administrator, and she calls with an investment idea that is clearly against company policy or IRS rules—perhaps buying a collection of old coins, for example. The administrator tells her that collectibles—and old coins are considered collectibles—are prohibited transactions within an IRA, so she can't legally do so. If the administrator is uncertain about the request, he or she will bump it up to the in-house expert. If the answer is sill unclear, the question will go to the custodian.

If Jo has chosen her administrator well, the firm will have the in-house expertise to save her the time and expense of having to consult with the custodian on relatively routine matters.

CLASSIFIED CASE STUDY

Guidant Financial

Tips From Guidant Financial:

The term "self-directed" can be misleading when talking about retirement investing. Many investment firms would have you believe it simply means choosing which mutual funds to invest in for retirement. Fortunately, it means much more. Self-directed investing can include investments in both traditional investments, like stocks & mutual funds and non-traditional investments, like real estate and businesses. You can have the control to truly diversify your retirement funds in any number of investments. A truly self-directed retirement plan creates opportunity for investors to stick to their core competencies…to invest in what they know and understand.

Typically, you need to decide also have to choose which type of investments you want to purchase before you decide which type of self directed IRA you'll need. If all you want to do is invest in stocks, bonds and mutual funds…then call a stockbroker. However, if you want to invest in real estate or paper assets like notes or tax liens on top of securities – a self directed IRA custodian or facilitator is probably your best option.

Interviewing Prospective Administrators

Choosing any service provider is a mix of objective and subjective evaluations. Services offered could end up being no more important to you than a company's hours of operation or whether your contact person has an annoying habit of chewing gum on the job. At the same time, there is a core list of questions that should be presented to every prospective administrator that quantifies what they have to offer. Jo has such a list. She's also added a few questions that she hopes will either instill confidence in the honesty and integrity of each company or sound a warning alarm.

Hopefully, she'll end up with enough objective information to eliminate the chaff and sufficient subjective observations to whittle the remainder down to a few good contenders.

1. **What kinds of transactions can you handle?** This first question will tell Jo if she's in the right ballpark. She already has a general sense of the types of investments that interest her. She knows for sure that she wants to invest in real estate and precious metals. She is also pretty certain she wants to buy and sell mortgage notes and maybe even own a partnership share of a business, although that might be a few years away. She's learned that most self-directed IRA administrators can handle real estate transactions and mortgage notes, but she's interested in finding an administrator who can handle all her investments for her, since the idea of changing administrators down the road really doesn't appeal to her at this point. Questioning prospective administrators up front about those transactions will quickly tell Jo whether she should scratch them off her list or proceed to the rest of the questions.

2. **What is the typical turnaround for funding a transaction?** Some firms handle so many clients that days or weeks can pass between the time a transaction is ordered and when it is actually executed. This can cost Jo

opportunities. Some investments, like tax liens, for example have to be paid for within a day of the purchase and IRS rules say that she can't front the money from her personal account and pay herself back later from the IRA.

3. **What are the credentials of your staff?** Finding an administrator with on-staff lawyers, CPAs, and real estate professionals would be a plus for Jo. At the same time, unless they have experience, special training as IRA advisors, and participate in a program for ongoing education, Jo may want to look elsewhere. Laws change, and the IRS continually issues rulings that clarify the interpretations of its rules and regulations. Above all, Jo will want to make sure that the individuals who convey those rules have the latest information.

4. **How long have you been in business?** This question can be a red herring. A young company may not have a clearly defined track record, and it may not have all the wrinkles ironed out of its procedures. At the same time, this is a business where service and attention to detail are paramount. The principals may have brought a wealth of experience to the new enterprise and have the resources available to help you.

    By contrast, a long-established company may offer a larger staff with more diversified experience; yet, it could also be so large that Jo might end up feeling like she's nothing more than a social security number and an annual fee to the staff.

5. **Is the company involved in any current, ongoing, or pending litigation?** Obviously, with this question, Jo wants to determine if her assets are safe with this administrator. Before she moves on, she'll also want to make note of a few related issues too. Evasive answers to any of these questions should sound a warning alarm.

     a.   Are you bonded for theft and fraud?

     b.   Are you insured for errors and omissions?

     c.   Do you provide annual audited reports?

     d.   What are your financial resources?

     e.   May I see your financial statements?

6. **Where do you go for answers to tough questions?** No one knows everything about everything, so if an administrator tries to tell Jo that he or she doesn't need to consult with experts because he or she *is* the expert, it might be time to move on to the next name on the list.

7. **Do you provide investment advice or training to your clients?** Jo is confident that she doesn't really need an administrator to help her screen her investment choices—at least not in the beginning. At some point, however, she's likely to be treading on new territory, and she likes the idea of having an administrator who is readily available to answer her questions and give her a little guidance now and then. She isn't completely certain that she will go that route, however, as the extra hand-holding will likely be accompanied with higher fees as well. Since she is still weighing the pros and cons, she enters a tick mark next to the administrators who answer in the affirmative.

8. **Can you provide automatic sweeps?** In Jo's current IRA account, her unused money is automatically swept into a money market savings account at the end of each day. This means that her money is never sitting completely idle while it waits for her to choose a new investment.

9. **How are your fees structured?** It's rarely wise to buy any product or service based on cost alone. Nevertheless, if one administrator or another deviates from the norm by any substantial amount, Jo will be alerted to ask more questions.

Jo's current IRA costs her less than $100 a year in administration fees. By comparison, self-directed IRAs usually generate administrative fees that range anywhere from a few hundred to over a thousand dollars a year for a $100,000 account.

> **TIP:** IRS rules prohibiting the comingling of IRA and non-IRA funds do not prohibit Jo from paying her administrative fees with funds held outside of her IRA. Many people choose to go that route, because it keeps the fees from becoming a slow leak on their tax-sheltered funds.

The fees for a self-directed IRA are generated at both the administrator level and the custodian/trustee level. To get a complete picture of the costs, Jo will want to ask about both.

Typically, custodians charge a fee for each transaction and may also charge an annual fee for holding the assets as well.

While there are only two basic fee structures for administrators, fee-based and asset-based, the way they package and label them creates a seemingly limitless array of options. To complicate matters, some administrators offer a hybrid fee structure, in which they mix and match both fee-based and asset-based fee schedules.

With a *fee-based* administrator, Jo will be charged either a flat annual fee or a separate fee for each service or transactions, in addition to the fees charged by the custodian/trustee. For example, each purchase or sale of any asset, wire transfer, registration, or re-registration of an asset or distribution will generate a fee from both the custodian and the administrator. Sometimes an administrator will even charge extra for incidentals like postage and photocopying over and above the stated fees, so it's a good idea to ask ahead of time how these things are handled.

An *asset-based* administrator may charge Jo an annual fee, based on either the total value of the assets in her account or on the number and type of assets held in the account. Jo will have to determine which method each asset-based administrator uses and give careful consideration to how she plans to invest her money to know which one is best for her.

If Jo chooses an administrator with a *hybrid* fee structure, she will likely be charged a lower annual fee than with an asset-based structure, along with set fees for certain transactions or services. She'll have to do a thorough analysis to determine if this type of fee structure will cost her more or less over the long haul.

Regardless of whether she chooses a fee-based, asset-based, or hybrid fee administrator, it will be important for Jo compare all the fees from all sources. Surprises are rarely a good thing with financial transactions, and unexpected costs are nothing Jo wants to be faced with when she executes her first investment. Last, but not least, she'll want to find out if she will be charged a termination fee when, and if, she decides to move her assets to a new administrator.

CLASSIFIED CASE STUDY

Company: Equity Trust Company
Location: Equity Trust Company is
a family-run business in Cleveland,
Ohio. More information can be found
one at www.trustetc.com or contacted
by phone at (440) 323-5491.

Services: Equity Trust Company is a non-depository trust chartered by the South Dakota Banking Commission. As a trust company, Equity Trust can provide its clients with a wide array of trust services, including serving as an IRA custodian and as a trustee for individuals, corporations, institutions and employee benefit, stock ownership and retirement plans.

Advice from Equity Trust:

Five important questions for a client to ask a prospective administrator:

• Are they an administrator or custodian, there is a huge difference in regulations between the two. (Custodians are highly regulated.)

• How long have they been in business?

• How are they regulated?

• How is the account protected?

• *How easy is it to do with business with them/what type of support do they offer?*

10. **Where are you located? What are your hours of operation?** Some people like to conduct business face-to-face. For them, choosing an administrator in their local area could be important. Jo, on the other hand, is used to doing business with people thousands of miles away. Still, she may want to know that she has the option of sitting down with her administrator if she undertakes a particularly complicated investment or if she ever has a problem with her account.

11. **Can I access my account online? Can I make changes to my account and submit transaction instructions online?** One of the benefits of the living in the 21st century is the convenience of being able to conduct business from the comfort and convenience of your own home 24/7. This is particularly important to Jo, given the long hours she works at her new job.

Adding It All Up

When Jo finished interviewing and investigating the administrators on her list, she spent a day comparing the answers she received. When she had a handful of companies she liked, she reviewed their locations and found that one of them was located a few blocks from her office. Convenience clinched the deal.

With the decision about a self-directed IRA administrator made, Jo treated herself to a celebratory dinner with a friend. In the morning, she filled out the papers to open the account. Her new administrator guided her through the process of issuing the rollover instructions to her 401(k) plan and the rollover was completed with three days to spare.

CHAPTER FIVE

Jo's Backup Crew

None of us is as smart as all of us.

–KEN BLANCHARD

Over the next several years, Jo plans on investing in everything from basic residential income property to loaning money on mortgage notes. She'll start with investments she has some experience and a reasonable comfort level with and gradually progress to more complex and higher-risk investments.

Even in the beginning, when she's working well within her comfort zone, she's not naive enough to believe she can do it all on her own. Certain jobs will require specialized skills—the kinds that require years of education and experience to master. That's why she's built a network of qualified professionals.

Since Bill got her thinking of herself as general contractor for her retirement extreme makeover, she's switched from referring to them as her Golden Rolodex® (because of the value she places on their expertise) to calling them her subcontractors. It helps her to keep focused on her goals.

Most of her relationships with her subcontractors date back to the days when she bought her first home. Now it's time for the years spent nurturing her relationships with them to really pay off. Each of them will play a vital role in increasing her profits and keeping her on the straight and narrow where the IRS is concerned.

Real Estate Agent

Jo has been working with the same real estate agent for over 10 years. A good part of the agent's job will be to flush out investment opportunities for Jo, but she'll do much more than that.

She'll give Jo a hand with her due diligence by gathering together much of the information Jo will need, like a list of selling prices for similar properties and the going rate for rentals in the area, for example. She will also write up the contract and handle the contract work, negotiations with the seller, and other purchase-related tasks. Even if Jo finds a property on her own, she can hire her agent to represent her on the sale or simply to assist her from the sidelines.

Working with a real estate agent can add a bit of expense to a transaction, but it might well be one of the best bargains available, given what it would cost to hire out the work item by item.

Licensed Home Inspector

There's no doubt about it. Jo is more than capable of handling property inspections on her own. She's very knowledgeable about construction and whatever she doesn't know, a very close friend of hers does.

That being said, Jo is buying this property within her IRA. More than in any other circumstance, she wants to be absolutely certain that the property is both sound and worth every penny she will have to pay for it. That's why she'll hire the services of a licensed home inspector.

Sure, it will cost her a few hundred dollars. But, if the inspector discovers a major problem, saving Jo from a bad deal will make the inspection fee look like pocket change.

Title Insurance Company

When the title for real estate passes from owner to owner, any and all encumbrances to the title pass with it. The purpose of title insurance is to convey an assurance to the new owner that the title is free of liens and other defects. That assurance is backed up by insurance that says that if the title company makes a mistake in researching the property's history, they will pay to clear up the problems.

Typically, the purchaser of the title insurance in a real estate transaction selects the title insurance company. Depending on local custom, the seller or the purchaser of property may pay for title insurance as part of the deal; this is usually a negotiable item. In truth, there are probably only small differences between one title company and another. Nevertheless, Jo is on a first-name basis with the employees of the title company she used for her previous real estate purchases, so she will ask her real estate agent to use the company of her choice. Rarely does any one party to a real estate transaction have a preference, so the seller will probably agree. If so, Jo will have one less thing to worry about, knowing that the work will be completed on time and in a quality manner.

Title insurance is an often overlooked but critical part of any real estate transaction. Old Spanish land grants going back to the 1500's; claims by Native American tribes, outstanding tax liens or warrants, previously deeded ground, air or mineral rights, all can have a critical impact on a buyer's ability to enjoy newly purchased real estate without undue worry. Title insurance guarantees that a buyer takes land with the assurance that if anything crops up in the future, the Title Insurance Company will fix it, either by clearing the title or by paying back to the purchaser the full purchase price of the property if the title cannot be cleared.

Self-Directed IRA Administrator

This book already discussed the functions of an administrator and how important it is for Jo to choose one who is backed up by a team of experts in the field. If Jo is wise, she will nurture this new relationship as carefully as she has with her other team of professionals. Jo's administrator, after all, is the one who makes sure that everything with her account runs smoothly.

Property Manager

Finding a property manager to prepare the property for rental, find a tenant, and then collect the rent and manage maintenance issues will be a snap for Jo. She already has an established relationship with the property manager she used for the rental property she owned for five years. If Jo were  new to the business, however, or if the property were out of her local area, she could ask her real estate agent or IRA administrator for recommendations.

Loan Officer or Mortgage Broker

It is perfectly legal for Jo to obtain financing for the purchase of assets inside her IRA. As always, there are certain IRS rules that govern that financing, which we'll go into in Chapter Eight. Those restrictions could limit Jo's choice of a lender as well, so Jo will want to allow plenty of time to locate a suitable lender if and when she makes the decision to go that route.

More than likely, she will start her search for a lender with her own bank, where she is already known. If she finds that their underwriting policies do not permit loaning money on IRA assets (or if the terms are less than satisfactory), she has other options too. She can contact a mortgage broker or begin calling the professionals in her Golden Rolodex® for recommendations until she finds a lender she's comfortable adding to her list of trusted subcontractors.

Lawyer

Hopefully, you're getting the picture that keeping on the right side of the IRS is absolutely crucial when it comes to investing IRA assets. As important as that is, let's not get so focused on IRS rules that we forget about the other important jobs Jo's attorney will do for her.

Let's assume that Jo is lucky and her attorney has plenty of experience in all the areas she's going to need. In real life, that may not be the case. So maybe you'll need to line up a couple of different attorneys, so you can call on the right expert for the job.

The need for a lawyer with tax and IRA experience is a given. That way, if Jo is ever uncertain of the advice her administrator dishes out, she's got someone to call for a second opinion. An attorney with strong real estate and contract law experience ranks a close second—especially if Jo becomes involved with mortgage notes and real estate options. When and if Jo wants to purchase tax liens, she might want to ask her lawyer to check the legal postings for potential leads on available properties and then to help her with the due diligence.

A transaction doesn't have to be complicated to require an attorney. Even for something as straightforward as buying residential real estate directly from the property owner, Jo's lawyer should draw up the contract or at least review the one prepared by the seller. Sometimes she may want her lawyer to act as an escrow agent as well.

Again, the services of an attorney cost money; sometimes, a lot of money. But, in the end, a good lawyer is cheap insurance against making costly mistakes. And, because of his or her legal network, your attorney can be an excellent source for locating investment opportunities too.

Accountant

Jo's finances have reached the point where a good tax accountant with lots of IRA experience is an absolute must. The accountant will also be a valuable resource when Jo gets ready to invest in a business or analyzes the cash flow of complex investments.

Will Jo need each and every one of her subcontractors on each and every investment? Of course not. Some she will call more often than others. But she has a solid crew of professionals lined up for those times when anything short of an expert simply won't do.

CLASSIFIED CASE STUDY

Advice From Equity Trust:

The financial powers of IRAs are tremendous, and most people want to control their own financial future—that is where we help our clients. With self-directed IRAs you can harness the power of IRAs and invest in what you know best, whether you want to invest in stocks, real estate or private placements.

One of the biggest mistakes you see an account holder making is titling his investments incorrectly. Instead of being titled in a person's own name, it has to be titled in the custodian's name for the benefit of the IRA owners. For example: Equity Trust Company Custodian FBO (for the benefit of) IRA owner's name.

LEGAL TIP: When hiring a real estate broker, property manager, mortgage broker, lawyer, accountant or inspector, always make sure that the professional carries "Errors and Omissions" liability insurance, otherwise known as professional malpractice insurance. If you have a problem with an uninsured professional, you may have no financial recourse to recover your damages. If the professional is insured, then at least you can recover up to the limits of the liability policy to ameliorate your damages and losses due to professional negligence.

CHAPTER SIX

Managing Risk

Take calculated risks. That is quite different from being rash.

–GEORGE PATTON

After years of managing her finances, investing in the stock market, and owning rental property, Jo considers herself a reasonably savvy investor. Her expertise didn't come without a few missteps, however. Along the way she took some chances. She ended up regretting some of them. Of course, every mistake comes with a lesson, and the most important lessons pertain to something we'll be talking a lot about in the coming chapters: the risk-reward relationship.

Beware the Pundits

You'll often hear investment experts (most often someone with something to sell) utter profundities, like "The greater the risk, the greater the potential reward." Perhaps you're picking nits, but you'll find this particular theory troublesome. It implies that risk and reward share a fixed relationship, which is simply not true—at least, not beyond the glare of the casino lights.

It's easy enough to quantify the odds associated with games of chance. Sometimes they are even posted on the rolling marquee. They're based on fixed rules of mathematics, so before you walk through the door, you know the risks—or at least you should. You know the potential reward. You know what you stand to lose if the risk doesn't pay off. By contrast, neither the risks nor the potential reward for an investment are fixed or even assured.

Although the degree of risk can vary from extremely low to hair-raising, some element of risk is an ever-present factor in any investment. Potential reward, on the other hand, can range from zero to windfall.

You read the last sentence correctly, and it's so important that we'll state it again: Potential reward can range from zero to windfall. That's because sometimes a potential reward never existed in the first place, as can be the case with fraud or faulty analysis. Then, there is the investor who gets really lucky and the investment outperforms the most optimistic projections.

This disconnect is why you tend to think of risk and reward as the two wings on an airplane. The pilot needs both of them to get the plane off the ground and safely back down again. If they're not carefully matched or if either contains structural deficiencies, the flight will be doomed before takeoff. Only a pilot who is also a fool would try to fly a craft without carefully inspecting them before each and every flight.

Greater Risk Does Not Always Equal Greater Reward. Never Trust. Always Verify.

In other words, potential profit may be more illusion than fact. Likewise, risks that initially seem reasonable, on closer investigation, may turn out to be anything but. Both potential profit and risk must be identified, verified, and accurately evaluated. Like the offer Jo received from her neighbor.

He has an apple tree in his backyard, and he has told Jo that she is welcome to help herself to all the apples she'd like. All she has to do is walk across the street to get them, so Jo might think this is a pretty good offer—until she discovers that the fruit is long past its prime.

Let's assume, though, that she has verified that they are the brightest, shiniest, reddest apples ever. The only problem is that getting to the apples involves a bit of risk. Perhaps speeding traffic zipping up and down the street. Or a thunderstorm that makes stepping outside feel like a sword dance. They would have to be mighty good apples for Jo to be willing to venture across the street to snatch one under those circumstances. Or maybe Jo will decide to get her apples from the local produce stand if there is a big, toothy, snarly dog loose in the neighbor's backyard.

What reward—or potential reward—would it take to get Jo to try making friends with the neighbor's dog? Bigger apples? More exotic apples? Maybe a tree that produces fine Belgian chocolates instead of apples? How about one that drops $100 bills on the ground every morning? Once she knows how much she's willing to risk, Jo needs to verify the true nature of the fruit before committing herself to the venture.

How much reward justifies how much risk is a question that only Jo can answer. And since this is a book about investing retirement savings, the question warrants serious consideration.

If Jo wants to pick from the money tree to feather her retirement nest, she needs a three-step strategy:

- To find the rare one that sits in a wide-open, grassy meadow.

- To find a way to tame the snarly dog that guards the trees.

- And, perhaps most important, to learn to recognize the snarly dogs that cannot be tamed at all.

It may be true that there is a decided shortage of easy-picking money trees, but it is also true that most dogs can be tamed—if you know how to go about it.

Taming Risk

Any discussion of risk must begin with a discussion of the most personal of subjects: risk tolerance. Some people actually jump off a platform 130 feet above a canyon floor with nothing but a glorified rubber band attached to their waists. Others think twice before climbing aboard a Ferris wheel at the state fair. For the purposes of our discussion, we'll go for the middle ground. We'll assume that if you're reading this book, you've graduated beyond Ferris wheels. At the same time, we'll assume that, at least  where your retirement savings are concerned, you're somewhere short of bungee jumping. We'll hope you're not likely to blow your wad on the pass line.

Jo has a moderate risk tolerance. She enjoys a leisurely Ferris wheel ride once in a while and even an occasional roller-coaster ride. Most of the time, she prefers the rides that fall somewhere in between. Regardless of which ride she's on, however, she avoids unnecessary risks. The same thing is true of her investments.

There are three ways to tame the risk in any venture. First and foremost is something called *due diligence*, which is another way to refer to doing your homework. Next in line is having a plan—or a sound financial basis—for any investment. Finally, there are ways to fine-tune the structure of the deal to mitigate risk. Let's look at each one individually.

Due Diligence: Exposing the Facts

It's time to visit our good friend Dick again. He's got an interesting story to tell about one of his investments, and you might see yourself or someone you know in it.

Dick was watching television one night when the phone rang. It was his brother-in-law calling to give him a hot tip on a ground-floor opportunity. A reliable source at work had heard that the company was about to be bought out by its biggest competitor. When it happened, the stock would double almost overnight. As they hung up, his brother-in-law chided him for his low risk tolerance and told him he'd be a fool not to jump in on this once-in-a-lifetime opportunity.

Well, Dick is no fool, so he dashed to his computer, logged onto his brokerage account and entered an order to buy a thousand shares when the market opened in the morning. He went to bed feeling prouder than proud that he'd taken a bold step toward wealth.

Poor Dick. He couldn't have been more wrong. Over the next weeks and months, the stock drifted lower and lower, and no buyout materialized. When it was down to less than half the price he paid for it, he sold his shares, cursed his brother-in-law, and grumbled about how the average person can't make any money in the market.

Dick may never have made any money on that particular stock, but he could have kept from losing money, which is at least as important. How? By exercising *due diligence.* Simply put, that means to *diligently* work to learn everything possible about the investment before diving headlong into it. It sounds simple enough, doesn't it? While the concept is simple, actually doing it is anything but. Not for the stock market. Not for real estate; and not for any other investment. It takes effort, and it takes a certain level of skill.

Some people, like Jo, have the expertise required to conduct most of their own due diligence. Others don't. Some are willing to learn. Others won't. Whether you're in the *can* category or in the *can't* or *won't* category, sooner or later, you're going to need the services of an expert. Fortunately for Jo, she's got the crack team of subcontractors we talked about earlier.

Every transaction that Jo will execute within her self-directed IRA will involve one or more members of her team of professionals. Some of their functions will be routine administrative activities, like issuing or receiving funds or filing paperwork with the appropriate governmental agencies. Other times, her experts will help her to locate investment opportunities. By far, their most critical contribution to Jo's plan to retire rich will be to help conduct due diligence. This includes everything from evaluating the inherent risks and potential rewards for each investment to helping Jo protect herself from fraud.

Plan: Have One and Stick to It

There's an old question that asks, *if you don't know where you're going, how are you going to know when you get there*? There's a similar truth about investing: If you don't know why you're in an investment, how will you know when to get out?

If Jo has already completed her due diligence, and a particular investment appears to offer an acceptable reward for an equally acceptable risk, the next question she'll need to answer pertains to the exact dollars involved. That's where planning comes into play. Businesses have business plans that lay out a destination and a route for getting there. Investments are a sort of business, so shouldn't they have something similar?

Without a plan, Jo doesn't know what price she is willing to pay for an investment and at what point she expects to realize a profit. If all goes well, she'll still need to make decisions about when to sell and at what price. Unless she ties her due diligence to her plan, it will be tough for her to make informed decisions. That could mean missing a critical opportunity to take a profit and instead facing an unnecessary loss.

So what should be in Jo's investment plan? At the very least, it needs to contain a bare- bones outline of the investment and a financial analysis of it. The summary will tell her how she intends to enter it, manage it, and ultimately exit it—all of which will be influenced to a large extent by the analysis she and her subs did during the due diligence phase of the project. The financial analysis will include ROI estimates and, for some investments, cash flow analysis.

Having a plan is one thing. Sticking to it is another. That's where discipline comes in, and lack of discipline can be as costly to Jo's bottom line as careless research. This is one area where Jo has no one to depend on other than herself. She's the general contractor. Everyone else is taking orders from her, so it's not likely that they can do much more than act as her conscience if she veers from her plan. Whether or not she listens to her conscience ultimately remains her decision, however.

Structure: Modifying the Framework

The wonderful thing about real estate- and contract-based investments, such as mortgage notes, is the ability to vary the structure of an investment to compensate for a weakness in one area or another. You'll get into this in detail a little later, but this book can lay the groundwork for that discussion with this example.

Remember when you wanted to buy your first car? Chances are your credit history was neither good nor bad. It was nonexistent. After being turned down by three car dealers, you made that dreaded telephone call to your folks. You needed a cosigner for the loan. Why? Because the dealer's credit department needed to mitigate the risk of loaning you money to buy the car. They needed to restructure the loan so that someone with both a good credit history and sufficient assets to attach would be on the hook along with you in case you failed to repay the loan.

Many of the investments discussed in the coming chapters will lend themselves to similar restructuring. Sometimes the simple act of changing the terms of a transaction can move that transaction out of the loser column and into the winner column.

CLASSIFIED CASE STUDY

Advice from Allstate Mortgage & Investments:

Another benefit of using private investors is the ease in which an existing client can obtain additional funds. A perfect example is a client who has a low credit score. The property he or she was seeking to borrow against is a 5-acre parcel with a mobile home. With the customer's low credit he or she would be unable to obtain financing through the conventional lenders or banks. Using a private investor who is set up with a self- directed IRA accounts can secure the financing for this client. (However, due to the Dodd-Frank Act's new regulations in regards to private investing, this is harder to do than before. This act will be discussed in depth in the next chapter.)

The real benefit comes when the client wants to borrow additional money. The existing investor agrees to loan the additional funds requested. The title company must prepare a modification of the mortgage, adjusting the loan amount for the balance on the existing plus the additional amount requested. The title company then sends the modification to the IRA office for approval. Once the modification is approved, the IRA office wires the money to the title company for funding. This is a simple solution to what could have been a difficult and time-consuming proposal. This case is very similar to a customer having a line of credit at the bank. When he or she needs additional money, it takes more time to receive it in regards to the Dodd-Frank Act. With this investor, he or she can advance additional funds within a few days due to the LTV, staying under 65% and without having to start the whole process over again.

Guarding Against Fraud

Anytime money is involved, you can bet there's a ne'er-do-well looking for an opportunity to take his or her unfair share. If that sounds cynical, consider these numbers. In 2010, the FBI received reports of financial corruption on more than $11 billion in fraudulent loans, which is down from 2009. What's equally alarming is that the FBI believes that a majority of all fraud losses involve industry insiders.[1]

Mortgage fraud is generally divided into two categories: misrepresentation of the borrower and misrepresentation of the property. In short, buyers will sometimes overstate their net worth or conceal a less-than-favorable credit history to obtain financing they would not otherwise receive. Sellers, on the other hand, will sometimes overstate the value of an asset or conceal defects in it to obtain a higher price than the asset would otherwise fetch.

In either case, the responsibility falls to Jo to ensure to the best of her ability that all of the information she is provided is accurate. These numbers make clear exactly why Jo relies on her team of professionals every step of the way— especially in any area where she feels uncertain of her own abilities to sort out fact from fiction.

However, since the real estate market meltdown between 2006-2007 in the Great Recession, it has become very apparent that banks, financial institutions and their representatives have engaged in an ongoing pattern of fraud and misrepresentation regarding Real Estate Investment Trusts (REITs), mortgage foreclosures and inadequate proof of ownership of mortgages and/or notes. So it's a "Buyer Beware" scenario when dealing with mortgage fraud here, too. More on this to come…

---

1   http://www.fbi.gov/stats-services/publications/mortgage-fraud-2010

Understanding the Law

The Dodd-Frank Act: Why It Affects Your Self-Directed IRA

What is the Dodd-Frank Act?

America's economy crashed when the Great Recession of 2008 occurred. The housing market declined, the stock market suffered, and businesses all across the country shut down due to the biggest financial crisis since the Great Depression. The U.S. government bailed many large companies and most of the auto industry's losses with billions of taxpayer dollars, so government officials decided to manage the financial industry better in the future. The Dodd-Frank Act was created to keep America's financial industry intact and prevent another market crash.

President Obama signed the Dodd-Frank Wall Street Reform and Consumer Act, better known as the Dodd-Frank Act, on July 21, 2010. The act was named after Senator Chris Dodd and U.S. Representative Barney Frank, who sponsored and promoted the legislation. These new laws instated major regulations—243 new rules in total—on the financial industry to boost its deflated market and prevent the economy from having another financial meltdown.

The **three** major components of the Dodd-Frank Act include:

- Regulating banks (especially the risky ones)

- Implementing new rules and procedures for financial institutions (and how they conduct business), and

- Protect consumers from undertaking huge loans and being misled by creditors and lenders.

The bill contains 16 areas of reform and created new councils to regulate the financial industry, such as the **Financial Stability Oversight Council**, **Federal Insurance Office**, and the **Consumer Financial Protection Bureau**. The SEC, also known as the **Security and Exchange Commission**, adopted 95 of the act's new rules and is more proactive about what goes on between businesses and consumers.

One of the main components of the Dodd-Frank Act is bank regulation. If a bank gets "too big" and misleads its consumers with outrageous fees and obscure documents, then it may be asked to increase its reserve requirement, which is the money saved up and usually not used for lending or business costs, so the bank doesn't conveniently "run out of money". Banks will also be ordered to shut down quickly before they run out of money. The **Volcker Rule** prohibits banks from owning, investing, or sponsoring hedge funds, which are non-bank financial firms. This rule only allows trading when it's necessary for the bank to conduct business, but doesn't allow them to "swap trade".

When derivatives (a contract that is determined by fluctuations in the underlying asset between two or more parties) become risky, the SEC steps in and requires them to be transacted in public. However, certain banks, hedge funds, and energy companies are exempt from derivative oversight, but qualifying for any of these exemptions is difficult to do.

The **Federal Insurance Office** also monitors risky insurance companies and their business transactions. Some huge insurance companies, such **AIG** and **Lehman Brothers**, had to be bailed out for billions of dollars and was one of the contributing factors of the Great Recession. Affordable insurance, as well as less hidden fees and being ripped off by companies, is now offered.

Credit-rating agencies, another contributing factor of the Great Recession, are also monitored by the Dodd-Frank Act, as well as credit-reporting agencies, credit-card debt, and payday and consumer loans. The agencies that either loaned out money or mislead consumers about their credit ratings were blamed for being an influential catalyst of the Great Recession. The SEC now has the power to check up on agencies and de-certify them if they give misleading ratings or break a new protocol.

This act now controls how money is lent and spent to ensure that powerhouse companies don't risk money and demand to be bailed out again. Credit agencies and banks are also forbidden to give misleading advice to consumers or allow them to take on a loan that they can't afford. The Great Recession uncovered flaws in the financial industry, so the government is trying to fix the system.

How does this affect me?

Essentially, the Dodd-Frank Act revamped how money is borrowed and lent in America's economy on every level. However, the best effect of this act is the surplus of consumer protection. The **Consumer Financial Protection Bureau** protects consumers from bad business practices, such as risky lending or hidden fees. Credit agencies gave people high credit-score ratings when their scores were actually very low, which lead to bankruptcy and other dilemmas. The new bureaus now help consumers understand confusing policies and contracts better, but they can only borrow loans if they meet certain guidelines.

For example, if you wanted to buy your first home, then you'd have to go through a more difficult process to determine whether you can take out a loan or not. You would need a higher credit score than what was acceptable in the past and see which loan options are available to you. It's much harder to purchase a car, home or any other expensive item now.

Some people see this process as a ridiculous restriction. In some scenarios, this is true; loaning agencies now deny loans too quickly to average Americans. However, it does save people from taking on a loan that they may not be able to afford. Regardless of different situations, it's important to understand how the Dodd-Frank Act affects you, such as making investments and receiving loans. Before you venture into a new business or life decision regarding your self-directed IRA, consider these changes; there are actions that used to be considered acceptable but now aren't.

What do these changes mean for private investors and advisors?

When it comes to investments, the government has made it harder for people to invest because the Dodd-Frank Act attempts to eliminate most risky situations. Investment managers must now register with the SEC and be inspected periodically to see if they are following procedures. They must meet many standards so they can conduct business. The new rules limit mortgage options and access to credit, which means average consumers can't purchase big-ticketed items as easily now. The act's new mortgage financing regulation took effect on January 10, 2014.

As for private investing, the rules still apply. Private investors, such as ordinary people who choose to invest into real estate or the like, are subject to new regulations. Their private investment advisors must also undergo registration and strict regulations as well. The Volcker Rule also makes it harder for private investors to borrow money for their investments. Because banks were involved with too many risky transactions, their abilities to lend money are now limited.

What does this mean for private mortgage loans?

To the average person, the Dodd-Frank Act may seem like it doesn't affect his or her personal life, but in reality, this act affects everyone. It's much more difficult to receive loans now, especially for investing in a business or owning a home. The Consumer Financial Protection Bureau (CFPB) implements the new rules for the mortgage industry as well. The strict regulations of borrowing and lending loans are good and bad at the same time; it's good for financial institutions so they keep in line, but it's bad for consumers because it doesn't promote growth for new businesses and investments. It's essentially stopping the economy from growing.

The **Mortgage Reform Act** made several changes to the "high-cost mortgage" regulations in the **Home Ownership and Equity Protection Act** (HOEPA). The purpose of theses changes was to lower the pricing threshold for loans that are considered high cost. The new limitations that are set in place ban prepayment and balloon payments, late fees that are limited to no more than four percent of the amount, and expand the pre-loan counseling required under HOEPA. The government is in favor of borrowers and lays heavy regulations on creditors, banks and other financial institutions.

When you finance your home, the government monitors the entire process, such as mortgage options, eligibility standards and even your payment schedule; essentially, the government plays a micro-management role to make sure borrowers understand how much money and responsibility they are undertaking and that they make their payments on time.

However, there are a few exclusions to the Dodd-Frank Act in regards to mortgage financing, such as the **three-property exclusion** and **one-property exclusion**. The **three-property exclusion** exempts sellers who finance the purchase of three or fewer properties in a 12-month period. The property must be owned by the seller, didn't construct the property, and meet certain loaning requirements. The **one-property exclusion** is less restrictive and may be used if the seller is only financing one property within 12 months.

But if a person doesn't qualify for any of those exclusions, then sellers should be wary about what loans they offer buyers. As for borrowers, it's still a long and difficult process to obtain loans for big purchases. However, they'll be able to understand the fine print better when signing mortgage contracts and borrowing loans.

What does this mean for your self-directed IRA?

Investing in real estate and promissory notes will be much more difficult now in relation to the Dodd-Frank Act. Investing in real estate, or another type of investment, cannot be as easily done as before. You have to meet special requirements and keep up with new regulations. If you wanted to sell a property, business, or anything else, then you must follow the act's new guidelines. Although having a self-directed IRA is a longer process now, you can still manage to invest your money wherever you want to. There are practical ways to execute what you want to do with your money and where you want to place it. If you study the laws and follow the rules, then you will still be able to accomplish your intended goals, no matter what new act or rule is now instilled.

Conclusion

There is some controversial debate about whether the Dodd-Frank Act is an overboard approach to deal with the financial crisis or if it's truly going to benefit America's economy. Some people believe that it inhibits investors from conducting business, lays too many rules on financial businesses and institutions, and doesn't encourage economic growth. Others believe that it will protect investors and customers by cutting down unnecessary risk.

Another group of people think that the regulations are enough because they feel Wall Street takes too many risks and expects to be bailed out by public tax dollars. Either way, the instilled Dodd-Frank Act now changes how the economy flows, from financial powerhouses to the individual man. It's important to fully understand what the Dodd-Frank Act changed and focus on how it will benefit you as the consumer. Banks were hitting borrowers with so many fees and misleading them about mortgage loans. Now, you're protected. If you study the new rules and regulations, then you can still find a way to have a self-directed IRA for your retirement years.

Glossary

Securities and Exchange Commission (SEC): The SEC now controls how banks conduct business

Consumer Financial Protection Bureau (CFPB): This new bureau closely watches the mortgage industry and instills specific guidelines. Consumers and borrowers are also protected by this bureau

Office of Credit Ratings: This office, headed under the SEC, closely watches credit-rating agencies. They must undergo random inspections and not mislead consumers with false credit scores.

Financial Stability Oversight Council & Orderly Liquidation Authority: This office can cease and assist banks that are "too big to fail".

Hedge funds: non-bank financial institutions

Commodity Futures Trading Commission (CFTC): regulates risky derivatives like credit default swaps

Federal Insurance Office (FIO): This office watches insurance companies to keep them in line and not mislead customers

Whistle blower provision: If someone reports information about financial corruption and insider trading, then he or she will receive a financial reward.

PART THREE

Building Blocks to Retiring Rich

"If you have built castles in the air, your work need not be lost; that is where they should be. Now put the foundations under them."

–HENRY DAVID THOREAU

CHAPTER SEVEN

The Allure of Real Estate

The best investment on earth is earth.

- LOUIS J. GLICKMAN

If there is a common thread that runs throughout mankind, it is probably the quest to own a piece of dirt. Sometimes it's a lust for acres and acres of dirt. Sometimes a modest plot fulfills the desire. On occasion, satisfying the visceral drive to own the place called home whets the entrepreneurial appetite as well. But why? What makes real estate such an alluring investment? Perhaps it is the belief that there's money to be made on anything that is almost universally coveted. Someone once said that the only thing that will always be there is land. Barring a nuclear war, we suspect that is a truism. Death and taxes will also always be with us, but that's beyond the scope of this book.

Entrepreneurs are an inventive sort, which probably explains why trying to bring order to any discussion of real estate investments ends up feeling like a three-dimensional puzzle best solved with a sledgehammer. In lieu of a sledgehammer, we're going to resort to a few arbitrary definitions as we delve a little deeper into the question of why and how people invest in real estate.

Why Real Estate?

Other than buying a home as a hedge against inflation, which falls beyond the purview of this book, there are essentially three classes of real estate investments. Each one is defined by the motivation behind the purchase. They are listed here in the order in which they will be discussed in the following chapters.

1. **Rental income:** For centuries, people have exploited the landlord-tenant relationship to build real estate empires. And for centuries it has been true that, if properly structured, the income generated from the landlord-tenant relationship can pay the operating expenses and return a positive cash flow too.

2. **An expectation of future value:** Some people are driven to buy real estate because of the generally held belief that real estate most often increases in value over time—a process we call appreciation. If you buy the property early enough and hold it long enough, common wisdom says that you can reasonably expect to cash in on some degree of appreciation. Of course, real estate does not always appreciate. In some cases, it has been known to decrease in value. But, unlike stock in a company, it would be exceedingly unlikely that its value would drop to zero. This has been clearly borne out since the real estate market came crashing down on a national basis. After a period of uncontrolled and explosive growth, the real estate investment bubble burst, leaving many investors and homeowners "upside down", that is owing more in mortgages than the property was realistically worth. This led to a nationwide crisis in mortgage foreclosures, bank failures, bad loans and bankruptcies that still have not quite recovered from the Great Recession. It also resulted in multiple lawsuits by various state attorney generals going after banks and mortgage companies for fraud and other complaints.

3. **Quick profit:** Finally, every real estate investor fantasizes about finding a prime piece of real estate at a bargain-basement price. For sure, it doesn't happen often, but when a parcel can be bought at 20 percent or more below its current market value, there's plenty of room for an immediate turnaround and quick profit—if all goes well.

If the question of why makes up the first dimension of our 3D real-estate puzzle, then the second and third dimensions must be the twin components of how and where.

Traditional Versus Nontraditional Real Estate Sources

Categorizing the methods used to acquire real estate can be approached in a number of different ways, depending on who is doing the sorting. Length of holding period is often used to distinguish between investing for future appreciation and flipping for a quick profit, for example. Another approach is to differentiate based on the type of transaction, like options versus purchase contracts. Still another way to slice and dice them is on the basis of the channel through which the real estate is purchased, such as a real estate broker or a tax-lien sale or foreclosure sale.

For the purposes of our discussion, we're going to divide them into two baskets. We'll begin with what we'll call traditional real estate transactions, because they are the least complex and lowest risk. Then we'll work our way up to more complex and higher-risk investments—the ones we'll lump into the nontraditional category.

TRADITIONAL	NON-TRADITIONAL
• Real estate broker-assisted	• Real estate options
• For sale by owner	• Foreclosure, tax liens, REOs

Traditional Real Estate Transactions

Buying real estate through traditional channels involves essentially six steps. The fine details of each step may vary depending on state law and local custom. Yet, the mechanics remain pretty much the same whether you're buying commercial or residential property or whether it it's funded by IRA assets or nonretirement savings.

Step 1: Write up an offer. In most states, an offer to buy real estate must be in writing. When Jo is ready to make an offer on a property, she will have her real estate agent prepare a real estate purchase contract. If she's buying directly from an owner/seller, she'll have her real estate agent draw up the contract. In the first case, her agent will present the offer to the seller. In the latter case, she can either present it herself or ask her agent or attorney to do it for her.

LEGAL TIP: Purchase contracts can be in various forms. Some states have forms prepared by the statewide Real Estate Brokers association; some have forms prepared by the lawyers' state Bar Association; some have jointly prepared forms (agreed forms by the Brokers and the Bar). When possible, use a jointly prepared form if one exists in the state where the property is located. Forms prepared solely by Brokers associations tend to protect the Brokers more than the parties to the contract. Always have a Real Estate lawyer prepare or review the contract before signing.

When it comes time to enter the name of the buyer, Jo will simply enter the name of the IRA instead of her own.

Jo's offer to purchase the property will include any stipulations that qualify her interest in purchasing it. These are known as *contingency clauses* and typically identify things like repairs and inspections that need to be completed, and also might say that the purchase depends on her ability to obtain satisfactory financing. At the time of the initial offer, the buyer (in this case, Jo's IRA) will give the real estate agent or seller a check to make it a binding contract. This check is sometimes called a *binder* or *earnest money*, because it demonstrates that Jo is earnest and sincere about her intent to purchase the property. The check will be attached to the contract and will not be cashed unless and until both parties reach an agreement.

Step 2: Negotiate the deal. It's rare for the seller to accept a buyer's offer the first time around. More often, the seller's real estate agent returns to the buyer with a counteroffer. The counteroffer might include an amended asking price that is higher than the buyer's initial offer, but lower than the original asking price. Sometimes the seller will meet the buyer's offering price, but will reject some of the contingencies. Jo will have the option of accepting the counteroffer as it is presented or writing up a new purchase offer and starting the negotiation process all over again. If they fail to reach an agreement, Jo gets her earnest money back and is free to walk away from the property without penalty.

LEGAL TIP: There are many things that can be negotiated in a contract to purchase; a buyer should consider all of them. Things like who pays for title insurance, needed repairs, disclosed and undisclosed defects, etc. When a property is subject to Homeowners Association or Condo Association controls, other requirements may enter into the mix. Always find out what restrictions exist on use, changes or modifications to the property, permitted holiday decorations and time frames, etc. as well as obtain all regulations, condo documents, etc. and carefully review them before you sign the final contract. Once you have purchased the property, you cannot claim ignorance of these and they can have a substantial effect on your ability to use the property as you wish. For example, some associations or condos limit the number of times you can rent a unit to different people or within a given time frame. Many states now require that a property owner disclose all known defects to prospective purchasers as part of the contract; failure to do so can result in the voiding of a sales contract.

Step 3: Sign the purchase contract. If all goes well, Jo and the seller will eventually reach an agreement on the terms of the sale. When both sets of signatures are on the purchase contract, it's a done deal. If Jo backs out of the contract without cause after this point, she will lose her earnest money and may be liable for reimbursing the seller for damages.

Step 4: Conduct the inspections. In addition to the pest inspection required by some states, Jo will conduct two more inspections of the property. One is scheduled immediately after the contract is signed, typically within the first two weeks. While Jo is free to conduct this inspection herself, she believes that the extra cost of hiring a licensed home inspection professional is good insurance. If material problems are discovered during either the building inspection or the pest inspection, negotiations can be reopened to resolve any issues to the satisfaction of both Jo and the seller. Once again, if they fail to reach an agreement, the contingency clauses pertaining to inspections free Jo to cancel the contract without penalty.

The third and final inspection Jo will conduct takes the form of a walk-through of the property immediately prior to signing the closing documents. The purpose of the final walk-through is to confirm that all conditions of the contract have been met and that the condition of the property has not changed substantially since the original inspection. If she cannot attend the final walk-through herself, Jo can have her real estate agent or another designated party do it for her. As with previous inspections, if problems are discovered, Jo will enter into a new round of negotiations that will either resolve the issues to both parties' satisfaction or result in a canceled contract.

Step 5: Close the deal. After the purchase contract was signed and while Jo was busy attending to the inspections (and possibly arranging financing), the real estate broker forwarded the purchase contract and earnest money check to the title insurance company. The title company places the money in its escrow account and proceeds to prepare the legal documents and keep an accurate accounting of the fees and other expenses for both Jo and the seller.

One of the most important functions of the title company is to conduct a title search to ensure that the property is free of any liens or encumbrances, including taxing authority liens. When the title search is complete and the title is deemed to be clean, the title company issues title insurance to the buyer. If somewhere down the line a defect in the title is discovered, the title insurance protects Jo's investment by assuming responsibility for any and all costs to clear the title. In a worst-case scenario, the title insurance will reimburse Jo for the entire investment.

When the title company completes its work, it will present the documents to the IRA administrator for acceptance and approval and will arrange an appointment for the closing. In some states, the buyer and seller both appear for the closing. In other states, they appear separately or can even close by mail. Regardless of which variation is followed, when Jo and the seller have both signed the documents that finalize the sale, the seller will be presented with a check (or a receipt for a wire transfer). At this point, Jo's IRA owns the property.

Step 6. Record the transaction. The job not being complete until the paperwork is done is never truer than in the case of a real-estate transaction. Once the transfer of ownership is complete, the title company and IRA administrator each have one more essential responsibility. The title company will record the deed (and mortgage note, if Jo has obtained financing for the purchase) at the courthouse, to ensure that Jo's interest in, ownership of, and rights to the property become part of the public record. At  the same time, the IRA administrator will file the required forms with the IRS to record the addition of the asset to Jo's IRA. *Now* the transaction is complete.

Non-traditional Sources

If you examine the steps of a traditional real estate purchase carefully, you'll notice that each has one and only one purpose: to limit risk. Without signatures and earnest money, for example, either party could walk away from the deal and leave the other party high and dry. Without inspections, the seller could conceal defects that affect the value of the property. Without title insurance, the buyer might end up with a worthless title. The list goes on. The point is that the process includes built-in safeguards that a careful investor can use to reduce risk.

With non-traditional sources, such as foreclosures and tax-lien sales, some of those steps are missing or compressed. For example, negotiations may take the form of bidding against other buyers, as in the case of an auction. Likewise, inspections may run the standard course or may not be possible at all, as in the case of some tax lien sales.

The steps will vary, depending on the type of purchase, who the seller is, and sometimes by locale. In each case, it will be up to Jo to examine the process and find points at which she can insert her own safeguards. But two steps that must always be included, and again it is Jo's chore to ensure that they are, are title insurance and the recording of the title at the local courthouse. Beyond that, if Jo remains flexible and alert, she may be able to use some of these nontraditional sources to give her IRA balance a healthy boost.

CLASSIFIED CASE STUDY

Advice From Equity Trust:

Here's a real-life example of a rental property investment one of our clients, a realtor and real-estate investor, made in his self-directed IRA – in his own words:

"I partnered with two other individuals to purchase a 104 unit apartment complex for $2.5 million. For my part I had to provide $50,000. I had nearly $30,000 in two IRA's and a 401 (k) I was rolling over from a previous employer. Equity Trust Company walked me through the rollover and account activation procedures, helped me consolidate my accounts, and cut the check to the partnership in record time! I raised an additional $20,000 from other sources to round out the $50,000 and my partners and I were able to close on the complex on time. The complex has been cash flow positive since day one despite requiring over $43,000 in capital improvements. We are now over 95% occupancy and I am making as much as $2,200 / month –100% TAX FREE FOREVER thanks to Equity Trust Company- 88% annual return!"

CHAPTER EIGHT

Becoming a Landlord: Investing in Income Property

Once we rid ourselves of traditional thinking, we can get on with creating the future.

–JAMES BERTRAND

Sizing Up the Job

Skill Level: Do-It-Yourself

The worth of a piece of real estate can be judged in terms of its market value or its usefulness to its owner. A vacant lot may hold promise for future value, but has little intrinsic value unless and until it is either sold or developed. A building, on the other hand, has current and immediate usefulness. The owner can occupy it or generously offer it to someone else to occupy for little or no cost. More commonly, property that is not owner-occupied becomes income property.

IRS rules pretty well eliminate options one and two for IRA-held assets. The account holder cannot occupy it; nor can the use of it be given away or offered at bargain-basement prices. Personal residence and benevolence, then, must be reserved for non-IRA assets, which narrows down the options for how an IRA-owned asset can be used.

Fortunately, holding rental property in an IRA can make good sense. It lends itself to the only two real estate investment strategies that work within an IRA. It can be held for future appreciation and generate rental income in the interim. If Jo does her homework well and calculates her cash flow assumptions accurately, the income should exceed the expenses. Net result: net income and an ever-increasing account balance. With that goal in mind, Jo has chosen income property as her first self-directed IRA investment. Let's find out how she'll put the project together.

Calling in the Subcontractors

Jo comes to this transaction with a decent amount of experience as a landlord. During the time she held the rental property, it generated a steady positive cash flow. When she sold it, she almost doubled her money, thanks to the recent surge in real estate prices. That was before she learned that she could save thousands of dollars in capital gains taxes by owning it within a self-directed IRA. Using her IRA this time around will involve fundamentally the same principles and processes. The primary difference will be the addition of a new professional to her team of experts—the IRA administrator.

How much expert help any real estate transaction requires depends on the buyer's (or seller's) experience and the complexity of the deal. That said, there are a few professionals that will be part of the team on every transaction.

The IRA administrator's duties include everything from making sure that Jo's investments remain on the right side of the IRS rules to issuing wire transfers to accurately recording deposits to filing IRS reports. Consequently, she'll be called in early on each investment and will remain involved for as long as the asset is held within the account. Because of the Dodd-Frank Act, the administrator will monitor how everything is complete, including the payment schedule.

Jo's real estate broker ranks at the top of the list, right next to the account administrator. When Jo gives her the go ahead, she'll kick off the search for a property that meets the criteria Jo has outlined. If Jo finds a lead on her own, she'll hire her agent to assist her with the due diligence. In either case, the agent will provide Jo with data on the property's market value, real estate taxes and insurance estimates, going rates for rent in the area, crime rates, and anything else Jo asks that is within the agent's ability to deliver. If she's brokering the deal, she'll also coordinate the negotiations between Jo and the seller, and interface with the title company and perhaps Jo's attorney, accountant, and property inspectors.

This book already talked extensively about the role of the title company. It bears repeating, however, that title insurance is an essential component of each and every real estate transaction. Sometimes, claims against a title aren't recorded or aren't recorded correctly. With title insurance, clearing problems that emerge after closing become the responsibility of the title insurance company—not Jo.

Establishing the true condition of the property is an essential part of due diligence. It takes two different types of inspectors to make that determination. Typically, a licensed pest inspector gets called in first. The pest inspector's job is to look for signs of termite or other pest infestations. If indications of an infestation are found, Jo will have the opportunity to either cancel the deal or require the seller to treat the infestation and repair any damage associated with it.

Next comes the licensed home inspector. This is not the time for Jo to become penny-wise and pound-foolish by attempting a do-it-yourself inspection. The job of the home inspector is to assess the safety; structural and functional integrity of the foundation; the roofing, plumbing, electrical, and mechanical; and heating and air conditioning units—in other words, the big-ticket items (and a few small ones too) that can add up to equally big costs for Jo if she fails to identify problems during the narrow window of opportunity in which she can reopen negotiations. The risks are far too great to get hung up over a relatively nominal fee, especially since the inspection often ends up paying for itself. Few houses are perfect, and the inspection report can provide Jo with the leverage she needs to return to the seller with a revised offer, contingent upon the repair or replacement of deficiencies identified in the report.

LEGAL TIP: The inspection is critical to a decision whether or not to purchase a given property. Make sure the inspector looks at conformity to current code requirements in addition to the structural integrity of the property. This can avoid a costly problem down the road. Let's say your inspector tells you the property is good and you close. A few months later you decide you want to make an alteration. Code Enforcement comes out and says you need to rewire the entire property because of deficiencies from the previous owner (such as un-permitted, defective or un-inspected wiring modifications). At worst this could destroy the value of your investment; at the very least you may be headed for years of costly litigation against the former owner and/or your inspector for failure to disclose.

LEGAL TIP: Any structural or infrastructural modifications to a property that are done, such as converting a basement into a rental apartment, adding another bathroom, putting in a new heating plant or air conditioning unit, adding a new electrical line etc., all can result in loss of the Certificate of Occupancy ("C of O") if done without complying with the local building codes and obtaining a permit. Without a C of O you are not entitled to occupy or use the property until corrected). In many jurisdictions, violation of the C of O can result in fines that accumulate on a daily basis until complied with. Speak with your local Building Department before you do anything to determine the requirements you must meet in advance.

Above all, Jo will not use an inspector who is recommended to her by anyone who stands to gain from a rubber-stamp endorsement of the property—even her real estate agent. It is true that she and Jo go back a long way. Jo considers her a friend, as well as a business associate, and wants to keep it that way. By avoiding any potential conflict of interest, Jo will be able to sleep at night, confident that the property has received an objective inspection, that the report accurately reflects the inspector's findings, and that her interests have been protected.

In addition to the regulars, a few other professionals play equally critical roles, even though they may not be called in on every job. Their functions can range from convenience to confidence building to a nonnegotiable requirement, depending on the circumstances.

Anytime Jo purchases a rental property, she'll have to decide who is going to collect the rent, have the furnace repaired and the grass cut, and act as mediator between feuding neighbors. She could hire a friend or relative (but not an excluded family member, of course). She might be able to hire her IRA administrator or even her real estate broker. Or she could hire a professional property management service.

Each comes with its own set of pros and cons, and to a large extent, the choice boils down to personal preference.

Whether or not Jo needs to call in her attorney depends on the complexity of the transaction. If a real estate broker represents Jo, and there do not appear to be any complicating factors associated with the deal, she may forgo, including her attorney. If, on the other hand, she is buying the property from an owner/seller, she'll want her attorney to draw up the purchase agreement. It goes without saying that anytime a transaction deviates from the standard, she'll call on him to protect her interests.

Because Jo has a background in financial analysis, she probably won't require the services of her accountant to evaluate the cash flow assumptions for a single-unit rental property. If she pursues anything out of the ordinary, however, it might be money well spent to at least have him look over her analysis to make sure she hasn't missed anything significant. A mistake at this point can make the difference between a positive cash flow and a negative one.

LEGAL TIP: Always make sure that any property you buy is FULLY insured (casualty, fire, flood) to its full fair market value, and re-evaluate this number annually. Changes in the surrounding market, crime rates, tax rates, permitted land use, etc., can increase or decrease the fair market value. In the event of an insurance or casualty loss, if you do not have the property fully insured you stand to suffer a substantial loss financially. The way property insurance is structured, if you insure it for less than full fair market value the carrier will only pay a portion of your loss based on the ratio of what you insured it for compared to its full market value, not the full amount of your policy. In other words, if you have a $100,000 insurance policy on a property worth $200,000, in the event of a total loss the carrier will only pay out a portion of the $100k policy; not the full amount.

LEGAL TIP: Before purchasing property insurance, always check out the insurance company through your state's insurance commission for complaints, track record regarding claims, rate increase history, etc. This applies to your own home or property as well as to your investment properties.

Nuts and Bolts

Aside from the IRS restriction that says neither Jo, nor any prohibited party, can use property held in Jo's IRA, she can pick from virtually any type of real estate that appeals to her. She previously held a single-family rental unit. She could choose a duplex or other multifamily unit, or she might want to buy a vacation rental—perhaps a lakeside cottage or even an ocean-view condo. When Bill first suggested the self-directed IRA and explained its workings, that was her first thought. There's a secluded lake nearby, where she'd eventually like to own one of those rustic log homes. Using her self-directed IRA to buy it strikes her as a great opportunity to use the seasonal rental income, which is typically higher than residential rental rates, to pay for the property. If she can swing it within her Roth IRA, she can even take it as a tax-free distribution when she retires. She hasn't ruled out the idea, but she's not limiting herself to it either.

In addition to vacation homes, Jo is interested in looking at single-family homes, condos, and maybe even commercial properties, if good prospects show up. Those were the marching orders she gave her real estate agent, along with certain stipulations concerning areas of most interest, price range, condition, and above all, a potential for a positive cash flow and future appreciation. Two weeks have passed when Jo finally receives the anticipated phone call. Her agent has located two properties that might interest her.

The first is a single-family brick colonial in a middle-income planned community. The second is an upscale condo near downtown. Both show potential for being good moneymakers—at least on the surface. Jo has friends who live near the colonial, so she is familiar with the construction quality and the community amenities. By contrast, the condo is in a high-demand area that is popular with young professionals. It has even more amenities and a breathtaking view of the city as well.

According to the real estate agent, both sellers are very motivated. In real estate language, that means they'll entertain any reasonable offer and sometimes some not-so-reasonable ones.

Within a few days, Jo has viewed both properties and is busy poring over numbers. She's decided that she'd be willing to pay up to $170,000 on the colonial and up to $190,000 on the condo, and she's worked up a spreadsheet to evaluate the cash flow and estimated ROI on both properties based on these purchase prices.

At this point, Jo has two prospective properties. Now it's time to pick the better investment between them. In doing so, Jo will consider future appreciation, estimate each property's annual cash flow, and factor in area vacancy rates, which can turn a good investment into a bad one in short order. Hopefully, when she's done, a clear winner will emerge.

After analyzing competitive selling prices, she has formed an opinion of each property's market value. Each is lower than the asking price and perhaps even lower than what another buyer might be willing to pay for the same property. She's prepared for the seller to turn down the offer, because she and the seller have opposing motives. Jo wants to pay as little as possible, and the seller wants to collect as much as possible from the sale of the property. If they both remain flexible, they may be able to meet in the middle. How flexible Jo can afford to be will be determined by the results of her financial analysis.

In forming her opinion on each property's value, Jo considered future uncertainties. Her intention is to hold the property for a long-term investment. At the same time, unexpected events could prompt her to alter her plan. Paying top dollar for the property could force her into a position in which she must sell at a loss if she needs to unload it quickly. And taking a loss on her first self-directed IRA investment (or any subsequent one, for that matter) is exactly what she wants to avoid.

Cash flow was another factor Jo considered in settling on a purchase price for the properties. She's looking for two profit points on the property: one based on appreciation when she sells it and the other one based on the month-by-month, year-by-year cash flow. In short, the cash she invests to purchase the property needs to return a positive cash flow after the annual operating expenses are deducted.

Positive cash flow could be defined as anything greater than zero. Obviously, that's too vague to be useful. She needs a measurement that can be expressed in terms of a percentage. Jo's looking at the $20,000 difference between the purchase prices of the two properties. That's $20,000 more cash out of her IRA account if she chooses the condo over the colonial. Considering net income alone falls short of telling her if investing the extra money in the condo will return a commensurate profit. *Cash on cash return*, on the other hand, will do exactly that.

Cash on cash return: A calculation often used for analyzing return on real estate investments. It is computed by dividing net income by the total cash invested.

Cash on cash ROI = net income ÷ cash invested

Calculating cash on cash return involves two steps. First, Jo must compute the annual net income for the property. This is done by subtracting the annual expenses from the annual revenues, then the net income is divided by the total cash invested. The goal is to come up with a percentage that approaches double digits. High single digits can pass muster if the property also offers good appreciation prospects and a low vacancy rate.

The first thing Jo discovers as she begins her computations is that the rents in the area of the colonial are a little on the soft side. Her real estate agent explains that this is due to the relatively high vacancy rate in the area—at least compared to the condo. Even though she can get into the colonial for a smaller cash outlay, the lower rent could shortchange the cash on cash return for the property. The only way to find out is to finish the calculations.

For the colonial, Jo estimates that her annual operating expenses will run about $3,800 against a gross income of $18,000, returning a net income of almost $14,200. The condo, on the other hand, will return a net income of roughly $2,200 more—which it should, given that it's going to cost her $20,000 more to purchase than the colonial. (See Table 15.)

By dividing the net income by the purchase price on each property, we can see that the cash on cash return on the condo comes out only .3 percent higher than the return on the colonial. Taken alone, that might not seem like enough to tip the scales one way or another. Combined with a higher appreciation rate, it could.

Coming up with appreciation assumptions can be tricky business. Generally speaking, they are typically viewed as a continuing trend. So, if an area experiences an average appreciation rate of 8 percent over the past five years or so, if nothing has changed within the area, and if economic conditions have not deteriorated, it can be assumed that future appreciation will continue at approximately the same rate.

Problems arise with this methodology, however, if the rate of growth spikes when compared to a longer stretch of history. Even industry analysts can't come to a consensus on how long the double-digit appreciation rates we've seen over the past few years might continue. Nor can they agree on what will happen when and if the real estate market softens. If they can't be certain, how can Jo hope to be? *Note to readers:* In retrospect, the extraordinary market boom of the early and mid 2000's took a nosedive in 2007 and today, in 2015, fully eight years later, market values in most communities across the nation have not returned to their previous values. The potential investor needs to keep this in mind when making decisions.

Opting to err on the side of caution, Jo decides to treat the recent appreciation spike as an aberration and estimate the properties' future values based on the historic numbers before the real estate feeding frenzy started in the early 2000s. Accordingly, she plugs 5 percent for the colonial and 6 percent for the condo into her analysis. The resulting calculation shows Jo that the appreciation on the condo will likely outpace the colonial by almost 5 percent over a four-year period. Combining the cash on cash returns with the appreciation, the condo ends up yielding an annualized ROI of 15.2 percent (6.6 percent annualized appreciation plus 8.7 percent cash on cash), compared to 13.7 percent on the colonial.

Just in case Jo has any lingering doubt about which investment is likely to yield a better return, one more piece of data provided by her real estate agent clinches the deal. The vacancy rate for comparable single-family homes near the colonial is nearly 7 percent, whereas the vacancy rate for similar condos is running at the very low rate of 2 percent.

Table 15. CASH ON CASH ANALYSIS - COLONIAL VERSUS CONDO

	SINGLE-FAMILY COLONIAL	LUXURY CONDO
Average competitive price	$180,000	$200,000
Asking price	$190,000	$210,000
Purchase price	$170,000	$190,000
SF home income - $1,500 per month	$18,000	N/A
Condo income - $1,900 per month	N/A	$22,800
Utilities	Paid by renter	Paid by renter
Property tax	$1,190	$1,330
Insurance	$680	$760
Annual HOA fee	$300	$2,400
Property management fees	$1,632	$1,824
Annual expenses	$3,802	$6,314
Annual net income	$14,198	$16,486
Annual cash on cash ROI	8.4%	8.7%
Appreciation	5%	6%
Anticipated four-year appreciation	$36,636	$49,871
Anticipated sales price	$206,636	$239,871
Anticipated ROI on appreciation	21.6%	26.2%
Anticipated annualized ROI on appreciation	5.4%	6.6%

Satisfied that she has completed her due diligence and has a sound financial basis for the investment, Jo makes an appointment to see the condo one more time. This time, she'll go over it with a fine-tooth comb, looking for anything that might cause her to rethink her interest in the property. If it still looks like a good investment when she's finished, she'll touch base with her IRA administrator, give the rest of her subs a heads-up, then make an offer.

Funding the Purchase: Cash Versus Financing

Thanks to Jo's 401(k) rollover, she has enough cash in her traditional IRA to pay cash for the condo. But, what if she didn't? Or what if she wanted to diversify her holdings and didn't want to tie up so much of her IRA money in one investment? The answer to all those questions is that there is an alternative. She could borrow some of the money.

It is perfectly legal to obtain financing on an IRA-held asset. That said, this might be an appropriate time to review the difference between *can* and *may*. The IRS says that Jo *may* borrow money to purchase real estate within her IRA. Whether or not she is able to find a lender willing to underwrite such a loan, however, will determine whether or not she *can* do what the law allows.

When Jo purchased real estate in the past, she obtained a mortgage that gave the lender the right to foreclose on the property if she failed to make her payments and, if necessary, to attach her other assets as well. Lenders like it that way, because it discourages people from walking away from their properties when things get rough. Financing an IRA-held asset works a little differently.

By law, any loan made for property held in an IRA must be secured by the property itself, not by the IRA. This means that if the borrower (in this case, Jo's IRA) fails to pay back the loan as promised, the lender may take back only the property used to secure the loan and nothing more. It cannot attach other assets within the IRA or any of Jo's other assets. This limited recourse is why, until recently, finding a bank or mortgage company willing to underwrite such a loan was next to impossible.

The good news is that more and more lenders are modifying their underwriting policies to capture a piece of the growing self-directed IRA market. The bad news is that it will typically require a larger down payment and possibly come with the price tag of a premium interest rate compared to a non-IRA loan.

There's one more complication Jo will have to consider if she decides to finance the purchase. A little-known tax called the *unrelated business income tax* (UBIT). Here's how it works.

You've heard it said that every rule has an exception. The UBIT is the exception to the tax-exempt rule. Tax-exempt, in this case, refers to the fact that normally you don't have to pay taxes on the earnings inside an IRA until you take the earnings as distributions. And with a Roth IRA, you would never have to pay taxes on your investment earnings.

Originally conceived for nonprofit and charitable organizations, the UBIT is a tax on income generated from activities that are unrelated to the organization's primary business. A component of the UBIT, the *unrelated debt financed income*, or UDFI, applies to IRA income generated by financed assets.

The UDFI exempts the first $1,000 of debt-related income that applies only to the portion of the income generated by the debt. For example, let's assume that Jo owns an income property with an average adjusted basis of $100,000 (calculated by averaging the value of the property at the start of the year and the end of the year, after subtracting applicable deductions). The average balance of the mortgage is $20,000 (20 percent of the basis). The property generates a gross profit of $11,000 during the year. Because the first $1,000 is exempt, $10,000 will be used to calculate the UDFI. The unrelated debt-financed income is $2,000 ($10,000 x 20%), which will be taxed at the trust rate. In this example, the tax comes out to $332.

When it's time to sell the property, the UBIT will apply to the capital gains on the investment if debt has been associated with the asset at any time during the 12 months prior to the sale. Of course, the simple way to avoid the UBIT when the property is sold is to pay off the debt at least 366 days prior to selling it.

Renting the Property

It's been a month since Jo's offer on the condo was accepted, and she's about to close on the transaction. The house has passed all its inspections, including the final walk-through. Her IRA administrator has a copy of the paperwork from the title insurance company. In a matter of hours, she'll sign the papers, and Jo's IRA administrator will issue a wire transfer to fund the transaction, marking the end of the acquisition process. Jo's project, however, is just getting under way. All she's done so far is to spend money to buy a piece of real estate. Now she's got to turn it into a cash machine.

Jo's been anything but idle over the past four weeks. She's lined up insurance for the property and hired herself a property manager (PM). She'd considered the alternatives and eliminated her IRA administrator (too expensive), her broker (too busy), and a friend or relative (too much strain on the relationships at this point).

Jo brought the PM onboard as soon as the purchase contract was signed. Within two weeks, she had a few nibbles and a serious applicant. Now, the new tenant has passed a credit check, paid the move-in costs, and is ready to assume occupancy.

What you'll notice is that, aside from the involvement of the IRA administrator, this process very much mirrors any other rental property scenario. The PM will collect the rent, forward it to the administrator and handle the day-to-day business of managing the property. As vacancies occur, the process begins again.

Selling Income Property

Jo didn't buy the condo with the intention of turning it over for a quick profit. It was chosen as a long-term investment, so selling is the last thing on her mind. But sooner or later, every property changes hands. Anticipating that eventuality is part of the planning process discussed earlier.

The mechanics of selling a piece of real estate held in an IRA are very much the same as for selling any other piece of real estate—or selling any asset held in any IRA, for that matter. When Jo wants to sell stock in her IRA, she issues a sell order to her broker. When the order is filled, the cash is deposited in her account, and she can turn around and buy more stock or let the money sit idle for a period of time.

Likewise, when Jo gets ready to sell the condo, she will discuss her plans with her IRA administrator, then list it with her real estate agent. When the sale is complete, the funds will be deposited in her self-directed IRA. If the asset generated debt-based income during the 12 months prior to the sale, Jo will owe the UBIT on the capital gain, regardless of whether it was held in a traditional IRA or a Roth IRA. If not, the only tax the gain will ever generate will not come due until Jo begins taking distributions from her traditional IRA.

CHAPTER NINE

Becoming a Lender: Investing in Real Estate-Backed Notes

*The only man who sticks closer to you in
adversity than a friend is a creditor.*

–AUTHOR UNKNOWN

Sizing Up the Job

Skill Level: Craftsman

When you bought your first home, the closing officer probably presented a file of papers about an inch thick for your signature. Unless you paid cash for the property, the mass of documents included a mortgage and the mortgage note, also referred to as the trust deed or a promissory note.

The job of your mortgage was to secure the real estate as collateral for the loan. In typical legalese, it stated that the lender could take the property if you failed to repay the loan. But nowhere in the mortgage did it cite the details about when and how you were required to repay the loan. That was the job of the note.

Together, the two documents obliged you to repay a specific amount at a specific interest rate over a specific period of time and at specific intervals. Failure to meet the terms of the note would jeopardize your continued ownership of the property and your credit standing as well.

Collateral: Property used as security against a loan.

Primary market: When you sign a note directly with your lender, the transaction is said to take place on the primary market.

Secondary market: When one lender sells a note to another lender, the transaction is said to take place on the secondary market.

When money is lent and a note is signed between the buyer and the lender, whether it's at the time of the purchase or later when the property is refinanced, the transaction is generically referred to as *originating a note*. Originating notes is carried out on the *primary market*. Somewhere down the road, the lender will very likely sell the debt to another party on the *secondary market*. To make the acquisition attractive to potential note buyers, the seller typically discounts the note—meaning that it is being offered for less than the outstanding balance on the loan.

This book will explain how and why either party would want to do such a thing shortly. What's important to realize at this point is that your self-directed IRA can be used to invest in both the primary- and secondary-note markets. Before you get to that, however, this book needs to establish the scope of the discussion.

Senior Notes Versus Junior Notes

Real estate can have a number of different notes against it, which are classified according to the repayment priority of each. A *senior note* is the first lien against a property and has the first claim for repayment. By extension, a *junior note* is any debt claim that follows a senior note. If that sounds confusing, it won't for long. Jo's home is a perfect example.

Jo obtained a mortgage and signed a promissory note when she bought her house. This is the senior note. A few years later, she used the equity in her house to secure additional financing to remodel the kitchen. She accomplished this through what is called a *second mortgage*, although it's often referred to as a *home-equity loan* in ads and TV commercials. The resulting note would be classified a junior note, because its claim against the security (her home) is secondary to the senior note. Buying and selling secondary, or junior, notes falls into the high-risk investment category and has a questionable place in any but the most well funded IRA. That's why we will limit our current discussion to high-grade, real estate-backed senior notes.

> **Senior note:** A secured debt that will be paid first in the event of a foreclosure.
>
> **Junior note:** Any note that is secured after the senior note. There can be any number of junior notes, but only one senior note. In the event the borrower defaults on the loan, the holder of a junior note can file a claim for payment, but the claim will be paid only after the senior note is satisfied.

Repayment priority is not the only risk factor that separates low-risk notes from their high-risk counterparts. The terms of the note are every bit as important. Of course, the terms are already set by the time it comes on the secondary market. For better or worse, they were negotiated at the time the note was underwritten and include the amount to be repaid, the interest rate charged and the repayment terms. Sometimes the creditworthiness of the borrower can introduce additional risk too.

Together, these factors determine where the note falls on the risk continuum and influence how much of a discount the note will command to make it attractive on the resale market.

To understand how these factors impact the value of a note, let's define each one and then see how a buyer and seller might use them to establish the discount on a note.

- **Loan-to-value ratio (LTV):** A calculation derived by dividing the balance of the loan by the market value of the property. It is used as a measure of risk for a note. The lower the result of the calculation, the lower the risk to the lender.

- **Borrower's creditworthiness:** An evaluation of the probability that the borrower will repay the loan according to the terms of the note. To a large degree, this is a subjective evaluation, although objective data, such as income and credit history, are considered too.

- **Interest rate:** A percentage of the balance of the note charged by the lender and paid by the borrower.

- **Term of the loan:** The life span of the note. Notes can be written for virtually any duration, from days to months to years. Mortgage notes are typically written for 5-, 10-, 15-, 20-, and 30-year terms. On the secondary market, the *term* of the loan refers to the length of time remaining in the life of the note.

CLASSIFIED CASE STUDY

Advice From Allstate Mortgage & Investments:

One of our clients wanted to borrow on their home to invest in some additional property. As their home had been quit claim deeded to them by their parents, they had no loan against it and this would be a straight cash-out deal. We met with them and started their loan the same way we would start any loan. They filled out a complete application, reviewed there credit and did some research on the value of there home. They had collection accounts, charge offs and low credit scores. The value of their home was $200,000 and they needed a loan amount of $120,000, which puts us at a LTV of 65%.

Based on the customers credit score, low loan to value and the urgency for a fast closing we suggested going with a private investor. We knew that going with a private investor we could close quickly and my client would have their funds by the deadline.

Once we found an investor to do the loan we had the title company prepare the closing documents. The documents were then forwarded to the investors IRA office. Typically when the closing documents are forwarded to the IRA office, the turn around time is 24-48 hours. They will either approve the mortgage, note etc. or they will advise us of any changes that will need to be made before the closing. If there are any changes that need to be made the title company will make the corrections and we will resubmit the documents to the IRA for approval. Once approved, we have the customers sign the closing documents and the money is then wired to the title company for funding. We were able to close this loan in 10 days and the customers purchased their second property.

Calling in the Subcontractors

Whether Jo is buying an existing note or originating a new one, her team of experts will perform very similar tasks. Early on in the process—long before she has a deal, in most cases—she will call in her IRA administrator, accountant, attorney, title insurance company, and real estate agent.  Why? Primarily because an ounce of prevention is worth a pound of cure. You may be thinking that the primary role of her team of seasoned professionals is to help her execute the transaction. They have another role, however, that is every bit as important. They are going to help sniff out the first scent of danger, so that Jo can walk away before she is contractually committed to an investment she may live to regret.

What kinds of things will they be trying to detect? The attorney is looking for a legitimate seller and contractual language that protects Jo's interests, for starters. If Jo feels uncomfortable with her own assessments, her accountant will help Jo analyze the cash flow assumptions of the deal. The real estate broker will help Jo pull together the numbers to feed to the accountant. The title insurance company will perform a title search to make sure that the note she is considering buying is the senior note on the property and that there are no defects to the title. A copy will be forwarded to Jo's attorney for review. The IRA administrator will give Jo the information she needs to make sure that all transactions follow both IRS rules and the administrator's company policies.

Assuming that the pending transaction passes its various legal, financial, and due diligence inspections, Jo will give her attorney the go-ahead to coordinate the rest of the process. He will order an escrow account to be established with the title company and see that a full title search is completed and title insurance written. He and the IRA administrator will review all of the final documents before Jo signs them.

In the meantime, Jo will be searching for one more subcontractor to add to her team. As a lender, she'll need someone to collect the borrower's payments—a mortgage servicer. She'll probably be able to locate a reliable one by asking her experts. Certainly between her accountant, lawyer, and administrator, one of them will have worked with a mortgage servicer they can recommend. When she's chosen one, she'll add this new professional to her Golden Rolodex° and put him or her in touch with the IRA administrator, since they will be working together for the duration of the note.

Of course, when the transaction is complete, her experts will each send Jo a bill for their services, which Jo will gladly pay because she knows that without them, the risk factor for the investment would have grown exponentially.

CLASSIFIED CASE STUDY

Meet Jean—a 74 year-old widow who lives in Florida. She opened her self-directed IRA two years ago at the urging of her son. She has chosen to use the assets in her account to underwrite mortgage notes through a mortgage broker.

When my husband died, I inherited his IRA, which I rolled over into a bank IRA in my own name. That was a big mistake, because I had them [the bank] invest it for me. With the stock market, you never know where it's going to go. It goes up; it goes down. I lost money.

The self-directed IRA is great for me because my interest rate is locked in. Sure, I could face a foreclosure, but the mortgage broker I use does all the screening for me. And all the loans I make are within a fifty-mile radius. That way I can see what I'm lending my money on.

Most of my loans are for five years. I never loan more than 50% of the value of the property and the interest rate is usually around 13 percent – sometimes more – with a pre-payment penalty. I've never carried a loan for the full term.

I was thinking about getting long-term care insurance – just in case. But the premiums are almost $1,000 a month. Between my small pensions, Social Security and the locked-in interest income from the self-directed IRA, I figure that if anything happens I'll have enough coming in to cover my expenses.

I hope I never need a nursing home, but I know I'll be okay, if I do.

Buying Paper

Skill Level: Craftsman

Once upon a time, people deposited their money at a local bank or savings and loan where it earned compound interest for as long as it stayed on deposit. The banker used the funds on deposit to make home loans to the community. Every month, homeowners mailed or walked their mortgage payments to the bank, and sooner or later, the loans were paid off, either when the houses sold or when the borrowers finished making all their payments.

Ten years ago, when Jo was ready to buy her home, she obtained a mortgage from her bank, just like in the old days. In some areas, it would have been called a deed of trust, but it accomplished the same thing. It established the house as the collateral that secured her loan. But the mortgage itself  did not stipulate the repayment terms. She signed a separate mortgage note, which spelled out the terms by which she promised to repay the loan.

Then one day, Jo received a letter in the mail advising her that her mortgage note had been sold to a New York banker. A week or so later, she received a new payment book and instructions about where to send future payments. So much for a lifelong relationship with one banker.

What happened with Jo's mortgage note is very common. Bankers and mortgage companies routinely package a group of notes they hold into a portfolio and sell it at a discount on the secondary market to raise cash so they can make new loans. While the small investor is hardly in a position to buy one of these portfolios, someone like Jo certainly can buy an individual real estate-backed note if it suits her purposes.

Along about now, you may be wondering why she would want to buy just the note, if owning income property in a self-directed IRA is such a great way to grow her account. To understand Jo's interest in real estate notes requires that we first understand a little more about them.

Loan-to-Value Ratio (LTV): The Lower the Better

Our good friend Dick made his last payment on the mortgage note for his home a few years ago. Shortly afterward, he retired, sold the house, and moved to his vacation home in the country, where he lives full-time. He didn't need the cash for his house, so when he put the house up for sale, he stated that he was willing to carry the loan for a qualified buyer with 20 percent down.

At the closing, he netted a nice cash payment and began collecting 6 percent compound interest on the balance of the loan. Current CD rates were 3 percent lower, so it was a premium deal for him. Now, two years later, a lake-view property down the road from his country home has come on the market at a price Dick can't pass up. The only problem is that he's short on cash at the moment, since most of his money is tied up in various investments. If he can find a quick buyer for the note on his old house, though, he might be able to raise enough cash to cover the purchase. The question is, How much can he get for the note? That depends on several things.

According to the risk-reward relationship theory, the higher the risk of a note, the more potential reward the note needs to offer to make it attractive to an investor. In this case, the risk is that the borrower might default on the loan, and the lender could end up owning the property. If that happens, the lender will be in a world of hurt if the balance on the loan is more than the market value. That's why lenders want a healthy down payment from the buyer at the time the note is written.

By contrast, if the balance on the loan is well below the property's market value, the lender is fairly assured that he or she can sell the foreclosed property and still net a profit out of the deal. Clearly, whether a lender is writing a new note or buying an existing note, the lower the loan-to-value ratio (LTV), the less risky the investment. Let's look at how the numbers add up in Dick's case.

> Balance on Dick's note: $200,000
> Market value of the property: $270,000
> LTV = 74%

In general, investors consider an LTV of 75 percent, as the maximum acceptable level for a salable note. To demonstrate how a prospective buyer of Dick's note would look at his offering, let's compare it to a note that Jane has for sale at the same time.

> Balance on Jane's note: $150,000
> Market value of property: $270,000
> LTV = 56%

If the borrower defaults on Dick's loan and the buyer of his note has to sell the property again, he stands to make as much as $70,000 on the deal. But, if the borrower defaults on Jane's note, the note buyer could sell the property and pocket perhaps $120,000. This is in addition to the principal and interest collected during the period the note is held.

If Jo were looking for a note to purchase, which deal do you think would be of more interest to her? If LTV were the only factor to be considered, the choice would be a slam dunk. But there's more to valuing a note than a low LTV ratio.

Borrower's Credit History: Caution Equals Less Risk

When Jo loaned her cousin Shirley money to buy a lot for a vacation home, Jo knew what she was getting into. She'd known Shirley her entire life. She knew her work history and that when Shirley's husband had been ill a few years earlier, Shirley had taken a second job until he was back on his feet to make sure the bills got paid. In short, she knew that Shirley would do whatever it took to make sure the loan was paid back.

If Jo decides to buy a real estate note, she won't have the advantage of knowing the borrower as well as she knows Shirley. So, unless Jo is foolishly looking for the chance to experience the foreclosure process, she'll want to look long and hard at the probability that the borrower will actually pay off the note—or, more to the point, that at some point he or she will stop paying altogether.

There are never guarantees where repayment is concerned. Even responsible folks with sterling credit can run into a spate of ill fortune. But in today's real estate market, some lenders have relaxed the qualifications  for homebuyers to the point where salaries are often stretched to the max to meet financial obligations. A run-of-the-mill bump in the road can cause them to fall behind on their payments. Sometimes they get over the rough patch. Sometimes not.

So how does Jo protect herself? By finding out everything there is to know about the history of the note. We can assume that Jo has already determined the value of the property through a competitive market analysis and that she knows the balance on the note, so she has established the LTV. What she doesn't know is when the note was originated and for what amount. That information can be found on the note itself, which was filed at the courthouse, or with the county recorder, at the time it was signed. Once she has the answers to those two questions, she'll have some idea as to how committed the borrower is to the property. The more equity a borrower has accrued in the property, the lower the likelihood that he or she will risk losing that equity by defaulting on the loan.

The current lender should be able to provide Jo with the borrower's payment history. Privacy laws protect credit information without the express consent of the borrower, so it is unlikely that she will be able to check the borrower's credit rating herself. But, again, the current lender should be able to provide Jo with the borrower's credit rating from the credit check that was completed at the time of the original loan application. It may not be current, but sometimes you work with the tools available.

The Role of Credit Ratings

Each of the three agencies uses a unique scoring model, which can result in a slightly different rating number for the same individual, depending on which agency is used. There are sufficient similarities, however, to make a few general comments.

Credit ratings are given as FICO® scores that range from 300 to 850. Lenders use a borrower's FICO® score as an underwriting criterion in determining if a borrower will be approved for a loan and at what interest rate the loan will be written. In general, a borrower with a FICO® rating above roughly 700 or better will pay a lower interest rate. Borrowers with a credit rating below 600 will typically pay a slightly higher interest rate than those over 700, and a borrower with a rating below 500 will pay the most. Given that interest rate structure is one way that lenders manage risk, there is a lesson in those numbers that Jo can use to determine if she considers a borrower on a given note to be an acceptable credit risk. Unless the LTV is exceedingly low and she is willing to own the property, she probably wants to hold a note only for a borrower with a FICO® score of 700 or higher.

Interest Rate: The Higher the Better

As you discovered in the discussion on credit ratings, borrowers with good credit typically pay lower interest rates than borrowers with poor credit. That's because, aside from loaning money only to people who don't need it, one of the most  effective ways to manage risk is through the interest rate structure.

Interest generates the income that makes a lender willing to underwrite a loan in the first place. When a lender decides to take a chance on a borrower with less than sterling credit, the lender will often cover potential downstream problems with guaranteed upstream income. In other words, the lender will charge an interest rate that will generate sufficient income now to keep him or her operating in the black if the borrower defaults later.

During the years that Dick owned the note, he collected more than $28,000 in principal and interest. If the interest rate had been just one percent higher, that number would have increased to $32,000 and change. That's an additional $4,000 cushion if the borrower defaults. It follows, then, that a note with a higher interest rate would command a higher price (and lower discount) than a similar note with a lower interest rate.

Term: the Shorter the Better — But Not Too Short

The ideal investment can probably be defined as one that returns the highest possible return in the shortest time period. Why is time a factor? Because money tied up in one investment cannot be put to work on a new opportunity if one presents itself—one that might offer a higher ROI than the existing investment. As disappointing as passing up golden opportunities can be, there is another reason that time can be a real profit killer: inflation.

Although most people think of inflation as an increase in the cost of goods, it has a more sinister effect on investments. It actually weakens the investment dollar. Here's how. Let's say that in 1995 Jo invests $100,000 for ten years and earns an ROI of 8.6 percent. At the end of the term, she cashes out for $215,892. A profit of $115,892 sounds pretty good until you factor in time.

Let's assume that we experienced an average annual inflation rate of 3 percent during the ten years Jo held the investment. By the time she collects her $215,892, it only has the buying power of $160,644 in 1995 dollars. That reduces her 8.6 percent ROI to a mere 6 percent.

Time can have another downside where holding a note is concerned. This book talked about the potential for default as being the biggest risk and noted that even a creditworthy borrower can hit on hard times. The longer Jo holds a note, the more opportunity there will be for a good investment to turn sour.

Jo has two ways in which she can reduce the term of any note she chooses to hold. The first, of course, is to buy a note with an acceptable term. The other is to hold the note for as long as she is comfortable doing so and then offer the note for sale to another investor. How good a job she did in choosing the note in the first place will become apparent when it comes time to sell it. If she chose a well-structured note at an appropriate discount, she'll reap an acceptable ROI.

If not? She'll learn a valuable lesson for the next time. Hopefully, it won't prove to be a costly lesson, because this is Jo's retirement money we're talking about.

If long-term notes equal greater risk, does it follow that short-term notes equal less risk? The short answer on short-term notes is, not always—balloon payments being a case in point.

> **Balloon payment:** A lump-sum payment due at the end of a loan. Balloon payments are usually structured as part of a short-term loan, sometimes referred to as a *bullet loan*. A bullet note can be written in either of two ways. The most common requires periodic payments throughout the term of the loan, followed by the final balloon payment. Alternatively, the payments can be deferred to the end of the term, at which time the borrower pays the balloon payment, covering both interest and principal.

The way homeowners generally deal with a balloon payment is to refinance or sell the property before the due date. If the borrower fails to do one or the other and doesn't have the cash to meet the payment, he or she could be forced into default. Again, unless Jo is willing to risk dealing with a foreclosure, she'd be wise to walk away from a note that includes a balloon payment in the near future. Note investors generally define near future as within a year or two.

If the note is sufficiently discounted, Jo might be tempted to snatch it up and try to resell it before the balloon payment comes due. The risk in such an approach is that there probably is a reason that the note is priced so favorably—like maybe no one else wants to gamble on it either.

Nuts and Bolts

Let's take a look at how Jo might fare on a hypothetical mortgage note transaction with the following terms:

Loan balance	$ 64,000
Property value	$ 100,000
LTV	64%
Interest rate	6%
Term	10 years

Assume that the borrower has an excellent credit rating and perfect payment history on the loan. A competitive market analysis of comparable homes in the area confirms the estimated market value of the house and that the area is continuing a slow, but steady year-over-year appreciation.

As with any real estate transaction, Jo contacts her title insurance professionals and has them run a preliminary title check. Her attorney reviews the deal and gives her the nod to proceed. This is a vanilla mortgage note acquisition deal, so she's confident that there is no legal conflict with IRS rules, but she gives her IRA administrator a heads-up about the pending transaction. If the administrator detects a problem, she will let Jo know before she crosses the point of no return. In this case, the administrator confirms Jo's take on the situation. When everything has checked out to Jo's satisfaction, she offers the note holder 70 percent of the value of the balance. That's a little below the standard of 75 percent for a pristine deal, but she wants to err on the side of caution, since this is her first note transaction. It turns out that the note holder is in immediate need of the cash, so he accepts her offer.

One Note, Four Possible Outcomes

Let's fast-forward a bit and assume that the buy side of the transaction has gone without a hitch, and Jo now owns the note. Now what? There are four possible outcomes, only one of which is fully within her control.

Outcome A: Jo Holds the Note for the Balance of Its Term

Tying her money up for 10 years is not Jo's first choice for an outcome for this investment. Granted, the principal will be drawn steadily downward, but at an excruciatingly painful rate when she considers the other investments she will have to let pass her by while the note matures. As you probably know from watching the equity in your home grow, it's typically many years before the lion's share of your payment switches from interest to principal. Speaking of interest, it will add to her IRA balance each and every month. So, this outcome might not be entirely bad.

If Jo did hold the note for its full term, she would collect $21,264 in interest income. Combined with the principal reclaimed through the monthly payments, her income from the investment would total about $85,264. After deducting the price she paid for the note ten years earlier, she would net $40,464. That's almost as much as the note cost her in the first place—90 percent, to be exact. There's just one little problem. She had to hold the note for ten years to get there. That works out to an annualized ROI of 9 percent. If that amount is adjusted for inflation, the ROI turns abysmal.

Outcome B: Borrower Pays Off the Loan

Let's say the homeowner sells the house a year after Jo buys his mortgage note. Over the course of the 12 months she held the note, Jo will have collected interest payments totaling $3,411 and another $4,400 in payments toward the principal. When the sale on the house closes, she will also receive the outstanding balance on the loan, which amounts to approximately $59,000. After we deduct the $44,800 Jo paid for the note from her total income ($67,411), she nets $22,611 out of the deal, earning her an annualized ROI of 5 percent. Of course, the numbers would vary depending upon how long Jo holds the note before the borrower sells. Bear in mind, however, that in this day and age, the average homeowner only stays in a home for about six years. The greatest likelihood, then, would be for the outcome to fall somewhere between Outcome A and Outcome B—unless, of course, disaster strikes.

Outcome C: Borrower Defaults

Companies downsize. They close up shop. Sometimes they move their jobs offshore. People get sick. Marriages dissolve. It would be impossible to list all of the hardships that can befall a homeowner. Even a person with perfect credit and a flawless payment history can run into a rough patch that ends up lasting longer than anyone thought possible. If the borrower on Jo's mortgage note turns out to be one of them, all is not lost for Jo; quite the opposite, in fact.

To demonstrate how it works, let's assume that a year after Jo buys the mortgage note, the borrower stops making the payments. Because Jo's note is secured by the real estate mortgage, Jo can foreclose on the loan, take title to the property, and do with it as she pleases. What she pleases, of course, is to sell it at its full market value. In this case, full market value is $69,000 more than she paid for the note in the first place, as you see in Table 16.

Table 16. FORECLOSED NOTE PROFIT ANALYSIS

NOTE VALUE	
Market value of property	$ 100,000
Loan balance	$ 64,000
LTV (loan-to-value ratio)	64%
Note discounted price (70% of balance)	$ 44,800
PROFIT ANALYSIS	
Jo's Cost	**$ 44,800**
Selling price after foreclosure	$ 106,000
Interest income (1 year)	$ 3,411
Principal pay-down (1 year)	$ 4,405
Total income	$ 113,816
Jo's profit (total income less cost)	$ 69,019
Annualized ROI	154%

Of course, these figures do not account for the cost (and aggravation) of going through the foreclosure process and selling the property. However, even after covering those expenses, Jo will very likely be well compensated for her aggravation.

Outcome D: Jo Resells the Note

What if this homeowner turns out to be the exception to the rule? Perhaps the house is in the same neighborhood where he grew up, went to school, and married his wife. Maybe he can't think of another place in the world where he'd rather live. He just might remain in the same house for 20 or 30 years.

After a few years of holding the note, Jo might become impatient waiting for him to sell the house so that she can collect the loan payoff. Or maybe she believes she bought the note at such a good price that she can turn it over in short order and capture a nice profit. Let's consider how that scenario would pan out for Jo.

In the year since Jo bought the note, the value of the house has appreciated by $5,000, and the loan balance has decreased to $59,183. Together, that brings the LTV down to 56 percent, a drop of 8 percent since Jo purchased it. Remember that investors want an LTV below 75 percent, so when she puts it on the market, she quickly finds a buyer at a 25 percent discount off the loan balance.

When all is said and done, Jo receives $44,387 from the sale of the note and $7,816 from interest and principal payments from the 12 months she owned the note. Deducting the price she paid for the note returns a profit of $7,816 or 17.6 percent. That's almost double the annualized return from holding onto the note for ten years—with a lot less risk.

Table 17. RESOLD NOTE PROFIT ANALYSIS

UPDATED NOTE VALUE	
Market value of property	$ 105,000
Loan balance	$ 59,183
LTV (loan-to-value ratio)	56%
Note Discount Price (75% of balance)	$ 44,387
PROFIT ANALYSIS	
Jo's Cost	$ 44,800
Income from sale of note	$ 44,387
Interest income (1 year)	$ 3,411
Principal pay-down (1 year)	$ 4,405
Total income	$ 52,203
Jo's profit (total income less cost)	$ 7,816
Annualized ROI	17.6%

Notes for Sale: Where to Find Them

Jo starts her search for a mortgage note where she usually starts any search—on the Internet. After a few minutes of searching, however, she realizes that the challenge of weeding out the legitimate brokers from the gimmicks and scam artists is going to take more time than she has available. Instead, she turns to her personal and business network.

She mentions her interest to her lawyer, accountant, real estate broker, coworkers, friends, and family members. She passes out her business cards to them and asks them to ask around. Certainly, one of them knows someone who is carrying a mortgage note. More to the point, certainly one of them knows someone who wants to unload a mortgage note for ready cash. It takes a few weeks, but she finally receives a call from her accountant. He has a client who needs to raise some quick cash.

If the call from her accountant hadn't come, Jo could have set about calling some of the larger real estate brokers or real estate attorneys in her area. Whether she deems it wise to cast her net beyond her own personal and professional network is a question only Jo can answer, and it depends to a large extent on how comfortable she feels about her ability to detect investment hucksters when she sees them.

Originating Notes

Skill Level: Master Craftsman

A while back, Jo's cousin Shirley asked Jo if she might be interested in loaning her $15,000 to buy a plot of land in the mountains where Shirley and her husband planned to build a cabin for weekend getaways. When they found the land, they had assumed that with their good credit, getting favorable financing would be a simple matter. What they discovered, instead, was that most lenders wanted to charge almost 4 percent above the home mortgage interest rate for a loan on undeveloped acreage. A discussion with Jo over Thanksgiving dinner ended up with an arrangement that benefited Jo and Shirley alike.

At the time that Jo made the loan to Shirley, she just happened to have $20,000 in treasury notes that were about to mature. By lending Shirley some of the money at a fair interest rate, she could bump the earning capacity of the money upward by an extra 2 to 3 percent. It was a win-win deal, especially since Jo knew Shirley well enough to have a clear assurance that the risk of default was exceptionally low.

There are other ways to become a real estate lender too. Every day, all across America, property owners sell their real estate and offer to provide financing on the transaction to a qualified buyer. Why would they do that instead of taking the cash in hand? Often to avoid the capital gain tax hit they would face for selling the property and receiving a lump-sum payment at closing.

Generally speaking, a single person can earn up to $250,000 profit on the sale of his or her primary residence and owe no capital gains tax. For a married couple, the limit is doubled. But every penny of the gain above that amount and all of the profit on the sale of a second home or investment property are taxable. If the seller doesn't have an immediate need for the cash, one way to lessen the tax burden of the transaction is to accept payments from the buyer—at a fair interest rate, of course—for some period of time.

Most seller-financed loans are not spread out over 20 or 30 years like loans from banks and mortgage companies. Instead, the seller typically offers a bullet loan, as we discussed earlier. A bullet loan typically has a short term—perhaps five to seven years or so—with a balloon payment due at the end. If the buyer plans to remain in the house longer than that, he or she has the option of obtaining conventional financing anytime within the term of the loan. Alternatively, he or she can sell the property and pay off the loan. In either case, the seller has enjoyed interest income from the property and a steady paydown on the principal.

But, what if Jo lacks property to sell and still wants to underwrite a mortgage note? Certainly, she could purchase an existing note, as we discussed earlier. Or, she could find a homebuyer or real estate developer or anyone else with a need for cash and a piece of real estate to pledge as security for the loan.

Along about now, you might be asking, *why?* Why originate a loan when it's a relatively simple procedure to buy one that's already in place? The question is best answered by remembering why Jo switched to a self-directed IRA in the first place. She wanted more flexibility and control over her retirement savings investments.

Being able to choose between underwriting a new loan and purchasing an existing note on the secondary market is an example of that flexibility.

Think of an existing note as a house that's already constructed. Everything about the house is perfect, except that it's in Ohio and you have your heart set on a view of the ocean. There are no oceans to be had in the Buckeye State, so it might be time to start looking for a different house. It's that way with notes. The terms of an existing note cannot be modified. But a new note can be constructed exactly the way you want it, giving you better control in managing the balance between risk and reward.

Nitty Gritty

Let's see how Jo would put that flexibility to work in the case of a borrower who has signed an $80,000 purchase contract on 20 acres of plowed-under cornfield adjoining his property. The contract is contingent upon his lining up suitable financing. Suitable in this case means that he wants to obtain a blanket mortgage on a rental property he owns and the additional land.

> **Blanket mortgage:** One mortgage that uses two or more properties to secure a real estate-backed note. If the borrower fails to pay back the loan according to the terms of the note, the lender has recourse against all of the property securing the loan.

He tells the mortgage broker that the market value of the rental is approximately $150,000 and that it is owned outright. He wants to borrow $160,000 to cover the purchase of the land, subdividing the land into ten, one-acre home sites and running

utilities to the site. The other ten acres will be reserved for an access road and as a buffer between his property and his new neighbors.

The day after he signed the sales contract, a local builder came around looking to buy the land from him for $100,000. The borrower has done his homework, and he knows that once the lots are subdivided and improved, he can wholesale them out for $40,000 or more each. Selling them one at a time could yield double that. Why should he give the extra profit to the builder, when he can keep it for himself?

In the end, the builder agreed to pay $30,000 for each of the ten lots after the subdividing is complete. He tells the mortgage broker that he only needs the money for 10 to 12 months, because he's certain that he can have everything complete in about 8 months. He's added the extra 4 months as cushion.

He goes on to explain that his bank has offered him an 80 percent loan on the rental with an interest rate of 5.64 percent, but won't approve a blanket loan on the two properties. That leaves him $40,000 short on what he needs for the project. He's hoping to find a lender who will write a blanket mortgage so that he can raise the additional money without having to carry two separate loans.

The broker does some figuring and suggests a loan that would amortize on a 20-year schedule, resulting in a monthly payment of $1,147 for principal and interest and a balloon payment for $156,000 on the first anniversary of the loan. When the borrower gives him verbal agreement on the terms, the mortgage broker calls Jo to see if she's interested.

Table 18. BLANKET MORTGAGE NOTE ANALYSIS

Market Value of Rental Property	$ 150,000
Market Value of Vacant Land	$ 80,000
Total Market Value of Combined Assets	$ 230,000
Loan Balance	$ 160,000
Term	12 months
Interest Rate	6%
LTV (Loan-to-Value Ratio)	69%

LTV

The first thing that Jo will look at with any note, new or existing, is the loan-to-value ratio. In this case, it is 69 percent. Since Jo typically would not be interested in any note with an LTV above 75 percent, this is acceptable. She also notes that if the borrower defaults on the loan, she'd find herself in possession of a rental property that is worth almost as much as the loan balance. She knows someone who might be interested in buying the land if she ends up owning it, so she feels the loan is sufficiently secured, assuming that everything checks out as the owner has represented.

Interest Rate

When Jo loaned money to her cousin Shirley, she was free to offer her a great deal on the interest rate. The amount they settled on was higher than Jo was able to get even in a long-term treasury note at the time and yet lower than a bank or mortgage company would have charged Shirley. Whether it was a wise financial decision could be debated, but she was satisfied with the amount and happy to be able to do her cousin a favor.

When Jo originates a mortgage note within her self-directed IRA, she will lose the freedom to use her financial success to do favors for family members—or anyone else, for that matter. That is because every investment within an IRA must be undertaken with the primary goal of benefiting the IRA. That premise is the basis for the tax advantages proffered by the IRA legislation. Breaking the rule means risking the loss of the IRA's tax advantages.

It stands to reason, then, that if Jo loans our would-be land developer the $160,000 he needs to develop the acreage next door, she will have to do so at the market rate for a similar loan through a bank or mortgage company. The mortgage broker can advise her as to what the competitive rate is for this type of loan, or her accountant or real estate broker can research the information for her. For the purposes of our example, we'll assume that it is somewhere between 5.75 and 6 percent. The IRS requires that the terms of the note must meet or exceed that amount to protect the tax-sheltered status of Jo's IRA. Based on that requirement, she settles on 6 percent to be on the safe side.

Term

The length of the loan is a more difficult matter. The borrower insists that he can finish the project in less than one year and does not want a financial commitment beyond that date. His reasons have more to do with his personal aversion to debt than anything else, but Jo makes him an offer that suits her thinking anyway.

For Jo to agree to underwrite this loan, she will require that the borrower increase the term of the loan to at least three years. Five would be better. She will have her attorney insert a clause in the contract that stipulates that if the loan is paid off within the first twelve months, the owner will owe a prepayment penalty equal to the balance of the first year's interest.

Why three years instead of one? Because Jo wants to make sure she isn't setting him up for disaster if things don't go as smoothly as he expects. Granted, he's already added a couple of months to his time line, but what if the builder goes out of business or gets caught up in bureaucratic red tape on the subdividing process? The borrower could end up having to find a new buyer, and that could take anywhere from a few days to a few years. The last thing Jo wants is to force the borrower into foreclosure for being optimistic.

There's another reason for stipulating a longer-term note, and it's the same reason Jo wants to include a guarantee of 12 months of interest even if his project wraps up early. It takes time, effort, and money on Jo's part to write the loan in the first place. She wants to be guaranteed at least a minimum return of 6 percent on the deal to make it worthwhile. Hopefully, she'll end up carrying the loan another year or so beyond that.

Borrower's Credit History

Originating the loan also provides Jo with more control over the creditworthiness of the borrower. Not everyone looking for mortgage financing is as good at paying his or her bills as Shirley is at paying hers. By putting herself in the driver's seat, Jo can set the qualifications for loan approval and choose only the cream of the crop among borrowers. To accomplish this, she will require a credit report, employment check stubs or W-2 forms, and income tax returns.

If the borrower is married, she'll require that both spouses sign the note. If the borrower scoffs at the request, she'll take that as a sign that he or she may have something to hide.

When it comes to choosing a borrower who is a good credit risk, the downside—and everything does have its downside—is that a new borrower comes without a track record. By contrast, an established loan comes with the borrower's payment history. Unknowns increase risk. Yet, it may be a risk Jo is willing to take if the terms of the note are exactly to her liking.

Three Essential Documents

With a real estate-backed note, the property itself is the security for the loan. If the assets pledged are anything less than represented, it will decrease the value of the security and increase the risk of the investment. So, assuming that the borrower accepts Jo's terms, she has three more steps she will want to take to minimize her risk on the deal.

Appraisal

Jo will have already asked her real estate agent to compile the selling prices of similar houses, as well as both developed and undeveloped acreage in the area, so she's reasonably comfortable that the borrower has accurately represented the market value of both properties. However, individual  houses have individual strengths and weaknesses. A professional appraisal will point out both and establish the actual value of the house as accurately as possible, without actually putting it on the market.

Title Insurance

The homeowner/borrower has represented that he owns the rental property free and clear—that there are no liens on the property and that this loan will be in senior position. Owner representations are one thing. Proof is another. To get that proof, Jo will order a title search and insurance to make certain that a prior claim does not jeopardize her right to payment in case the borrower fails to pay back the loan according to the terms of the note.

Casualty Insurance

Real estate notes generally require that the property owner carry homeowner's insurance to protect against the risk of loss by fire or other casualty. Jo wants to go one step further and require that she be named as a coinsured on the policy. This way, if the property does suffer a major loss, she will be assured that the homeowner does not take the check from the insurance company and leave her to enforce her claim through the legal system.

CLASSIFIED CASE STUDY

Meet Doug—he owns a business. About three years ago, his CPA recommended that he open a self-directed IRA. All of the partners in the firm had moved to self-directed IRAs and he felt that it would be a good move for Doug, too. It's worked out so well that Doug's mother, his wife and his in-laws have all made the move to self-directed IRAs, too.

I started my retirement plan when I was 30 years old. Initially, I was putting in $30 a month and investing in the stock market. When the market tanked in the late '90s, I was losing more money every month than I was putting in the account.

A few years ago, I met a mortgage broker who works with private lenders. I've been working with him ever since I opened my self-directed IRA. He does the screening then I check out the property before agreeing to the deal.

I would say that the most important thing for a mortgage note lender to do is to match the legal description of the property to the physical address. I heard about a fraud case a few years ago where an investor was shown one property and the actual property he was loaning money on was a little shack down the road. That's pretty easy to avoid these days with the tools available on the Internet.

Not all mortgage brokers work with private lenders. The best way to find one is through a real estate agent. They know which brokers are open to working with you.

Borrowers Wanted: Where to Find Them

Shakespeare wrote that if you lend money to a friend, you're likely to lose both. Jo has been lucky that her friendship with her cousin Shirley hasn't suffered under the burden of doing business together. Would she do it again for another relative or perhaps a friend? Possibly. But what if she didn't want to risk losing a friend over money? Where else would she look for a borrower she might be interested in underwriting?

Mortgage brokers are always interested in developing new sources of funding for clients who come to them in search of favorable financing. Once she establishes a mortgage broker contact, Jo can lay out her terms and wait for the broker to match the right borrower to her loan. One plus for working with a mortgage broker is that he or she will handle the loan origination chores such as obtaining credit reports and financial statements.

Alternatively, if Jo has sufficient money to work with, she could contact builders and developers. Sometimes they need short-term financing for managing cash flow when projects overlap.

Finally, she has the option of running a classified ad in her local paper or in trade publications. She needs to be prepared, however, for the barrage of solicitations that will almost certainly follow.

A Cautionary Note About Real Estate Investment Trusts

When the real estate market tanked in 2007 and the investment bubble burst, a great deal of the fault could be laid to Real Estate Investment Trusts (REIT's), and the brokers and banking concerns that packaged and sold them. Basically, an REIT is created by taking literally thousands of mortgages, both residential and business, and combining them into a trust package. These packages were then sold within the market of major lenders as investments. The problem was that many of the lenders and their attorneys took shortcuts in packaging the trusts and in transferring them, often without actually having true legal possession of the documents, which represented an individual mortgage. When the real estate market started to reflect reality and not wishful thinking, many owners found themselves "upside down", that is, owing more on the mortgage than the property was worth. They started defaulting on their mortgages *en masse* and this created a huge backlog in Courts all over the country of mortgage foreclosures.

When some homeowners started fighting the foreclosures in court, it came out that the banks did not have, in many cases, the required transfer documents of the mortgages and notes which had been packaged into the REIT's to enable the banks to legally foreclose. While most courts bent over backwards to protect the banks and lenders, it also resulted in a number of fraud cases being filed against the lenders by various state Attorney Generals; in a few cases homeowners were actually relieved of their mortgage obligations as a penalty to the lenders.

Florida was a classic example of this on a local basis; not only were a number of lawyers who specialized in representing the lenders in foreclosure cases found to be engaging in fraudulent conduct (and were disbarred) for filing foreclosures without the required documents, some national lenders and major banking houses actually collapsed under the burden of improperly documented mortgages and notes, bad loans which never should have been made at all, and other banking violations. Some seven years later, the courts are still trying to dig their way out of the backlog.

When considering investing in an REIT, extreme caution must be utilized because of this ongoing problem. Because of this we do not recommend investing in REITs at all as simply being too risky. You have no way of determining whether the REIT actually holds adequate and sufficient proof of ownership of the thousands of notes and mortgages that comprise the REIT. The risk and aggravation is simply not worth the gain.

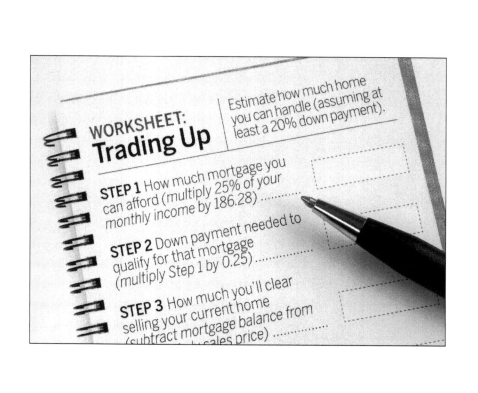

WORKSHEET:
Trading Up

Estimate how much home you can handle (assuming at least a 20% down payment).

STEP 1 How much mortgage you can afford (multiply 25% of your monthly income by 186.28) ....

STEP 2 Down payment needed to qualify for that mortgage (multiply Step 1 by 0.25) ....

STEP 3 How much you'll clear selling your current home (subtract mortgage balance from ~~~~~~ sales price) ....

CHAPTER TEN

Buying Options: The Ultimate In and Out Transaction

The best way to predict the future is to invent it.

–ALAN KAY

Sizing Up the Job

Skill Level: Craftsman

For each transaction that's been discussed so far, Jo's self-directed IRA acquired ownership of either a parcel of real estate or the debt secured by a parcel of real estate. Her objective with each was to purchase the asset at a lower price than she expected to be able to sell it for at some point in the future. In the interim, each transaction generated rental income—either from the use of the real estate, when she became a landlord, or from the use of her IRA money, when she became a lender.

Real estate options rarely offer rental cash flow. Properly researched and structured, however, real estate options offer Jo another type of investment to use to build her retirement security.

The concept behind real estate options is really quite simple. But first, let's establish what an option is not. It is not a purchase of real estate. To be certain, it can lead to the purchase of real estate, but by signing an option agreement, the buyer is only purchasing the control over a piece of property—not title to the property. Specifically, the buyer is purchasing the *exclusive right* to buy or sell a piece of property at an agreed-upon price on or before an agreed-upon date.

Exclusive right to buy means exactly what it sounds like. The seller relinquishes the right to sell the property to any other buyer for the duration of the option. At the expiration of the option contract, the buyer has the choice of exercising the option to purchase the property according to the terms stipulated in the agreement or not purchasing it at all. In the meantime, the property owner retains the right to use the property in any manner he or she chooses, providing it conforms to the law and the terms of the option agreement. The seller also continues to be responsible for keeping up the property, paying the taxes, and maintaining insurance on it.

Wilma's Bungalow

An option contract can be as simple or complex as the parties choose to make it, but every option agreement contains two elements that set it apart from a purchase agreement: option consideration and an expiration date or condition. The option consideration seals the deal, and the expiration date or condition establishes when or under what circumstances the buyer's option to purchase the property at the agreed-upon terms expires.

On the surface, that might sound like a pretty one-sided deal. Only a fool of a seller would willingly agree to take property off the market based on an iffy statement of intent from a buyer, right? Wrong. To understand why an option can be beneficial for both parties, let's examine a fairly straightforward transaction.

Jo's great-aunt Rose lives in a sleepy, little community about ten miles from Jo's house. Over the past few years, a boom in industrial development has spurred a parallel explosion in real estate values in many of the neighboring communities. Rose's community has lagged behind the others, but news that a large electronics manufacturer will build a new facility nearby will likely change that.

A few days after the announcement, Jo is visiting her aunt when they notice Rose's next- door neighbor, Wilma, outside supervising the hanging of a "for sale by owner" sign in the front yard. On a hunch, Jo wanders out to talk with the neighbor and discovers that Wilma has decided to sell her house because she thinks the exactly the same thing about the announcement that Jo does—that the neighborhood is destined for change. The big difference is that Jo sees it as good for property values, and Wilma sees it as the beginning of the end for the quaint little community.

When Jo gets home, she calls her real estate agent and asks her to find out what happened to real estate values when major employers moved into similar communities. She also asks for competitive sales data for homes in Rose's neighborhood and in particular for two-bedroom bungalows.

Based on the information Jo receives from her real-estate broker, she estimates that real estate values should experience double-digit gains in each of the two years following the opening of the manufacturing facility. In addition, although Wilma's house is one of smallest and oldest in the neighborhood, it appears to be priced almost 10 percent below its current market value. Taken together, that data would suggest that within two years of the opening of the manufacturing facility, Wilma's house could be worth 22 percent to 34 percent above the asking price.

Convinced that the property has the potential to return a sufficient ROI, Jo approaches Wilma with a proposition. By the time they are finished negotiating, Jo agrees to buy a three-year option to purchase the house at the full asking price of $81,000. She will pay the seller $10,000 at signing and another $10,000 on the first and the second anniversaries of the signing. The balance of $51,000 will be due when Jo exercises her option to buy.

Two years after Wilma and Jo sign the option agreement, Jo's IRA administrator issues the third check for $10,000 to Wilma. The electronics manufacturer has been in operation for a little less than a year, and the market value of the house has jumped by almost 47 percent—well ahead of Jo's expectations. It's time for Jo to start thinking about finding a buyer for Wilma's house.

That's right, finding a buyer. You see, Jo never intended to actually own the house; at least not for very long. Her plan from the beginning has been to find a buyer for the property and do a simultaneous close. That means that she will exercise her option to buy the house and sell it to another buyer either on the same day or very close to it.

Jo phones her real estate agent and gives her the go-ahead. Based on recent sales activity, Jo tells her agent that she wants to ask 10 percent above the home's current market value of $119,000. A month later, the real estate agent brings her an offer to purchase  the house at $115,000. After a little negotiating, she and the buyer agree on a price of $125,000. Jo gives Wilma a 30-day notice that she's ready to exercise her option, as required by their contract. A week after Jo wraps up the purchase of Wilma's house, she closes on the deal with her buyer. For her effort, Jo made $44,000 and an ROI of 147 percent on the $30,000 she paid to the seller during the term of the option.

Benefits to the Seller

You may have wondered why the seller would have taken this deal. Wouldn't she have been better off waiting for a cash-in-hand buyer? She could have wrapped up the sale in a matter of a few weeks or months instead of allowing Jo to tie up the property for two years and potentially three. It turns out that Wilma understood very clearly how her agreement with Jo would benefit her.

Option Consideration: A Bird in the Hand

First and foremost, the contract states that Wilma would receive $10,000 as the first installment of option consideration. It was hers to keep, along with each of the future installment payments, even if the Jo ultimately chose not to purchase the house. The form and value of the option consideration was for them to decide. Wilma might have agreed to accept the title to Jo's sports car or an all-expense-paid trip around the world. Or she might have required bigger or more frequent cash payments. In this case, $30,000 over the course of three years suited both Jo and Wilma fine.

A Buyer for a Hard-to-Sell Property

Sometimes a property languishes on the market for months or years with nary a nibble from a prospective buyer. Other times, the property generates initial interest, but some element of the sale (often the seller's demands or a fault with the property) quashes buyer enthusiasm in short order. Regardless of the reason a property fails to sell quickly, the longer it remains on the market, the greater the likelihood that the seller will accept an offer of an option to buy. With Wilma, the motivation boiled down to timing.

The day she hung the "for sale" sign in her front yard, she was angry and frustrated about the announcement of industrial development in the area. But the truth is, she really wasn't convinced that she was ready to leave. Jo's proposition allowed her an easier transition to a future that she knew was inevitable.

For 10 years, Wilma had spent her winters at her second home in Florida and summers in this house, which had been her home for the past 40 years. Every year, it gets a little more difficult to keep up two houses, but she's not really quite ready to give it up either. She doesn't like the changes she sees coming, but comfort in knowing they'll probably come a little at a time over a few years. She figures that by the time Jo is ready to buy the house, the time will be right for her too.

In the meantime, she'll collect $10,000 for sure and potentially another $20,000 in option consideration that she won't have to give back if Jo changes her mind. Furthermore, she's fairly certain that if Jo is willing to fork over that much money, she'll try very hard to find a way to complete the transaction.

Tax-Deferred Income

The IRS doesn't classify option consideration as income until the property sells or the option expires. This is Wilma's primary residence, and its sale price will be far less than the $250,000 tax-free threshold the IRS allows. If, on the other hand, this was Wilma's second home or an investment property, tax-deferred payments might have played a significant role in her decision to take Jo's offer.

Benefits to the Buyer

Jo wasn't looking for an option to buy real estate when she went to visit her Aunt Rose. But she knows enough to jump on an opportunity when it presents itself. A real estate option offers unique benefits that allow her to act quickly to lock in an opportunity without fully committing herself to a future course of action.

Time to Decide

In a sense, the option agreement that Jo entered into with Wilma was somewhat speculative. Based on the announcement that thousands of new jobs would be moving into the area and the research that her real estate broker did for her, Jo had every reason to expect that over the short term, real estate prices in the area would increase. Expectations can turn out to be substantially different from reality, however. Or as Yogi Berra said, "It's tough to make predictions, especially about the future."

By taking out an option on Wilma's property, Jo bought the time to allow her predictions about the future to be proven before she committed herself to the purchase.

Option Consideration: Good Insurance

Paying the option consideration benefits Jo as well as the seller. Sure, she stands to lose the whole amount if she decides not to go through with the purchase, but not paying it could expose her to greater risk.

Let's look at what would have happened if Jo and Wilma had agreed to enter into the same purchase option contract, except that Wilma had not required payment of an option consideration at signing. Wilma doesn't need the money until she's ready to move, so they might have agreed that Jo could wait and pay the full $81,000 when and if she decided to exercise her option on or before the expiration date three years out.

Based on their agreement, Jo would have paid for all of the legal work to execute and record the contract. Over the next two or three years, Jo would have been tickled to death as she watched the value of the real estate rise. Then just about the time that Jo was getting ready to exercise her option, what if Wilma announced that she'd changed her mind about selling? If you think resolving the problem would have been as simple as Jo taking Wilma to court to enforce the terms of the contract, think again. Clearly, the contract states that Wilma agreed to sell Jo the property. A judge, however, will require more than that.

An expression of intent is not sufficient when a contract is held up for the scrutiny of a court. The law requires that for a contract to be enforceable, it must demonstrate that the agreement benefits both parties.

Regardless of whether or not Wilma receives option consideration from Jo at the time they sign the contract, their arrangement most definitely benefits Jo. She has frozen the price of the property and taken it off the market for up to three years, while retaining the right to walk away without penalty. That's great for Jo, but what benefit does Wilma gain from the arrangement?

Unfortunately for Jo, the court won't equate Jo's expression of interest in buying the house as a true benefit to Wilma, especially given that the contract gives Jo what the law calls a *free look* provision.

To understand the free look provision, compare an option contract to a purchase contract. With a standard purchase contract, the buyer looks at the property and then makes a firm commitment to buy the house. If the buyer later fails to follow through with the purchase of the house, the seller retains the buyer's earnest money and, in some cases, can sue the buyer for additional damages.

By contrast, an option contract allows Jo to keep looking from the day she signs the contract until the day she either exercises her option to buy or walks away from the purchase—without penalty. That's a free look, and the law says that a free look benefits only the buyer. Now, if the option agreement is fronted with a nonrefundable option consideration, Jo no longer gets a free look. The playing field is leveled, and both the buyer and the seller, Jo and Wilma in this case, gain benefit from the contract.

To put the discussion into legal terms, our law recognizes that in order for a valid contract to exist, first there must be agreement of the parties as to the terms of the contract. Next, there must be mutual "consideration" to each party. "Consideration" is, as we have stated, a benefit to each party. Consideration can be a promise for a promise, an act for a promise, or an act for an act. It can also be an agreement to refrain from doing something, such as Wilma agreeing not to sell her home to another party before Jo's option expires. Jo paying money to Wilma is certainly a valid consideration in exchange for a promise by Wilma not to sell to anyone other than Jo within the option period. The parties must sign the agreement evidencing their consent. Contracts can also be made to benefit one or more third persons who is [are] not a signatory to the contract. This is known as a "third-party beneficiary contract".

One critical thing regarding real estate; it is basic law that for any contract concerning real estate to be valid, it needs to be in writing and signed by the parties to the contract. Legal formality is not a requirement; contracts signed on napkins have been held valid in court, so long as the other requirements of contract law were met (mutuality of agreement on the terms, consideration paid and consent of the parties).

In our example here, Jo is paying money to Wilma in exchange for Wilma's promise to sell her home to Jo within a specified period of time for a specified amount of money. When Jo and Wilma reduce their agreement to a written document, they both sign it and Jo makes the first payment to Wilma, a valid, enforceable contract has been entered into and Jo's ability to enforce it in a court of law is now secured.

The option consideration, then, is good insurance for Jo, because it gives Wilma benefit from the contract. If Wilma later refuses Jo's attempt to exercise her option to buy the house, it ensures that Jo's claim has legal standing in court.

Limited Risk

If an ideal investment is one that returns the highest return in the shortest period of time, the second-best investment must surely be the one in which the investor can control potential losses. That is exactly what an option accomplishes, by leaving an exit door open until Jo expressly decides to close it.

Consider what might have happened to the value of Wilma's house if the manufacturer had made a last-minute decision to move to different location. Or what if the manufacturer opened as planned, but failed to stimulate the migration to the suburbs that everyone, including Jo, expected? Every rule has an exception, and there is nothing that says that what happens in other communities has to happen in every community.

In either case, Jo would have thanked her lucky stars for years to come that she chose an option over an immediate purchase of Wilma's house. As for the money she paid Wilma, Jo would not have been happy to leave cash on the table, but that would have been a far better outcome than being saddled with a piece of real estate that offers little or no hope of turning a profit.

Cornfield Redux

Remember the buyer who was looking for a short-term mortgage on the 20 acres of cornfield? He wanted to buy the land, subdivide, and improve it, then sell it to a local builder. Jo was interested in underwriting the note, because the dollars made sense on the deal he was trying to put together. If she ended up owning the property, she knew she could make money on it. If he paid off the note as agreed, the interest income would still return a reasonable ROI. But, let's look at how Jo will structure the deal if we rewind the tape and make Jo the buyer instead of the lender.

The seller is asking $90,000 for 20 acres of plowed under cornfield. At Jo's request, her real estate broker pulls together the competitive numbers on the property and comes back with the following information.

Urban sprawl is pushing real estate development beyond the city limits, pressuring farmers to abandon their fields and cash out of the farming business. The going rate for tillable acreage is $1,800 an acre. One-acre building lots are commanding anywhere from $60,000 to $80,000 on the retail market and half that to a builder. The land backs up to a stand of oak woodland with a creek running through it, so she estimates that it will bring a price at the higher end of the range.

Jo's cost for subdividing the land and bringing in utilities will run in the vicinity of $10,000 per lot, assuming that she subdivides ten lots and reserves ten acres for an access road and a buffer between the farm next door and the new building lots. This will give her a net profit of $270,000 or 300 percent on the purchase price of the land. So far, everything she has learned matches up with the assumptions of the original investor. It's time for them to part ways, however.

Jo isn't interested in buying the land. She only wants to control it for a period of time. Long enough to reap the potential gains from getting to the property first, readying it for building, and then wholesaling it out to a builder. And she wants to do all this while putting up a minimal amount of money.

Jo agrees to pay the seller $10,000 on signing and commits to completing the subdivision and rezoning processes. According to her real estate broker's figures, Jo estimates that the value of the property will have jumped from $90,000 to close to $180,000 once that is completed. If market conditions confirm those assumptions, she has the choice of exercising her option and taking profits. Alternatively, she could choose to move on to phase two.

Assuming that Jo opts to press on, she will pay the seller another $10,000 on the first anniversary of the contract and will then have one year in which to have utilities brought onto the property. When the improvements are complete, she projects  that the market value of the property will be around $450,000.

Now bear in mind that Jo has had some expenses along the way. First of all, she paid the seller option consideration of $20,000 over the past two years. Then she had the expense of surveyors and government red tape to subdivide the land into 11 separate parcels and an access road. During the second year, she spent serious money bringing in utilities. So where does that put Jo? After her roughly $100,000 for the improvements and $20,000 in option consideration, she sitting with a potential profit somewhere in the vicinity of $250,000.

Once again, Jo has a choice. She can pay the next installment of option consideration to the seller and hold onto the option, or she can exercise it and move on. When her real estate broker brings her updated figures, she detects that the upward momentum in property values is starting to weaken. Lots are staying on the market a little longer than they did a year earlier, possibly because interest rates are going up or possibly because of the growing number of units on the market. She decides that instead of paying the next installment, which this time around is $30,000, she'll look for a buyer.

Fortunately for Jo, her real estate agent has been nurturing her contacts with the local builders, and two months before the third payment is due to the seller, she brings Jo an offer from one of them for $430,000 for everything except the buffer. When the contract is signed, she visits the adjacent property owner and offers to sell him the buffer space for $30,000. He's happy to have the extra land between him and the new building going on around him.

Jo turns the signed contracts over to her attorney and 45 days later, the balance in Jo's self-directed IRA has been boosted by more than $300,000, a 37 percent total ROI or an 18 percent annualized ROI.

When Options Make Sense

Certainly there was nothing wrong with the way the original deal was structured. The buyer wanted to buy the land outright by obtaining a blanket mortgage on one of his investment properties and the parcel to be developed.

His numbers added up. The property had sufficient current and future value to justify the venture. He even had a buyer waiting in the wings for the property to go back on the market once the improvements were complete. The only thing wrong with the entire transaction was the amount of money at risk. That's where Jo's approach excelled.

In the original transaction, the buyer had $160,000 and his rental property on the table from the beginning. If Murphy's Law raised its ugly head, he stood to face a substantial loss. By contrast, Jo limited her risk by controlling her cash outlay.

Eventually, she actually had nearly as much money at risk as the original buyer, but it flowed into the transaction at a slower pace and only after reassessing the investment and external conditions each step of the way.

Not every real estate transaction lends itself to being structured around an option to buy. Bearing in mind that every rule has an exception, options typically make the most sense when you don't intend to hold the real estate. The idea is to write the option contract for a sufficiently long duration to allow you to exercise the option and dispose of the property in relatively close succession.

CLASSIFIED CASE STUDY
Advice From Sterling Trust Company

Two of our clients used their Roth IRA to invest in a piece of real estate (undeveloped commercial property) in 1998/1999, shortly after Roth IRAs were created. (Roth IRA contributions are not deductible, but after meeting a 5-yr holding period, the Roth contributions & earnings are tax-free…great news if the investment is anticipated to have a significant return.)

Each contributed $4000 in a Roth and each IRA invested (holding a 50% undivided interest) in this piece of property. Within a year, the local city passed a zoning ordinance that prohibited any more billboards from being placed and the piece of property was the last property to have a billboard. A billboard company ended up buying the piece of property for a staggering $600+k and each Roth IRA split the proceeds and pocketed a very handsome return – which will now be tax-free when withdrawn!

Aunt Rose's Golden Parachute

Jo's great-aunt Rose is getting up in years and low on cash. A friend recommended that she look into a reverse mortgage, which is a type of loan that converts home equity to either a fixed monthly income or line of credit. The problem is that she wants to leave the house to Jo and if she takes out a reverse mortgage, eventually the bank will own all or most of the house. Jo has a better idea: an option contract to buy Rose's house. Here's how it will work.

Rose and Jo's IRA will enter into two agreements. The first will be an option to buy Rose's house. The second will be a life estate that will give Rose the right to live in her home until her death or until she permanently moves out of the house.

The option contract will not specify an exact day for the option expiration. Instead, it will be triggered by a condition—or more accurately, by either of two conditions. The same two conditions that would end Rose's life estate: her death or permanent move from the house.

Based on the competitive sales information Jo's real estate broker compiled, they fix the sales price of the house at $104,000. As the option consideration, Jo's IRA will pay Rose a monthly option consideration installment beginning at the signing of the contract and continuing for as long as Rose lives in the house.

After having Jo's accountant look at Rose's financial situation, they agree to follow his recommendation that the payments start out at $200 a month and increase every year by 3 percent more than the cost of living allowance formula used by the Social Security Administration to compute the annual benefit increase. As is typical with a real estate option, the consideration will be applied to the purchase price of the home, so that when Jo exercises the option, her IRA will pay Rose (or

Rose's estate) $104,000 minus the total amount paid in consideration to date. Any appreciation on the house is Rose's bequest to the great-niece who took such good care of her in her old age.

This way, Rose gets both of her wishes granted. She will be able to remain in her home and to leave it to Jo when she's finished with it. Jo gets her wish too. She gets to help out her aunt and buy the asset within her Roth IRA, through a series of affordable payments and one lump-sum payment at the end. The difference between the market value when she sells the property and the price she paid for the house is pure profit.

Real Estate Options: Where to Find Them

Jo stumbled on the two of the real estate option investments we discussed while visiting her Aunt Rose. Sometimes it works out that way, but not often. We've talked before about tapping your personal and professional network to locate available real estate and real estate-backed notes. The same is true about real estate options—with one difference.

Typically, a seller would rather have a sale now than a prospect of a sale down the road. The first is all but signed, sealed, and delivered, and the other has considerably more uncertainty attached to it. The trick to finding opportunities for option contracts lies in finding a seller with the right motivation.

What makes a seller willing to accept an option contract? Diminishing choices combined with a pressing need, in most cases. So the next time Jo is ready to try her hand with a real estate option contract, she will probably call the people she thinks will have an inside track on a motivated seller: her real estate broker, attorney, and accountant.

They are the experts that help her to manage her financial affairs, right? That means they're in a position to know which of their clients might have real estate to sell and which sellers are in the most need of a buyer.

CHAPTER ELEVEN

Alternative Sources for Real Estate

I know the price of success: dedication, hard work, and an unremitting devotion to the things you want to see happen.

—FRANK LLOYD WRIGHT

Sizing Up the Job

Skill Level: Master Craftsman

Traditionally, most people start their search for real estate with the classified ads or a call to a real estate broker. Today, the Internet has joined the party, offering buyers the freedom to screen potential properties in the comfort and convenience of their own  homes. The snappy multimedia shopping experience that technology makes possible makes it fun too.

All of these are good choices for investors with limited time available to spend on screening investments and, certainly, anyone not willing or able to invest an above- average amount of effort in due diligence. For investors looking for higher potential profits who have the willingness to do the work necessary to tame the risks, foreclosures, REOs, and tax liens could be another option.

If Saturday morning infomercials that promise quick and guaranteed real estate riches from taking "the road less traveled," as Robert Frost called it, is all you know about these alternative sources for real estate, listen up. While the basic facts represented by these and other high-return real estate systems may be founded on fact, it is also true that anything that sounds too good to be true *probably is.* So let's set the record straight.

Investing in distressed properties can offer exceptionally high returns for a careful and industrious investor. So, let's kick this discussion off by defining the spectrum of real estate investments generally classified as distressed and then get on to just how much work we're talking about.

Real estate can be considered distressed using either of two criteria: condition or terms of sale. Sometimes the two go hand in hand. For the purposes of our discussion, we're going to concentrate on properties that have limped onto the market through the legal system, rather than by the freewill choice of the seller, and therefore come burdened with less-than-favorable terms of sale. The huge profit potential offered by investing in these properties comes from the same calculations that create the profit in any transaction: Buy low, sell high.

Bank foreclosed and pre-foreclosed properties can occasionally be purchased for 20 percent below market value. Tax-lien sales can go for pennies on the dollar. Yet, it is wise to remember that the rules governing these transactions are written and administered by the seller—typically, a bank, loan company, or government agency. With rare exception, the rules are nonnegotiable, restrictive, and put the buyer at a distinct disadvantage. You can make a lot of money by investing in the right property under the right circumstances. Just remember our risk-reward credo:

> ## Greater Risk Does Not Always Equal Greater Reward
> ## Never Trust. Always Verify.

Risk Management

Any investment transaction that involves courts, government entities, and the highly regulated banking system might be compared to wading with alligators for fun and profit. But armed with the right tools and a skilled team of expert subcontractors, there are ways for Jo to grab an alligator without sacrificing an appendage (or worse). All require a hefty amount of work and even more caution. Down South, they have a rather unique expression for this: "When you're up to your a** in alligators, it's hard to remember your initial objective was to drain the swamp."

Every real estate purchase entails an element of risk. You might think that paying too much would rank right up at the top of the list. Not so. Property condition actually rates higher, because the buyer can't possibly know if a property is undervalued or overvalued until the condition of the property has been accurately assessed. One of the difficulties with foreclosures and tax-lien sales, however, is that often the buyer cannot gain access to the property to conduct that assessment.

Almost without exception, it is sold in "as is" condition. The property may have been neglected and sometimes has been intentionally damaged. It might also still be occupied, so gaining access for inspection may not be possible. "As is" can mean other things also, like existing liens that will pass with the title to the new owner. This bears repeating: A foreclosure sale property does **not** include title insurance. Clearing the title is the buyer's responsibility and expense.

With so many unknowns, there are still a few things Jo can do to protect herself as a buyer. She can learn everything she can about the property and the property owner. The lender or taxing authority may not have conducted a full assessment of the property, but it doesn't hurt to ask to see any inspection reports or disclosures that might be available. She can pay to have a preliminary title search completed. She'll look for outstanding judgments and pending bankruptcies, which can be a risk with tax-lien sale properties in particular. She will conduct a thorough investigation into the market value of similar properties in the area and evaluate the community in which it is situated and economic risk factors for the area as well. All of this information will be used to determine how much she should bid for the property or if it is wise to bid on it at all. Finally, if she decides to move forward, she will make sure there is sufficient room between her bid and the estimated market value of the property to allow for the unexpected.

If you think you're up to the task, roll up your shirtsleeves, and we'll see how Jo manages to put together some of these deals.

Foreclosure: The Birthplace of Distressed Property

Human gestation takes nine months from conception to delivery; giraffes, roughly twice that, and elephants, almost two years. Likewise, the road to foreclosure often begins many months before it culminates in a legal process that results in the termination of a property owner's rights. How long the road is depends to a large extent on why and where it is being traveled.

Foreclosure: A legal procedure taken for the purpose of terminating a property owner's rights, usually due to default on a note or tax obligation.

Many people use the term *foreclosure* to denote a property that has been repossessed by the lender when the borrower has defaulted on a loan. Technically, it also applies to the final step in the process of exercising the rights secured by purchasing a tax lien. Both instances require the legal termination of the property owner's rights to the property and the transfer of those rights to the new owner. For the purposes of this discussion, however, we will use the term in its common, most generic, form—as it regards the repossession of property by a lender.

The Road to Repossession

As discussed earlier, a mortgage secures the property as collateral for a loan, and the note stipulates the repayment terms. When a borrower defaults on the repayment terms, the mortgage gives the note holder the right to take back the property and terminate the owner's rights to it. Whether the note is held by a private lender or a banking institution or whether the loan is insured by a federal agency like HUD (Housing and Urban Development) or the VA (Veterans Administration) makes little difference in the outcome for the property owner. It does, however, dictate how it reaches the resale market. The entire process from start to finish is often referred to as *repossession* or *foreclosure*.

Believe it or not, lenders rarely choose to foreclose on a property. Their business is lending money, not buying and selling real estate. So, if a delinquent borrower gives them half a chance, a lender will often bend over backwards to work with the borrower to avoid foreclosure. This is exemplified by HUD's Loss Mitigation Program,[1] which gives lenders incentives to avoid foreclosure. Some of those incentives include restructuring the loan to make the monthly payments more affordable, waiving payments for a period of time, and under some circumstances,

---
1   U.S. Department of Housing and Urban Development, MORTGAGEE LETTER 96-61.

even writing off the loss when the borrower sells the property for less than the balance due on the loan. These loss mitigation practices are not limited to government-insured loans, however. Commercial lenders have similar policies. All of them are designed to keep the lender from becoming a real estate investor.

Too often, however, the preventive steps taken by the lender fail, and the property owner defaults on the loan. Depending on the lender and state law, several months might pass before the lender makes the determination to reclassify delinquent to in default. But, once the determination is made, the three-step foreclosure process begins.

Pre-foreclosure Notification

The first step in the foreclosure process involves notifying the borrower of the bank's intention to enforce its right to foreclose. Aside from any private written notice provided to the borrower, state law may require the lender to make a public notification. Most major newspapers include a public notices section where these types of notices are listed. They can also be found in local business newspapers as well.

In addition to clearing the legal hurdles required before proceeding to the next step, the pre-foreclosure notification often prompts the property owner to contact the lender to discuss alternatives to foreclosure, which takes us to the second step, loss mitigation.

Loss Mitigation

As noted earlier, lenders have a number of options at their disposal to help borrowers through a rough patch without losing the investment they've made in the property. It's almost always in the best interests of both borrower and lender if they can remain flexible and work out terms that give the property owner a second chance to meet his or her obligations to the lender. But sometimes the property owner can't or won't accept the lender's help. When this happens, the lender has no choice but to begin the foreclosure process. The language contained in the mortgage will define whether the foreclosure process will be statutory or judicial, the primary difference between the two being that a judicial foreclosure requires going before a judge, whereas a statutory foreclosure does not. To be certain, a statutory foreclosure requires strict adherence to procedures laid out by the legislative statutes. Yet, it is faster and less cumbersome than its judicial counterpart.

Foreclosure

The final step in the process is the actual foreclosure on the property. If the lender is required to file a judicial foreclosure, a hearing before a judge will be required. Depending on the particular jurisdiction, a lender may follow a series of steps laid out by state and local law without the need to file a petition for a court order. Regardless of which process is followed, the law generally calls for foreclosed property to be sold at auction to the highest bidder.

Profiting on the Foreclosure Process

As callous as profiting on another's misfortune sounds, it's wise to remember that the investor does not cause the property owner's problems. To the contrary, in some instances, the investor can even help the buyer out of a difficult spot, as we will see shortly.

The foreclosure process is composed of three distinct steps: pre-foreclosure notification, loss mitigation, and foreclosure. Each step offers opportunities for an aggressive—and careful—investor, like Jo. Of the three, pre-foreclosure may well present the best chance for Jo to pick up an appealing property well below its market value.

Buying Equity

If Jo has spread the word throughout her personal and professional network that she's interested in buying such a property, she might hear through the grapevine of someone facing the prospect of foreclosure. If so, perhaps she can do herself and a hard-pressed property owner a favor.

The property owner is strapped for cash and facing the nasty prospect of foreclosure, but it has not yet reached his doorstep. If Jo approaches him directly with an offer to buy out his equity at a discounted price, he just might jump at the opportunity to be rid of the property and avert a credit disaster. Let's look at how the numbers add up:

Table 19. PREFORECLOSURE WORKSHEET

Market value	$ 150,000
Loan value	$ 90,000
Equity	$ 60,000
Jo's offer for the equity	$ 30,000
Jo's cost ($ 30,000 plus $ 90,000 to pay off the mortgage)	$ 120,000
Jo's equity	$ 30,000

If the property owner accepts Jo's offer of $30,000 cash to walk away from the house, Jo will pay off the balance on the loan and own a $150,000 home for $120,000. That's 80 cents on the dollar or a 20 percent savings on the purchase price. If Jo conducts careful due diligence and enters into an agreement that includes contingencies for inspections and guarantees that the seller can convey a clear title at closing, Jo has a potential winner on her hands.

Short Sale

For the sake of this discussion, however, let's assume that Jo doesn't get an inside tip on a pending foreclosure prior to the lender's initiating action against the homeowner. Instead, we'll assume that Jo has been keeping an eye on the public notices column of the newspaper and courthouse foreclosure notices. After weeks of watching, she finally finds a three-bedroom ranch in a nice family neighborhood that interests her.

Unlike the house in which Jo was able to buy the equity from the property owner, this house has no equity. In fact, the mortgage exceeds the property value by $10,000. After some preliminary scrutiny that convinces her that the property is worthy of further investigation, she'll do a thorough assessment of the property before approaching the property owner with an offer to buy the house.

Along about now, you may be wondering why she's even bothering to talk to an owner who owes more on the property than its market value. It's a good question that has a two-part answer: property appeal and short sale.

> **Short sale:** A real estate transaction where the sales price falls short of the outstanding balance on the mortgage.

Let's take short sale first. This was discussed briefly with loss mitigation earlier. It works like this. A lender will sometimes do almost anything to keep a property from going into foreclosure, even if it means taking a loss. In a short sale, the lender agrees to write off the portion of the loan that exceeds the market value of the property in exchange for a pre-foreclosure sale.

The hitch with a short sale is that most lenders, HUD and other agencies included, may require that the sale price equal at least 95 percent of the appraised value, so a short sale is not likely to offer Jo a means of negotiating a bargain-basement price. It can, however, be a way to achieve nominal savings and, sometimes just as important, it can make her the first buyer in line for an appealing property.

Table 20. SHORT SALE WORKSHEET

Market value	$ 150,000
Loan value	$ 160,000
Equity	-$ 10,000
Jo's offer for the equity: (95% of market value)	$ 142,500
Jo's cost ($ 30,000 plus $ 90,000 to pay off the mortgage)	$ 120,000
Jo's equity	$ 7,500

About Property Values

Let's consider the market value of two identical properties, both three-bedroom brick ranches in the same neighborhood. Property A is in pristine condition, has superb curb appeal, and not wanting for updating or renovation. It recently sold for $200,000. Property B has suffered from a decade of neglect and needs about $20,000 worth of work to return it to the condition of Property A. It is currently listed for sale at $170,000.

If asked which property is the better bargain, the answer may seem to be a slam dunk. Property B, right? If Jo purchases it for the asking price and does the repairs, she'll have $190,000 in a property that's worth $200,000. Maybe not.

If this is an investment property, Jo will need to consider the loss of income during renovation. She also needs to add in the time and effort the renovation will require on her part. Finally, she needs to bear in mind the potential for cost overruns on the renovation. Sometimes, paying the market price for a pristine property can make better sense than looking for a bargain. Sometimes.

Unfortunately, these are the types of decisions that defy a black and white answer. For Jo, however, the answer is clear, and she is quite interested in striking a short sale at or near the market value on the *right* property.

If she can interest the property owner in a short sale, Jo's next step is to contact the bank, because the decision on a short sale ultimately rests with the lender. If they come to an agreement, Jo will turn the transaction over to her team of experts. As always, she'll have conducted a thorough cash flow analysis and examination of the property. She will also have written contingency clauses into the agreement for inspections and conveyance of a clear title. You should also be aware that short sales, typically, can take considerably longer to conclude than other forms of real estate sales.

Foreclosure Sale

Once the lender has completed the statutory or judicial foreclosure process, the property can be offered for sale at a public auction, the specifics of which are again dictated by statute. Generally speaking, a foreclosure sale, sometimes called a sheriff's sale, begins with a minimum bid that includes the balance due on the loan, along with unpaid, accrued interest, attorney fees, and any and all costs incurred throughout the foreclosure process.

Often foreclosure properties do not sell at the foreclosure sale, because the minimum bid is higher than the market value, once all the extra charges are included. This only makes sense, because otherwise the owner would have sold it on the open market during the pre-foreclosure period, paid off the encumbrances and avoided the grief of enduring the foreclosure process and its lingering repercussions. Exceptions do occur, however, so if Jo succeeds in winning the bid at a foreclosure sale, hopefully, she has paid special attention to conducting due diligence, because this is one type of sale in which the property is always purchased in "as is" condition. In most cases, a deposit will be required at the time of the sale with full payment due within a matter of a day or two. The specifics vary, so it is Jo's responsibility to find out what the rules are and be prepared to follow them.

Finally, there is also the potential that the property may be occupied. Depending on the individual circumstances, this could mean that Jo's first action as the new property owner will be dealing with an ugly eviction process.

REO Properties

When a property fails to sell at the foreclosure sale, it reverts to the lender, and the mortgage ceases to exist. The property is then referred to as a REO, or "real estate owned," a term that reflects the fact that it is no longer mortgaged—it is owned by the lender.

Once the lender owns the property, it will clear the title, evict any occupants, and ready the home for going back onto the market by tending to essential repairs. When these steps are all completed, the bank will add the property to its published list of available properties.

Table 21. TYPES OF REO PROPERTY

• Detached single family	• Commercial property
• Duplex, triplex, and fourplex	• Office property
• Condominium	• Industrial
• Vacant land	• Agricultural

Like properties sold at a foreclosure sale, REO properties are typically sold in "as-is" condition, so Jo will need to accurately assess the condition of the property before she extends an offer to purchase it. In rare circumstances, a lender might agree to certain repairs, but most often the property will be priced to account for its imperfections.

REO properties have an advantage over some other alternative-source properties in that Jo will usually have access to conduct inspections. And even though the lender-turned-owner will have released the mortgage lien, it will remain Jo's responsibility to determine if the title is completely clear of defects or encumbrances.

Whether the owner of an REO is a financial institution or a government agency, the process of acquiring the property is roughly the same. Most have entire departments that exist for the sole purpose of liquidating REO holdings. This does not mean they are inclined to dump the property well below its market value. Lenders and government agencies, both, typically contract with real estate brokers to list and market the property and maintain an arm's-length distance from the buyer during the sale. Jo has the choice of dealing directly with the lender's broker or having her own real estate broker make the contact and represent her for the purchase.

Tax-Lien Sales

When a property owner has a mortgage, he or she usually doesn't have to worry about paying the property tax bill when it comes due. Each time a mortgage payment is received by the lender, a credit is applied to the interest due, followed by one toward the principal. The balance is paid into an escrow account and used to pay the property taxes and insurance. It all happens automatically, without any action on the part of the property owner.

This has not always been the case in recent years, however. A property owner has the option of paying the taxes himself without participation of the mortgage holder if he so desires. This reduces the property owner's monthly mortgage payment. This also means that there is always a possibility of falling into tax arrears (owing back property taxes). This can also happen inadvertently: a clerk at the tax collector's office can improperly key in a payment on your property, crediting the payment to another parcel; or your payment may get lost in the mail. Somewhere down the road, you get a tax deficiency notice and have to fight it. That's why it is always recommended, whether you pay the taxes yourself or your mortgage-holder pays it, get a copy of a paid receipt each year after the tax payment has posted, and do this for every property you pay taxes on and keep those receipts.

Once the mortgage is paid off, however, it's a whole other story, and sometimes taxes get overlooked. Or sometimes a property owner will die with no apparent heir, in which case the property sits idle, forgotten or ignored, and property taxes accrue. Whatever the reason, if property taxes don't get paid, the end result is the same. The taxing authority has the obligation to exercise its right to collect the debt due.

Every tax jurisdiction has a set of prescribed procedures that are employed to attempt to bring the account current. When those attempts fail, the property owner risks losing a property worth thousands of dollars—perhaps hundreds of thousands of  dollars—to an investor, like Jo, who is willing to put up a relatively small amount of money for the right to collect the taxes due or foreclose on the property.

In most jurisdictions, this is accomplished through the sale of a tax-lien certificate, which transfers authority for lawful recourse from the taxing authority to the purchaser. As the owner of the tax-sale certificate, Jo will have the right to collect lawful interest on the amount owed, to initiate the foreclosure process after the required waiting period, and to occupy, lease, rent, or dispose of the property once she completes the foreclosure process. Understand that there is a grace or redemption period involved here for the original owner to pay Jo the taxes and interest due before she can foreclose on the property.

Without question, buying tax liens offers the greatest *potential* opportunity for extreme profits when compared to virtually any other real estate investment. If done well, Jo can bolster her IRA account balance by double-digit annualized rates by incorporating them into her investment plan. But they come with a commensurate risk.

Nuts and Bolts

Because virtually every government entity collects taxes, tax sales can take place at virtually every level of government, and each one does it a little bit differently. Frequency, registration requirements, fees, payment terms, redemption periods, and even what you are bidding on can vary from jurisdiction to jurisdiction. So, Jo's first step is to call the courthouse or check the Internet for tax auctions in her area. We'll run down a few of the variables so she'll know what questions to ask.

Redemption Period

Generally speaking, the rules that govern tax liens require a waiting period of anywhere from a year to three years (and sometimes more) before the lien holder can foreclose on the property. This is called the *redemption period*, because the property owner retains the right to redeem the property by satisfying the tax lien during that time.

Fees and Payment Terms

Fees to participate in a tax sale are typically nominal, but some jurisdictions charge an annual fee to maintain your position as the lien certificate holder. Payment terms for a successful bid almost always require payment in full, by cash or certified check on the day of the auction. In addition, the IRS requires that all bidders receive a 1099-INT form, so it will be necessary to complete a W-9 form when registering for the sale.

Type of Auction

Some jurisdictions conduct typical auctions, in which investors bid the amount they are willing to pay for the certificate. With this type of auction, the bidding generally starts at an amount that includes back taxes, accrued interest, and various fees. The investors bid progressively higher amounts, with the certificate being awarded to the highest bidder.

In other areas, the auction determines the rate of interest the winning bidder will collect when the certificate is redeemed. In that case, the taxing authority determines the maximum interest rate allowed. The bidding starts there, and the tax certificate goes to the investor willing to accept the lowest rate.

Let's say that the opening bid is 18 percent and Jo wins the bid at 12 percent. If the property owner satisfies the lien, he or she will have to pay Jo the back taxes, all of her costs, plus 12 percent interest for the period of time Jo owns the tax-lien certificate. Her biggest opportunity for gains, however, presents itself when the owner fails to exercise his right to redeem the certificate, and Jo winds up owning the property for the small price of the tax-sale certificate. Let's see how it works in practice.

In the first example, assume that Jo purchases a tax lien on a property with a market value of $90,000 and a two-year redemption period. The property owner is $4,500 in the arrears on his taxes. As the winning bidder, Jo's cost is $4,500 for the certificate and another $500 in costs. The property taxes accrue at a rate of $1,000 a year, so if Jo is going to preserve her position as the only lien certificate holder for the property, she will have to pay that amount as it comes due during the redemption period. As it turns out, the property owner redeems the certificate after one year, but just before the next tax payment comes due. To do so, he will pay Jo her costs of $5,000 plus $331 in interest, which yields Jo an ROI of 6.6 percent.

Table 22. TAX LIEN PROFIT ANALYSIS

LIEN REDEEMED BY OWNER AFTER ONE YEAR	
Market value	$ 90,000
Tax lien cost	$ 4,500
Miscellaneous fees	$ 500
Jo's total cost	$ 5,000
Interest rate	12%
Interest income	$ 331
Total ROI	6.6%

Now let's see what happens if the property owner fails to redeem the certificate. In this tax jurisdiction, Jo can apply for a tax deed after the two years have passed, at which time title to the property is transferred to Jo.

During the two years she held the tax-lien certificate, Jo paid an additional $2,000 in property taxes, bringing her total investment to $7,000 on a $90,000 property. Her total yield explodes to a whopping 1,185 percent, or 593 percent on an annualized basis.

Table 23. TAX LIEN PROFIT ANALYSIS

LIEN REDEEMED BY OWNER AFTER ONE YEAR	
Market value	$ 90,000
Tax lien cost	$ 4,500
Miscellaneous fees	$ 500
Two years of property taxes	$ 4,000
Jo's total cost	$ 9,000
Interest rate	12%
Jo's equity after foreclosure	$ 90,000
Total ROI	1,185.7%
Annualized ROI	593%

This book needs to emphasize at this point that these are hypothetical examples created to demonstrate a process and are in no way intended to represent the expected returns on a typical tax-lien certificate transaction. That said, tax lien purchases have the potential to yield very high returns. But that level of *potential* reward does not come without risk to Jo's principal.

Managing Risk

Previous Liens and Bankruptcy

For example, if Jo buys a tax-lien certificate and later discovers that the property owner has a bankruptcy pending, an IRS tax lien against the property, or both, her certificate could end up being worthless. Why? Because

bankruptcy and federal government liens typically take precedence over property tax liens. As shown in the following example, the combined totals of the IRS lien and the debts listed in the pending bankruptcy actually exceed the value of the property, and Jo just bought $5,000 worth of unenforceable debt. By conducting thorough due diligence, Jo might have avoided the mistake.

Table 24. EFFECT OF SENIOR CLAIMS ON JO'S TAX-LIEN CERTIFICATE

Market value	$ 90,000
IRS lien for back taxes	$ 50,000
Lien for consumer credit judgments included in bankruptcy filing	$ 40,000
Jo's tax-lien certificate	$ 5,000

Due diligence cannot eliminate all risk, however. The property owner could file for bankruptcy after Jo buys the certificate. When that happens, some taxing authorities will notify the lien certificate holder and issue a refund for everything except the fees associated with the purchase. You need to know how the particular jurisdiction works in order to minimize your risks and potentially maximize your profits…due diligence.

Multiple Liens and Legal Descriptions

Jo also needs to be aware that one property can have more than one tax lien against it. To protect her claim position, she'll want to own all of them, which might sound easier than it actually is. Due to re-platting and previous conveyances, one parcel can have multiple legal descriptions. If one of them is overlooked in the research, an earlier lien could go undiscovered.

Inspections

Ideally no one would buy property that hasn't thoroughly inspected. Yet, in the case of a tax-lien certificate, Jo will probably be limited to a curbside look prior to bidding. Even though the property appears fine from that distance, two or three years later, she may attempt to capture those double- or triple-digit gains only to discover that interior or structural defects diminish the property's value and crush her ROI.

These are just a few of the most serious problems Jo could run into when she buys a tax-lien certificate. She might also run into absolutely none. The point is that she needs to approach the transaction with a full awareness of the potential problems and a willingness to work to mitigate the risks they present.

How does she do that? By learning everything there is to know about the property and the property owner. Researching the genealogy of the property with the county recorder is a good place to start. While she's there, she can obtain the property owner's name from the deed and then have her attorney determine if he or she is a party to a pending bankruptcy. She can pay to have a title search done on the property to discover if there is an IRS lien or any other title defect associated with the property. She can have her real estate agent research the property's value. In short, this is the time for Jo to pull together pretty much her entire team of expert subcontractors. When they have completed their work, she can make an informed decision to go forward or walk away.

Probate Sales

Estates very often include real estate. Frequently the real estate assets need to be liquidated during the process of settling the estate—especially if there is more than one heir.

Anyone involved in real estate investments for very long knows that the owner of a vacant property is typically more motivated to sell than the owner of an occupied one. Why? Sometimes it's a money issue. Even a property owned outright, with no debt associated with it at all, costs the owner hard cash every year to keep it insured, maintain it and pay the taxes.

In the case of estate-owned real estate, anticipation of a pending cash windfall can play a role too. And sometimes dealing with the property is a good old-fashioned annoyance that the heir(s) simply want to be done with.

Whatever the motivation, probate property that is destined for liquidation translates into a buying opportunity for an aggressive investor—often yielding deep discounts below market value.

Calling in the Subcontractors

Jo could subscribe to the local legal news to find probate property leads. Alternatively, she could simply ask her attorney to alert her to opportunities. Her real estate agent might even track the listing herself. Whichever route Jo decides to take, she'll  need to assemble the same professional assistance as she would for any standard real estate acquisition.

Nuts and Bolts

Let's start by stating the obvious. Not all real estate that passes into probate will be offered for sale. Sometimes it is bequeathed to an individual who wants nothing more than to take possession. Likewise, not all probate property destined to be sold will be disposed of during the probate process. Jo's greatest opportunity for savings, however, lies with all the rest—the ones that will be sold by the executor of the estate.

Depending on the power granted the executor of the estate and state laws, he or she may be authorized to act independently in the sale of the property. In some instances, however, the sale is subject to court confirmation. This requirement creates a further advantage for Jo, in that some buyers will turn their backs to any deal that gets that complicated.

So let's assume that Jo finds a probate property that interests her. Her real estate agent confirms that it is one that required court confirmation.

From this point on, the purchase will follow virtually the same six steps we discussed in Chapter Seven, except for the additional step involved with obtaining the court's approval. That all sounds simple enough, but buying probate property is not without a wrinkle or two.

Generally speaking, the seller of the property is required by law to disclose any known defects. In the case of a probate sale, the seller (the executor) probably doesn't know anything about the property, so disclosures would be meaningless. For this reason, everything we said about inspections in previous chapters should now be reread, highlighted, circled, and underscored.

LEGAL TIP: The laws pertaining to recourse against the seller for property defects are generally limited to information known by the seller. Except in rare instances, the court will likely rule that the executor of an estate was not in a position to know about the property's defects and, therefore, cannot be held liable for disclosure.

Obtaining the services of an experienced, licensed home inspector will never be more important. Once the inspection is complete, however, and the value of the property verified through competitive price comparisons, Jo should be able to proceed with a reasonable amount of confidence.

Wrapping It Up

This chapter discussed the two ways in which property can be classified as distressed. Obviously, a house that has suffered from years of neglect or abuse qualifies. Sometimes a hammer and nails and a coat of paint or some other physical  repair can restore the property to its rightful condition. If it can be purchased at a price that takes the necessary repairs into consideration, this can be a great deal for an investor.

Properties that have earned the distressed label due to less-than-ideal terms, as in the case of lien or probate sales, for example, are really no different. In fact, these properties, when carefully selected and properly priced, can offer every bit as much investment opportunity as a fixer-upper—and sometimes more.

CHAPTER TWELVE

Business Structures

Sizing Up the Job

Skill Level: Craftsman

So far this book has focused on investments in which Jo has acted relatively independently. Granted, she has involved her IRA administrator in every transaction and has called upon her subcontractors when she needed an expert for a particular task. Still, every decision was hers, and every  dollar invested came from her IRA. Even if she had chosen to borrow money to finance an investment, the asset would have secured the debt.

There could come a time when Jo wants to undertake an investment that is simply too large for her IRA to handle on its own. Or she might want to limit her risk by buying only a partial interest in an investment. Whatever her motivation, Jo has options that can broaden her investment choices by joining forces with other investors.

These options can be as simple a general partnership or as complex as a limited liability company (LLC), which in the total scheme of business organizations is not all that complex, as we will see shortly. First, let's review how Jo can and cannot use her IRA.

She can:

- Continue to invest in stocks, bonds, mutual funds, annuities, and other financial instruments.
- Buy certain precious metals.
- Start or buy virtually any type of business.
- Invest in virtually any type of real estate.
- Pay cash or obtain financing for the assets purchased.
- Rent or lease the property to any non-disqualified parties.
- Manage the portfolio of investments within the IRA.

She cannot:

- Transfer non-IRA assets to her IRA.
- Transact business with a disqualified party—including Jo herself.
- Loan money to, or borrow money from, the IRA
- Manage a business owned by the IRA.
- Comingle non-IRA assets with IRA assets.
- Use the assets in the IRA in any way.

Disqualified parties:

- Jo

- Jo's spouse, parents, grandparents, children, adopted children, and grandchildren

- Jo's administrator (or anyone with a fiduciary responsibility to the IRA)

- The administrator's spouse, parents, grandparents, children, adopted children, and grandchildren

- The spouse of any disqualified party

Keeping the restrictions in mind, Jo still retains notable flexibility in how she manages her retirement investments. In this chapter, we will examine two more choices: a business partnership and an LLC.

Business Partnerships

Any one of the investments already covered could have been executed within a business partnership between Jo's IRA and any non-disqualified party. For example, in Chapter Three, you explored a scenario in which Jo and her cousin Shirley form a business partnership. In order to stay on the right side of the IRS when forming a partnership, Jo needs to remember that her IRA's ownership interest cannot exceed 49 percent of the company. The same restrictions apply to disqualified parties and likewise to the combined total of the IRA's interest and the interest of any and all disqualified parties.

For example, Shirley, Jo's father, and Jo's IRA can form a partnership. But the combination of Jo's interest and her father's interest cannot exceed the 49 percent threshold.

All in all, a partnership offers some benefits, but it has its downside too. On the plus side, Jo can pool the assets of her IRA with other people to take advantage of investments she might not be able to swing on her own without getting financing. Unlike financed investments and LLCs, which we will discuss momentarily, partnerships are not subject to the unrelated business income tax (UBIT). On the downside, it does prohibit Jo from actively participating in the management of the business for as long as it is held within her IRA and exposes her IRA assets to greater liability compared to an LLC.

One problem with partnerships is that in the event of a business problem or even failure, the assets of the individual partners are subject to claims by creditors. This means that Jo's IRA may be in jeopardy if a creditor has a claim for more than the partnership has.

The Limited Liability Company (LLC)

A limited liability company might be described as a hybrid of a corporation and a partnership. It's simpler than a corporation, in that there are no statutory requirements for its structure and operation. At the same time, it has clear advantages over a simple partnership, in that the liability of the principals is limited to the amount of their investment. For example, if Jo's IRA invests $100,000 in an LLC, her total liability for debts and other claims against the LLC will be limited to that amount.

When an LLC buys an asset, like a business or a piece of real estate, the LLC (not the owners of the LLC) owns the business. To make this clearer yet, consider what happens if Jo's IRA purchases 100 shares of stock in a company listed on the New York Stock Exchange. As a shareholder, Jo does not own the factory that produces the widgets the company sells. The corporation owns the factory. She does, however, have an ownership interest in the value of the company. If the company files for bankruptcy protection, she may lose the value of her 100 shares of stock. But that's where her liability ends.

Again, a few rules guiding when Jo's IRA can and cannot participate in an LLC:

- It can buy into an existing LLC, as long as the combined total of the portion owned by her IRA and the portion of the LLC owned by disqualified parties does not exceed 49 percent.

- It can establish a new LLC with anything short of a 100 percent ownership interest, provided the balance of the LLC is not owned by a disqualified person.

An LLC, then, provides Jo with two important benefits. First, it protects the assets within her IRA from liability from other investments. Second, because the IRA itself does not own the assets held in the LLC, a properly established LLC can allow Jo to be named a non-compensated manager of its investments, without breaking the self-dealing rules. But, the UBIT tax will apply to the net profits of the LLC, above the $1,000 annual exemption. (See Chapter Eight for further information on the UBIT.)

Calling in the Subcontractors

As the investments Jo has explored have grown in complexity and risk, the more assistance she has needed from her team of experts. If she has chosen them well, they will continue to serve her well. But before she calls on them to help her establish a business structure in which she will make more substantial and higher-risk investments, it might be wise to reassess their areas of specialty.

Not all IRA administrators, attorneys, accountants, and even real estate agents are created equal. If Jo is not absolutely convinced of their expertise, it might be time to add a few new members to the team.

Never before, and perhaps never again, will her attorney's experience with contract and business law be more important. Avoiding problems, after all, is immensely less costly than resolving them. In this particular case, he has referred her to a colleague of his who specializes in helping clients establish and acquire businesses.

She'll be looking for a new area of specialization from her accountant also. Fortunately, a conversation with him revealed something she never knew about him before. It turns out that he used to work in mergers and acquisitions for one of the largest accounting firms in the country. So analyzing the return on business income will be right up his alley.

As valuable as her real estate broker has been to Jo in finding and researching rental properties and mortgage notes, Jo knows its time for a change. The time has come when she needs an agent with the experience and contacts for locating and screening business property worthy of Jo's time and IRA money. The list goes on. Each one of Jo's subcontractors deserves scrutiny now, before she decides that this is the time to move to the next level. This is especially true of her IRA administrator.

When Jo chose her administrator, the whole concept of a self-directed IRA was new to her. She had a plan in mind for how she intended to proceed and what investments she wanted to pursue. She may not have fully understood the complexities of each, however. Now that she's dipped her toe in the water, she's in a better position to ask the all-important question: Is her IRA administrator up to the task? Does she have the experience and access to the professionals that will allow Jo to take full advantage of the flexibility afforded under the IRS rules without inadvertently violating them in the process? Fortunately, another interview with her administrator answers the questions to Jo's satisfaction.

When Jo is satisfied with the answers and has brought on any new team members she needs, she gets down to the business of owning a business.

Nuts and Bolts

With any investment, Jo is balancing two sometimes diametrically opposing goals: to grow her money at the fastest possible rate and to preserve her principal at all costs. That is the very essence of the risk-reward paradigm. We've talked at various times about modifying the structure of an investment to reduce risk and preserve principal. Bumping up the interest rate for a questionable borrower and adjusting the term of a note are two examples. Inserting contingencies clauses into real estate purchase agreements is another. The LLC provides a structure that allows for additional risk mitigation.

Establishing an IRA LLC or buying into an existing LLC with IRA assets requires the involvement of a competent attorney. Once the attorney has drafted an LLC contract that includes all the elements dictated by law, however, the principals still have a bit of latitude in which to agree on the terms of their business relationship. To protect her investment, Jo will want to anticipate everything that could go wrong and structure the terms governing the LLC accordingly.

The IRS says that an IRA can participate in any LLC formed between qualified parties for any permitted investment purposes. It can be established for the purpose of investing in one specific asset, or it can be formed for the purpose of conducting a series of investments. Very often an IRA holder employs an LLC for purposes of creating a private real estate investment trust or REIT. It can also be used to purchase a business.

Real Estate Investment Trust (REIT): A business enterprise established for the sole purpose of buying, managing, and selling real estate holdings.

LEGAL TIP: If you are considering investing into any form of REIT, before you do so reread our comments in Chapter 9 about the mortgage crisis of 2007, the effects we are still feeling today. Make absolutely sure you do your due diligence in examining the mortgages and notes you intend to invest in to insure that you will actually be taking a foreclosable interest in the property. Do NOT invest in an REIT if your subcontractors cannot examine the mortgages and notes to insure their transferability and viability.

You learned earlier about liquid and non-liquid assets, with a liquid asset being one that can be quickly and easily converted to cash. An LLC falls into the non-liquid investment category and often a long-term one at that. Because it is a vehicle for pooling investor resources, the principals rarely have the freedom to pull their portion of the capital out at will. Once in, their commitment generally spans years rather than months. A lot of things can go wrong in that span of time.

What can go wrong within an LLC? Pretty much anything that can go wrong in any investment, with the added complications inherent in any activity involving more than one person. That's why every LLC agreement Jo enters into will include the following provisions.

Opt-Out Clause

Conflicts with management probably rank at the top of the list of potential problems. Whether it boils down to management style, personality clashes, or poor performance, being locked into a contract with no opt-out clause can feel like being trapped in a sinking ship with no escape hatch.

That's why an opt-out that specifies the points at which she can withdraw from the agreement is absolutely essential in an LLC agreement. As each predetermined point approaches, she'll have the option of assessing the arrangement and deciding if it's in the best interests of her IRA to proceed or if it's time to cut and run.

Right of Transfer

Even though this book talks about Jo owning her IRAs, in reality she does not actually own them. Technically, she established a trust and named a trustee. The IRA trustee owns the IRA for the benefit of Joanne Moneymaker, and the IRA owns the assets inside the account, like a stake in the LLC, for example.

That technicality is what gives Jo the benefits of her self-directed IRA. It also complicates matters on occasion. For instance, what happens if Jo decides to change administrators while her IRA is holding an interest in an LLC? The answer is, she can't, unless the LLC agreement includes a clause that provides for the right to transfer ownership to *another party*—in this case, to another trustee.

Capital Preservation and Equity

Before you move on, let's talk about one more element that Jo's attorney will include in the LLC agreement. It pertains to equity—or more to the point, how the equity is distributed when an asset is sold.

Equity is really nothing more than the difference between the fair market value of an asset and the debt owed on it. For example, if Jo owns a house with a market value of $200,000 and a mortgage of

$50,000, she has $150,000 in equity on the asset. If she owns it free of debt, she has $200,000 in equity. Now let's say that Jo paid $150,000 in cash for the same house and invested another $30,000 in materials and her own effort. Now that she's finished, it's worth $200,000 even though she only invested $180,000 in actual cash into the property. The additional $20,000 is called her *sweat equity*.

If she goes to the bank to secure a home equity loan on the property, the bank won't care what portion of the equity came from hard cash and what portion came from her own sweat. All the bank cares about is the market value of the house and whether there is an existing note against it.

Equity in an LLC is not quite that simple. First of all, the equity is divided into shares, based on who contributed what percentage of the capital. Some investors may also contribute personal effort that raises the value of the property. This is called sweat equity. Then, as the property is held for a period of time, the value of the property may rise for other reasons, like inflation or increased demand. This is called *appreciation equity*. Again, the bank doesn't care about such differentiations, but Jo, Dick, and Jane will when the time comes to cash in on the investment.

Now, let's look at the same property within an LLC and see how the distribution works. For this discussion, we'll assume that Jo, Dick, and Jane together form JDJ LLC, which later buys a property for $150,000. The agreement divides the company into three unequal shares. Jo and Dick will both contribute $50,000 for a 25 percent share for each of them. Jane will contribute $50,000 initial cash, plus $30,000 in materials and all of the work to fix up the property. This represents a 50 percent share of the equity, even though roughly 15 percent of it will be in the form of sweat equity. Let's further assume that the property sells for $200,000 immediately upon completion of the work.

Above all, right off the top, each investor expects to be paid back the hard cash they fronted for the start-up enterprise when the company is liquidated. Profit is great, but not losing principal is even more important. Next, Jane will want to be compensated for the tired muscles and scraped knuckles she invested in the project. And finally, they'll all want a proportionate piece of the profit pie. This can all be accomplished by spelling out the distribution rules in the contract, and that's one of the big reasons that Jo will use an experienced real estate and contract law attorney to draw up the agreement. Table 25 shows how the distribution works out in real numbers.

Table 25. JDJ LLC LIQUIDATION DISTRIBUTIONS - PRINCIPAL ONLY

SELLING PRICE $200,000	CASH EQUITY	SWEAT EQUITY	CASH EQUITY RETURNED FIRST	SWEAT EQUITY RETURNED SECOND
Jo	$ 50,000	$ -	$ 50,000	
Dick	$ 50,000	$ -	$ 50,000	
Jane	$ 50,000	$ 20,000	$ 80,000	$ 20,000
	$ 30,000			

To take the example a step further, let's assume the company holds the property long enough to gain some appreciation equity, then sells it for $220,000. You'll see from Table 26 that the amount each investor receives for his or her cash and sweat equity has not changed. The appreciation equity is paid out last and is divided according to the ownership interest of each investor.

Table 26. JDJ LLC LIQUIDATION - PRINCIPAL AND APPRECIATION

SELLING PRICE $220,000	CASH EQUITY	SWEAT EQUITY	CASH EQUITY RETURNED FIRST	SWEAT EQUITY RETURNED SECOND	APPRECIATION EQUITY RETURNED LAST	TOTAL EQUITY PAYOUT
Jo	$ 50,000	$ -	$ 50,000	$ -	$ 25,000	$ 5,000
Dick	$ 50,000	$ -	$ 50,000	$ -	$ 25,000	$ 5,000
Jane	$ 50,000	$ 20,000	$ 80,000	$ 20,000	$ 50,000	$ 10,000
	$ 30,000					

LLC Example

Let's go back and revisit the tilled-under cornfield one more time. If you recall, Jo underwrote a loan on the property for the retired farmer who wanted to subdivide the land and wholesale it off to a local builder. A little later, you looked at another way to structure that deal, in which Jo bought a three-year option to buy the property. After subdividing and improving the land, she exercised the option and sold it to a developer a few days later, netting a 37 percent ROI over two years.

Have you wondered how the builder made out with that project? Let's find out. For this example, we're going to assume that the local builder bought the land, subdivided it, and completed the improvements. He's now ready to start building and is looking for some investors to go in on the project with him. Jo, Dick, and Jane confer and decide go for it, provided the builder will agree to allow Jo's attorney write up the contract.

They agree that Jo, Dick, and Jane will each contribute $450,000. In exchange, each will receive a 17 percent stake in JDJ&B LLC. The remaining 55 percent will belong to the builder in exchange for his $800,000 investment and a commitment to manage the project from start to finish.

Along with a clause that allows Jo to transfer her ownership interest in the LLC to another IRA trustee, Jo's attorney will include an opt-out clause that allows Jo, Dick, and Jane the option of cashing out on the annual anniversary of establishing the LLC. The builder agrees to the term, because he is confident that his temporary cash flow shortage will be resolved by then and, even if it isn't, the value of the project will be sufficient for him to obtain financing by that time.

The contract will also spell out that the LLC will be dissolved when the last house sells, which the builder estimates will take approximately two years. At dissolution, Jo, Dick, and Jane will each receive their $450,000 first, followed by the builder's $800,000, bringing the total capital distributions to $2.15 million. The projected appreciation equity of $2.2 million will be divided into five parts: Jo's, Dick's, and Jane's 17 percent each and the builder's 55 percent divided into two equal parts of 27.5 percent each, one representing his sweat equity and one equaling his appreciation equity.

Table 27. JDJ&B LLC LIQUIDATION PLAN

	CASH EQUITY, PAID FIRST	SWEAT EQUITY (AS A % OF PROFIT), PAID SECOND	APPRECIATION EQUITY (AS A % OF PROFIT), PAID THIRD	REALIZED PROFIT	ROI
Builder		27.5%		$785,000	92%
Jo	$450,000		17%	$210,000	46.7%
Dick	$450,000		17%	$210,000	46.7%
Jane	$450,000		17%	$210,000	46.7%
Builder	$800,000		27.5%	$785,000	92%
	$2,150,000			$2,200,000	

Prior to entering into the deal, her real estate agent brought a comprehensive research package to Jo that included the competitive marketing data on the property in its unimproved and improved states, as well as a complete prospectus concerning the developer and this project in particular. After going over it herself, she turned it over to her accountant for review, discussed the investment with her IRA administrator, and consulted with her attorney about the terms they would require in the contract.

If the project progresses on schedule and the houses sell as quickly as the builder expects, Jo can expect to net a little more than 23 percent on an annualized basis. Her due diligence shows that the builder has a successful track record on similar projects, so Jo feels confident that, barring an unusual development, the projections should hold. In a worst-case scenario, she can bail on the one-year anniversary and take her principal with her.

A Word About Taxes

The unrelated business income tax (UBIT) applies to all LLC profits in excess of $1,000 annually. Not only does Jo need to deduct the estimated tax from these projected earnings figures, she will also need to retain sufficient cash within her IRA to pay the tax, because paying it from her non-IRA assets would constitute commingling her assets and render it a prohibited transaction.

CHAPTER THIRTEEN

Owning a Business

*Whenever you see a successful business, someone
once made a courageous decision.*

–PETER F. DRUCKER

Sizing Up the Job

Skill Level: Master Craftsman

The decision to go into business is one of the most
important decisions a person ever makes. It very
often entails a lifestyle change. Even if the owner
hires someone to run the operation, the business
itself usually ends up taking center stage from
the grand opening (or reopening, in the case of a
business acquisition) until the lock is turned on
the front door for the very last time. Every bit as
important is the financial risk involved. This is of
particular concern if the assets used were earmarked
for retirement.

Every business, new or existing, boils down to an idea for a product or service and customers for it. Everything else is where to locate, whether to incorporate or form an LLC or a general partnership, and whether to run it yourself or hire someone to do it for you. Prices, distribution, size, marketing strategies, policies, and procedures all come later.

If you start the business from scratch, most of those decisions fall to you. The wisdom of your choices usually shows up in the bottom line, which is exactly why you wanted to be in business for yourself to start with. When you buy an existing business, however, you're buying the results of another businessperson's decisions.

Why take that chance? Primarily for two reasons, pertaining to buying a business within a self-directed IRA. First, making a success of a start-up business is tough enough under the watchful eye and careful control of the owner, who has a vested interest in its success. Turning that control over to someone else makes the venture that much more risky. But, that is exactly how the IRS rules say it must be done. Remember that, in most cases, the IRA account holder cannot actively manage the assets within the account.

The other reason buying an existing business can make more sense than starting one within an IRA is that it sidesteps the money pit of start-up costs, as well as the typical lag time between establishing the business and turning a profit. Of course, we are assuming that any business you might buy in or out of your IRA will be earning a profit at the time of acquisition. This is retirement money you're talking about, and socking it into an untested idea or one that has delivered questionable results falls into the bungee-jumping risk levels we talked about earlier.

As vital as Jo's attorney and administrator will be to this transaction, it's hard to overstate the role of her accountant and an experienced business appraiser either. Jo can do everything right legally and still end up in a world of hurt if the numbers don't add up. Their job will be to take the due diligence documentation and attempt to shoot holes in it, a process we'll talk more about shortly.

If the assets of the business Jo ultimately considers include real estate, she'll be calling on a certified building inspector with experience in commercial properties. She'll also need her title company to conduct the title search and issue insurance, as well as to administer the escrow account.

The search will start, however, with a business broker who will help Jo find and screen prospective businesses. Once she has a good prospect, the real work begins.

Nuts and Bolts

The IRS imposes few restrictions on the types of businesses you can own within an IRA. It could be a large or small operation and fit into virtually any industry segment. It could be anything from a sole proprietorship to owning shares in a corporation (but not an S corporation). It could be a one-of-a-kind entrepreneurial novelty to a worldwide franchise. Some of the choices IRA administrators like to cite include, plus a few of our own:

• Office properties	• Apartment complexes
• Assisted-living facilities	• Medical offices
• Mini-storage facilities	• Industrial properties
• Retail, manufacturing, and service operations	• Hotels, motels, bed-and- breakfast inns, and other resort properties

Acquiring a business can be accomplished by buying the assets of the company or, if it is a corporation, by buying the company's stock. Each has its own pros and cons. When buying a corporation through the acquisition of stock, you're getting the entire entity—assets and liabilities. All of them. By contrast, when buying a sole proprietorship or partnership, the buyer and seller typically negotiate about what assets and liabilities will transfer to the new owner. This can be a huge advantage.

In either case, careful due diligence is essential. If you've ever bought a used car and later discovered the lengths to which a seller will go to hide imperfections to make a sale, you know how essential. The complexities of evaluating a prospective business acquisition make inspecting a hunk of metal, rubber, and plastic look like child's play. Jo's experts will know exactly what to look for, but here's a sampling.

Table 28. BUSINESS ACQUISITION DUE DILIGENCE - HIDDEN DANGERS

• Outstanding federal, state, or local tax liabilities	• Overstated revenues, earnings, or both
• Undisclosed debt	• Overvalued, dated, or defective inventory
• Uncollectible receivables	• Undefendable patents or licensing rights
• Pending legal actions	• Overstated real estate value
• Nontransferable contracts	• Overvalued equipment and fixtures
• Disgruntled workers	• Disputes with suppliers or customers

Table 29. BUSINESS ACQUISITION DUE DILIGENCE - WHERE TO LOOK

• The three Ls: loans, liens, leases	• List of bankers, auditors, and accountants
• Correspondence	• Court orders and legal settlements
• Independent audits	• Compensation schedules
• List of clients	• Employee agreements
• Organizational charts	• Employee benefit plans
• Disgruntled workers	• Articles of incorporation or partnership/LLC agreements

Jo can certainly purchase a business outright within her IRA, hire a manager to run it, and step aside until she's ready to sell it or retire and assume management responsibilities herself. The hands-off policy required by IRS rules can make that a pretty risky approach, but there's actually another reason that Jo probably won't want to do it that way. Unlike a nonrecourse loan used to secure debt within an

IRA, a claim against an IRA-owned sole proprietorship or partnership can result in a claim against her other IRA assets. The way to protect her other assets, then, is the LLC we discussed earlier.

One of the most important benefits of an LLC is that it offers a layer of liability protection between the principals of the LLC and claims against the company. In other words, Jo's personal liability for claims against the LLC will be limited to the capital she invests in it. She certainly stands to lose every penny of her investment if the company goes belly-up or if it is sued. But, if the LLC filing is prepared correctly, that should be the limit of her exposure. For that reason, any business or partnership activities that Jo pursues within her IRA will be undertaken within the structure of an LLC.

Before Jo tasks her attorney with drawing up an LLC agreement, she has to know who the other principals will be. She's discussed her ideas with a few people and ultimately, she and her brother, Ted, and their friend, Jane, come to an agreement.  At Jo's urging, Ted has transferred his IRA to a self-directed IRA also, so he and Jo will both be buying into the LLC with IRA funds. Jane will be using cash. They agree on a 30-30-40 split, with Jane holding the largest share. Because of Jane's diverse business experience and flexible schedule, she will also serve as the general manager of the investment, allowing Jo and Ted to sidestep any risk of turning the investment into a prohibited transaction. They're open to a number of different types of businesses, but they've told the business broker that they are looking for a company with real estate holdings, as well as a strong cash flow and verifiable profits.

Over the course of the next few months, the business broker brings them a number of potential businesses for sale. For one reason or another, they've eliminated all but one, but are now studying a custom metal fabrication shop. The owner has been semiretired for the past five years and is now eyeing full retirement and wants to see the operation continue without him. The current manager was personally groomed by the owner, but he isn't interested in buying out the boss. The owner sees opportunities for expanding the business and making it even more profitable and is looking for a buyer with the vision and energy to make it happen.

Jo's accountant and attorney have reviewed the documentation the owner provided and verified that the company's net income has steadily increased by an average of 30 percent annually and totaled $140,000 for the most recent year. The owner is asking $700,000 for the operation, which would bring the total cash on cash return to 20 percent. The business broker has assigned a valuation of $400,000 for the real estate, which includes two buildings, a parking lot, and a small adjacent vacant lot. Presently, only one of the buildings is in use. While the second building and vacant lot could be sold off (netting perhaps $150,000), the business broker recommends using them to house the expansion the owner has suggested. Deducting the value of the real estate from the total capital investment brings the cost of the business and equipment to $300,000 and yields a return on operations of 46.7 percent.

Assuming Jo and her partners follow the broker's recommendations and the company continues to return a consistent net income, their individual returns work out like this.

Table 30. CUSTOM METAL FABRICATING LLC - PROFIT ANALYSIS

	Ownership Interest	Capital	Net Income	Cash on Cash Return (Net income Divided by Total Capital)	Costs of Business and Equipment	Return on Operations (Net Income Divided by Cost of Business and Equipment)
Jo	30%	$ 210,000	$ 42,000	20%	$ 90,000	46.7%
Ted	30%	$ 210,000	$ 42,000	20%	$ 90,000	46.7%
Jane	40%	$ 280,000	$ 56,000	20%	$ 120,000	46.7%
Overall	100%	$ 700,000	$ 140,000	20%	$ 300,000	46.7%

LEGAL TIP: With the due diligence completed, Jo and her partners will want to obtain an independent valuation of the business from a business appraiser before issuing an offer to buy. Remember that the business broker who brought them the property stands to earn a commission when the sale closes, so his evaluations might not be totally objective. Avoiding any potential conflict of interest will help everyone to sleep better at night.

It might seem that Jo, Ted, and Jane have spent a significant amount of money on a property that might not even advance to the acquisition stage. That's the nature of business acquisition. The business broker did much of the initial work that allowed them to narrow their interest down to one promising operation. But at any point during the due diligence process, red flags might have been raised that sent everyone back to square one, looking for a new candidate. Money spent at this stage of the game is every bit as important as the money spent for the acquisition, which brings us to one very important reminder. IRS rules prohibit comingling Jo's and Ted's personal money with their IRA transactions, so they paid all of the costs of the presale investigations with funds from their IRAs and the cash Jane contributed.

While all of this has been taking place, Jo's attorney worked with both IRA administrators (Jo's and Ted's) and Jane's attorney to draft the LLC agreement to everyone's specifications. Once it was completed and signed, the LLC was funded according to each party's ownership interest. With that finished and a decision to move forward made, the process of buying a business is very similar to buying any other property. In this case, however, they have asked Jo's attorney to act as their agent to complete the deal. This means that he will work with the business broker during the negotiations and coordinate the inspections, title work, and escrow account funding for the LLC.

When the deal closes, the business will operate like any other business. They're free to withdraw their earnings periodically, or they can choose to reinvest them into the business. They could even choose to break up and sell off the assets of the business if doing so makes more sense than operating the business. When they are ready to sell the business, in part or in whole, the terms of their LLC will stipulate the order in which the funds are distributed. Alternatively, Jo, Ted, and Jane may choose to leave the proceeds from the sale of the operation in the LLC and start over again with another venture.

That's the beauty of a self-directed IRA. Jo's investment choices, from start to finish, rest with Jo and Jo alone. This is only one example of how Jo might structure the purchase of a business within her IRA. As long as she works with her IRA administrator to make sure that she conforms to IRS rules and her backup team of expert professionals to manage the risks, the possibilities are endless.

CHAPTER FOURTEEN

Buying Precious Metals

It's choice — not chance — that determines your destiny.

–JEAN NIDETCH

Sizing Up the Job

Skill Level: Do-It-Yourself

Throughout history, gold and silver have captured the eye, heart, and imagination. They've been used for everything from currency to adornment to medical and industrial applications. Because of the perennial demand for them, they're also a favorite of investors. In fact, many experts agree that a well-diversified portfolio contains precious metals along with the usual stocks, bonds, real estate, and cash.

Earlier, this book discussed the inverse relationship between inflation and the stock market. Typically, when inflation rises, stock prices drop, as investors anticipate that higher prices will cut into corporate profits and crimp consumer demand at the same time. The price of gold, on the other hand, tends to rise along with inflation, so including gold in a diversified portfolio can help bolster the portfolio's bottom line in troubled economic times. The market value of silver, platinum, and palladium, on the other hand, is largely driven by industrial demand, with currency, jewelry making, and collecting playing a lesser role.

Until recently, precious metals played a very small role in IRA portfolios, because the IRS prohibited investing in collectibles within an IRA, and for years, all precious metals, with the exception of Gold and Silver Eagles, were treated as collectibles. This limited IRA holders to a choice between the two coins. Platinum and palladium in any form was prohibited.

On one hand, investing in Gold or Silver Eagles was better than investing in no metals at all. On the other hand, the restriction meant paying a premium above the *spot price* for the commodities. The Taxpayer Relief Act of 1997 made it a whole new ballgame for investors with an affinity for precious metals, by excluding certain bullion and coins from the definition of collectibles as it pertains to prohibited investments within an IRA.

Spot price: The current market price for a commodity such as precious metals, petroleum, and agricultural products.

Specifically, investors now have the option of holding the following gold, silver, platinum, and palladium coins and bullion within an IRA.

Table 31. IRA-APPROVED PRECIOUS METALS

BULLION*		COINS**	
METAL	**FINENESS**		
Gold	.995	American Gold, Silver, and Platinum Eagles	Platinum Isle of Man Cat and Noble Coins
Silver	.999		
Platinum	.9995	Australian Kangaroo, Nugget and Koala Coins, Kookaburra	Mexican Silver Libertads
Palladium	.9995	Canadian Gold, Silver, and Platinum Maple Leafs	Austrian Philharmonic
If fabricated by an NYMEX- or COMEX-approved refiner and meeting the following minimum fineness requirements.		**The South African Krugerrand is not approved for inclusion in an IRA, because its fineness is only .916.*	

Nuts and Bolts

Jo has bought a few gold coins over the years, which she keeps in a safe-deposit box at the bank. IRS rules prohibit her from transferring those coins into her IRA, but she can instruct her administrator to purchase any qualifying coins or bullion. Although the administrator will fund the transaction and file the necessary paperwork to record the acquisition by the IRA, the assets themselves will be stored in an off-site vault operated by a repository that specializes in the storage of precious metals.

If Jo later decides to sell any of her precious metal assets, she'll follow the same procedure as with any sale of IRA assets. She'll provide written instructions to her administrator, the sale will be transacted, and the proceeds will be deposited in her IRA.

In recent years, the price of gold and other precious metals has skyrocketed to previously unheard of heights. In 2011, gold topped out at just under $1,900 / ounce; in 2015, gold has decreased to about $1,293/ounce. Precious metals not only fluctuate on a daily basis but also in individual markets (London, New York, etc.). You can check various sources on the Internet to get up-to-the-minute quotes on various precious metals and to see charts on trends.

Investing in permitted precious metals can be very volatile as these market swings have shown. Unfortunately, to our way of thinking, one of the pleasures of owning such metals is being able to feel them, look at their beauty and just simply enjoy them. When investing through your IRA, because of the custody requirements you are denied these pleasures. One way around this is to allocate some of your IRA to purchase with the custody rules followed; purchase some additional metals with your non-IRA funds and just keep those around for your enjoyment. Can you say King Midas?

PART FOUR

Weatherproofing: Making Wealth Last

"The future, according to some scientist, will be exactly like the past, only far more expensive."

—JOHN SLADEK

CHAPTER FIFTEEN

Planning for Distributions

I'm proud to be paying taxes in the United States. The only thing is — I could be just as proud for half the money.

–ARTHUR GODFREY

Whether you spend decades feathering your retirement nest or try to cram decades of preparation into a few short years, there's no denying the hard work, worry, and sacrifice that goes into taking care of your money. Every dollar saved is a dollar you can't spend elsewhere. Every investment made demands careful investigation and execution. Every decision depends on your own good judgment. Then sooner or later, the day will arrive when, like Jo, you will find out how close you came to reaching your goal to retire rich.

Maybe you'll discover that you've amassed sufficient wealth that you don't need the assets in your IRA to cover your living expenses. Or you may find that your savings are borderline at best, and making the funds last is going to require every bit as much careful work as acquiring it did. In either case, the last thing you want to do is to hand Uncle Sam a greater share than necessary. Every tax penny saved is that much more comfort and security during your lifetime and maybe for your heirs as well.

That means that once you retire, your goals really won't change from when we began this journey. You'll want to have your cake and to eat it too. Put another way, you'll want to use your wealth to benefit you every day of your retirement without depleting it—or better yet, while it continues to grow. If that sounds impossible, remember the lesson about compound earnings that Jo learned when she was eight years old. Reinvested earnings grew her balance, which increased the earnings, which grew the balance, and so on. So the longer you keep your money working and the slower you use it, the better your chances of making your money take care of *you* for a change. Of course, as always, there will be a few rules to keep in mind.

The discussion that follows can only sketch out the basics on the topic of IRA distributions. Every situation is unique, and the IRS has exceptions to many of its rules. The benefits of a consultation with an experienced financial advisor or tax attorney should be obvious by this point in the book, but the caution bears repeating. Seek professional guidance anytime you make changes to your plan and, especially when it's time to begin taking distributions. You'll see soon exactly how important that advice is.

LEGAL TIP: Contrary to popular belief, the IRS Tax Code is not created by the IRS; it is a creation of and tinkered with every year by Congress. It is simply impossible to say with certainty today what our tax burden will look like in ten or even 5 years, especially with all the talk about Social Security going bankrupt in a few years from now. There are literally hundreds of changes each year to the Tax Code and tax lawyers and accountants scramble each year just to keep up. So what we say here should be accepted with a grain of salt…each year you should meet with your tax accountant and possibly your tax lawyer to go over what has changed in the code and plan for the next year in terms of required distributions. This is only common sense. The costs of these consultations and any work needed afterwards are always deductible on your taxes.

Distribution Rules

Way back when Jo opened her first IRA, she entered into a pact with Uncle Sam. Under the terms of their agreement, the IRS delayed or dismissed the tax liability on her retirement savings and its earnings. In exchange, Jo agreed to adhere to a few rules about how she managed the money in her account.

The rules governing contributions were easy enough to follow. Avoiding touching the third rail of prohibited transactions took a bit more caution, but it, too, was doable. Complying with the rules for distributions is every bit as important if Jo wants to take advantage of the stretch IRA option.

The good news about the distribution rules is that, for the most part, they require little more than a calendar and a sharpened pencil (or pocket calculator)—and a reliable method for remembering to check the former and the willingness to use the latter. In other words, the calculations are straightforward enough that almost anyone should be able to handle them. But, for the rest of Jo's life, remembering to make them will be one of the most important financial responsibilities of her lifetime. That's because of the bad news about the distribution rules. The penalties for breaking them are huge. Before we get into that, though, let's run through a brief review of the differences between traditional and Roth IRAs.

Table 32. IRA FEATURES RECAP

TRADITIONAL IRA	ROTH IRA
• Contributions are usually made with pretax dollars.*	• Contributions are made with after-tax dollars.
• Distributions (contributions and earnings) are taxed as regular income.**	• Distributions (contributions and earnings) are tax-free.
• Minimum age for penalty-free distributions: 59½, but exceptions apply.	• Minimum age for penalty-free distributions is 59½, but exceptions apply.
• Maximum age for contributions is 70½.	• There is no maximum age for contributions. You may make contributions at any age, as long as you have earned income.
• Age at which you must begin taking MRDs is 70½.	• Roth IRAs do not include a requirement for mandatory distributions.

*Under some circumstances, contributions may not qualify as tax-deductible.

**Nondeductible contributions (and associated earnings) are tax-free when distributed.

Jo has two IRAs, one traditional and one Roth. For as long as she continues to collect earned income, she will make her maximum allowable contribution to the Roth IRA. If her adjusted gross income rises to the point where she is prohibited from contributing to the Roth IRA, she'll make the contribution to her traditional IRA until she reaches the age of 70½, when traditional IRA contributions are no longer allowed.

> Whether Jo contributes to her traditional IRA, to her Roth IRA, or to both, her combined totals for a given year may not exceed the annual limit. In other words, her combined contributions for both accounts cannot exceed $5,500 in 2015, although she may divide the amount up between them in any way she chooses.

In years when it makes sense to do so, she will also move a portion of the assets in her traditional IRA to the Roth IRA. It's a complex analysis to determine if and when it's better to pay taxes now versus later, so she'll rely on her tax accountant to help her make those decisions.

IRAs were never intended to provide a home for all of your savings. Imagine what a bind Jo would find herself in if she tied all of her money up in IRAs and then discovered that she needed a new roof on the house. Money to cover the unexpected bumps in the road, major purchases and vacations, for example, all need to be acquired, stored, and invested outside of an IRA, where they can be accessed without penalty. To make matters even more complicated, Jo also needs to contend with the different distribution rules for traditional and Roth IRAs. Yet, as always, knowledge is king. Once she's armed with a clear understanding of the rules of the game, she'll be able to judge which accounts should be tapped when and under what circumstances.

Pretty much everything having to do with IRAs and distributions can be divided into three time periods:

- *Early Distributions*: Before age 59½, when early withdrawal penalties apply (with a few exceptions).

- *Optional Distributions*: After age 59½, but before age 70½, when any amount can be withdrawn for any reason without any penalties (with one exception).

- *Mandatory Distributions*: After age 70½, when traditional IRAs are subject to a mandatory distribution schedule (with no exceptions).

Early Distributions: Before Age 59½

By now, it should be fairly well understood that making IRA contributions is pretty much like dropping an envelope full of cash into a lockbox. It goes in a lot easier than it comes out—until someone comes along with a key, that is. In this case, the "key" is the magical age of 59½. Six months after your 59th birthday, you can do pretty much anything with your IRA account that pleases you. Hopefully, keeping the bulk of it working hard at generating tax-free or tax-deferred income is what pleases you, but the choice is yours. Choosing to withdraw the money before turning 59½ is quite another matter.

Do you remember when you were a kid and you wanted money from your piggy bank? You turned it upside down and slid a knife up and down in the slot until the coins dropped out one at a time—and hoped  with all your might that your folks wouldn't walk through the door and catch you in the act of stealing from yourself. Trying to get money out of your IRA before you turn 59½ is pretty much the same, except that Uncle Sam has a foolproof way of finding out you've had your fingers in the bank. Your IRA administrator is required to notify the IRS of any withdrawals—early or not.

Unlike your parents, the IRS doesn't get mad when you tap into your savings early. But it does get even by levying a 10 percent penalty on early withdrawals. That's 10 percent of the amount withdrawn, plus taxes, in some cases. If tithing to the IRS isn't sufficient to discourage impatience and develop an appreciation for delayed gratification, you're free help yourself to your IRA savings and take what's left to use for whatever purpose you have in mind.

Fortunately, the federal government is not completely without heart and common sense. Even the IRS recognizes that sometimes life takes a left turn when it should have taken a right. For those situations, there is a list of exceptions to the early withdrawal penalty. Remember, though, that even if no penalty is imposed, taxes may still apply.

Exceptions to the Early Distribution Penalty for Both Traditional and Roth IRAs

- If you become disabled, distributions due to the disability will be exempt from the 10 percent penalty.

- You may use IRA funds to pay medical expenses that exceed 7.5 percent of your adjusted gross income (line 37 on Form 1040 or line 22 on Form 1040A).

- If you are unemployed, withdrawals can be made to pay for health insurance premiums.

- You may use money from your IRA to pay for the cost of higher education for yourself or your spouse, child, or grandchild

- You can withdraw up to $10,000 from your IRA to purchase a first home or for any one of your following relatives.

  - Spouse

  - Child

  - Grandchild

  - Parent

  - Spouse's parent

  - Any other ancestor

In fact, you and your spouse can each withdraw $10,000 for a total of $20,000, without penalty, provided that the money is used to buy the same house.

- You can withdraw excess contributions before the date on which the taxes are due to be filed (typically, April 15 or the due date including any extensions). The withdrawal of any income from the excess contributions will be subject to a 10 percent penalty and income tax.

- At any point in time, regardless of age, you can withdraw the funds in your IRA in a series of substantially equal annual payments, calculated to deplete the IRA over your expected lifetime or the joint lives of you and your spouse. This distribution method is called an annuity and requires that the distribution be no more and no less than the exact amount scheduled for withdrawal, based on the appropriate IRS-approved schedule. The payments must continue for at least five years after the first withdrawal or until you turn 59½, whichever is later. Failure to comply with the rules will subject the withdrawals to the 10 percent early withdrawal penalty.

- Upon your death, your beneficiary or beneficiaries can withdraw the funds from your IRA without penalty. While this may be an option, it is often not the wisest choice, as we will see in Chapter Sixteen.

Optional Distributions: After Age 59½, but Before Age 70½

During this 11-year window, you are free to withdraw any amount from your traditional IRA at any time and for any reason, without penalty. Of course, you'll still have to pay taxes on the distributions, because the contributions were tax-deductible at the time they were deposited. But, finally at long last, if you need the money, it's there for you to use.

Roth IRAs operate a little bit differently, in that they distinguish between qualified distributions and nonqualified distributions. In short, a qualified distribution is one that is both penalty- and tax-free. A nonqualified distribution is everything else. You may be thinking that since you made the contribution with after-tax dollars that any withdrawal after the age of 59½ should be classified as a qualified distribution. Unfortunately, it's not that simple. The IRS imposes a two-part test for qualified distributions.

To be considered a qualified distribution, a withdrawal must be made:

With funds that have been in your Roth account for more than five years

and

Under one of the following qualifying conditions:

- On or after the date you turn 59½.
- Because you are disabled.
- By your estate or to a beneficiary.
- To buy a first home (up to $10,000).

So, if you open your Roth IRA at age 58, a distribution taken at age 60 will be subject to a 10 percent penalty, unless you are disabled or one of the other qualifying conditions applies or if one of the exceptions listed above applies. A little more patience will solve the problem.

Required Mandatory Distributions: After Age 70½ (Traditional IRAs Only)

Once you turn 59½, you have the option of tapping your traditional IRA account without penalty. When you turn 70½, tapping it becomes mandatory. Unlike your Roth IRA, which includes no minimum required distribution, the IRS will levy heavy penalties if you fail to withdraw a minimum amount from your traditional IRA each and every year. To see the rules in action, let's first look as how Jo will compute her RMD the right way; then we'll see what happens if she does it wrong.

A little earlier, we made the bold statement that all Jo needs to compute her RMD is a pencil and a calendar. That wasn't 100 percent accurate. She also needs to know what numbers to work with, doesn't she? For that, she'll need the year-end statement from her traditional IRA account and the correct IRA distribution table. We'll assume for our example that Jo is single and, therefore, will use Table III (Uniform Lifetime). Table 33 shows each table and how to know which one to use.

Table 33. IRA DISTRIBUTION TABLES[1]

TABLE NUMBER	TITLE	FOR USE BY...
Table I	Single Life Expectancy	Beneficiaries
Table II	Joint Life and Last Survivor Expectancy	Owners whose spouses are: • more than 10 years younger **and** • the sole beneficiaries of their IRAs
Table III	Uniform Lifetime	Owners who are: • unmarried or • married and whose spouses are not more than 10 years younger • married and whose spouses are not the sole beneficiaries of their IRAs
Tables available by calling 1-800-829-1040 or visiting the IRS Web site: http://www.irs.gov; order Pub.590-B		

LEGAL TIP: Commencing in 2014, the IRS Publication 590, Individual Retirement Arrangements (IRAs) is being revised. Publication 590A will focus on contributions to both traditional IRAs and Roth IRAs It will also include the rules for rollover and conversion contributions. Publication 590B will focus on distributions from traditional IRAs as well as Roth IRAs. Always check the IRS. gov website for the most current publications and make sure you request both 590A and 590B. They, like all the other IRS publications are free for the asking…your tax dollars at work!

---

1   IRS Publication 590.

If Jo has more than one IRA, she would calculate her RMD separately for each account. She could then add the individual amounts together and elect to take the total distribution from one account or split it up between them in any way that suits her. In either case, these are the steps she will follow:

Table 34. JO'S YEAR ONE RMD CALCULATIONS

Step 1:	December 31, 2043, traditional IRA account balance	$ 600,000
Step 2:	Distribution period	27.5 years
Step 3:	Divide Step 1 by Step 2 $ 600,000 ÷ 27.5	$ 21,818 Due by April 1, 2045 (the year after Jo turns 70½)

Notes for year one calculations:

Jo turns 70½ in 2044, but her first distribution is not due until April 1, 2045. To make the calculations, she will look back to her December 31, 2043, account balance, but she will use 70½ for establishing the first distribution period.

Table 35. JO'S YEAR TWO (AND SUBSEQUENT YEARS) RMD CALCULATIONS

Step 1:	Previous year's closing account balance	$ 578,182
Step 2:	Distribution period	26.5 years
Step 3:	Divide Step 1 by Step 2 $ 578,182 ÷ 26.5	$ 21,818 Due by December 31 of the current year

Notes for year two (and subsequent years) calculations:

- *In 2045, Jo will be required to receive both her 2044 RMD, which is due on April 1, and her current year RMD, which is due on December 31. To make the calculations for the second distribution, she will start with her December 31, 2044, account balance.*

- *For simplicity's sake, I have employed an arbitrary calculation to figure Jo's year-end balances that assumes no growth or distributions other than the RMDs. In the real world, those values would vary widely from year to year.*

ACCOUNTING TIP: To compute the RMD, always begin with the balance on your December 31 IRA statement for the previous year and always obtain the current distribution period from the appropriate IRS table.

Table 36. TABLE III (UNIFORM LIFETIME)

For Use by:

Unmarried Owners, Married Owners Whose Spouses Are Not More Than 10 Years Younger, and Married Owners Whose Spouses Are Not the Sole Beneficiaries of Their IRAs

AGE	DISTRIBUTION PERIOD	AGE	DISTRIBUTION PERIOD	AGE	DISTRIBUTION PERIOD
70	27.4	86	14.1	101	5.9
71	26.5	87	13.4	102	5.5
72	25.6	88	12.7	103	5.2
73	24.7	89	12	104	4.9
74	23.8	90	11.4	105	4.5
75	22.9	91	10.8	106	4.2
76	22	92	10.2	107	3.9
77	21.2	93	9.6	108	3.7
78	20.3	94	9.1	109	3.4
79	19.5	95	8.6	110	3.1
80	18.7	96	8.1	111	2.9
81	17.9	97	7.6	112	2.6
82	17.1	98	7.1	113	2.4
83	16.3	99	6.7	114	2.1
84	15.5	100	6.3	115 and over	1.9
85	14.8				

Table 37 shows us that if Jo waits to tap into her traditional IRA until she is required at age 70½ and lives long enough, her account will be depleted in the year 2089, when Jo reaches the ripe old age of 115.

Table 37. JO'S TRADITIONAL IRA RMD WORKSHEET

12/31/2043 Balance: $600,00					
YEAR	**JO'S AGE**	**DIST. PERIOD**	**JO'S MRD**	**JO'S IRA YEAR END BALANCE**	**DUE DATE**
2045	70	27.5	$21,818	$578,182	04/01/2045
2045	71	26.5	$21,818	$556,364	12/31/2045
2046	72	25.6	$21,733	$534,631	12/31/2046
2047	73	24.7	$21,645	$512,986	12/31/2047
2048	74	23.8	$21,554	$491,432	12/31/2048
2049	75	22.9	$21,460	$469,972	12/31/2049
2050	76	22	$21,362	$448,609	12/31/2050
2051	77	21.2	$21,161	$427,449	12/31/2051
2052	78	20.3	$21,057	$406,392	12/31/2052
2053	79	19.5	$20,841	$385,551	12/31/2053
2054	80	18.7	$20,618	$364,934	12/31/2054
2055	81	17.9	$20,387	$344,546	12/31/2055
2056	82	17.1	$20,149	$324,397	12/31/2056
2057	83	16.3	$19,902	$304,496	12/31/2057
2058	84	15.5	$19,645	$284,851	12/31/2058
2059	85	14.8	$19,247	$265,604	12/31/2059
2060	86	14.1	$18,837	$246,767	12/31/2060
2061	87	13.4	$18,415	$228,352	12/31/2061
2062	88	12.7	$17,980	$210,371	12/31/2062
2063	89	12	$17,531	$192,840	12/31/2063

YEAR	JO'S AGE	DIST. PERIOD	JO'S MRD	JO'S IRA YEAR END BALANCE	DUE DATE
2064	90	11.4	$16,916	$175,924	12/31/2064
2065	91	10.8	$16,289	$159,635	12/31/2065
2066	92	10.2	$15,650	$143,985	12/31/2066
2067	93	9.6	$14,998	$128,986	12/31/2067
2068	94	9.1	$14,174	$114,812	12/31/2068
2069	95	8.6	$13,350	$101,462	12/31/2069
2070	96	8.1	$12,526	$88,936	12/31/2070
2071	97	7.6	$11,702	$77,233	12/31/2071
2072	98	7.1	$10,878	$66,356	12/31/2072
2073	99	6.7	$9,904	$56,452	12/31/2073
2074	100	6.3	$8,961	$47,491	12/31/2074
2075	101	5.9	$8,049	$39,442	12/31/2075
2076	102	5.5	$7,171	$32,271	12/31/2076
2077	103	5.2	$6,206	$26,065	12/31/2077
2078	104	4.9	$5,319	$20,745	12/31/2078
2079	105	4.5	$4,610	$16,135	12/31/2079
2080	106	4.2	$3,842	$12,294	12/31/2080
2081	107	3.9	$3,152	$9,141	12/31/2081
2082	108	3.7	$2,471	$6,671	12/31/2082
2083	109	3.4	$1,962	$4,709	12/31/2083
2084	110	3.1	$1,519	$3,190	12/31/2084
2085	111	2.9	$1,100	$2,090	12/31/2085
2086	112	2.6	$804	$1,286	12/31/2086
2087	113	2.4	$536	$750	12/31/2087
2088	114	2.1	$357	$393	12/31/2088
2089	115 and over	1.9	$207	$186	12/31/2089

The important thing to note is that the distribution period does not change relative to the size of her account, but the RMD will. Let's play a little "what if" game with Jo's money. What if Jo only has $100,000 in her traditional IRA when she reaches 70½? It will still last her until she's 115 years old, but her RMDs start off at $3,650 and wrap up at $34 in 2089.

Table 38. JO'S TRADITIONAL IRA RMD WORKSHEET

12/31/2043 Balance: $100,000					
YEAR	**JO'S AGE**	**DIST. PERIOD**	**JO'S MRD**	**JO'S IRA YEAR END BALANCE**	**DUE DATE**
2044	70	27.4	$3,650	$96,350	04/01/2045
2045	71	26.5	$3,636	$92,715	12/31/2045
2046	72	25.6	$3,622	$89,093	12/31/2046
2047	73	24.7	$3,607	$85,486	12/31/2047
2048	74	23.8	$3,592	$81,894	12/31/2048
2049	75	22.9	$3,576	$78,318	12/31/2049
2050	76	22	$3,560	$74,758	12/31/2050
2051	77	21.2	$3,526	$71,232	12/31/2051
2052	78	20.3	$3,509	$67,723	12/31/2052
2053	79	19.5	$3,473	$64,250	12/31/2053
2054	80	18.7	$3,436	$60,814	12/31/2054
2055	81	17.9	$3,397	$57,416	12/31/2055
2056	82	17.1	$3,358	$54,059	12/31/2056
2057	83	16.3	$3,316	$50,742	12/31/2057
2058	84	15.5	$3,274	$47,469	12/31/2058
2059	85	14.8	$3,207	$44,261	12/31/2059
2060	86	14.1	$3,139	$41,122	12/31/2060
2061	87	13.4	$3,069	$38,053	12/31/2061

YEAR	JO'S AGE	DIST. PERIOD	JO'S MRD	JO'S IRA YEAR END BALANCE	DUE DATE
2062	88	12.7	$2,996	$35,057	12/31/2062
2063	89	12	$2,921	$32,136	12/31/2063
2064	90	11.4	$2,819	$29,317	12/31/2064
2065	91	10.8	$2,715	$26,602	12/31/2065
2066	92	10.2	$2,608	$23,994	12/31/2066
2067	93	9.6	$2,499	$21,495	12/31/2067
2068	94	9.1	$2,362	$19,133	12/31/2068
2069	95	8.6	$2,225	$16,908	12/31/2069
2070	96	8.1	$2,087	$14,821	12/31/2070
2071	97	7.6	$1,950	$12,870	12/31/2071
2072	98	7.1	$1,813	$11,058	12/31/2072
2073	99	6.7	$1,650	$9,407	12/31/2073
2074	100	6.3	$1,493	$7,914	12/31/2074
2075	101	5.9	$1,341	$6,573	12/31/2075
2076	102	5.5	$1,195	$5,378	12/31/2076
2077	103	5.2	$1,034	$4,344	12/31/2077
2078	104	4.9	$886	$3,457	12/31/2078
2079	105	4.5	$768	$2,689	12/31/2079
2080	106	4.2	$640	$2,049	12/31/2080
2081	107	3.9	$525	$1,523	12/31/2081
2082	108	3.7	$412	$1,112	12/31/2082
2083	109	3.4	$327	$785	12/31/2083
2084	110	3.1	$253	$532	12/31/2084
2085	111	2.9	$183	$348	12/31/2085
2086	112	2.6	$134	$214	12/31/2086

YEAR	JO'S AGE	DIST. PERIOD	JO'S MRD	JO'S IRA YEAR END BALANCE	DUE DATE
2087	113	2.4	$89	$125	12/31/2087
2088	114	2.1	$60	$65	12/31/2088
2089	115 and over	1.9	$34	$31	12/31/2089

Also, remember that Jo's traditional IRA distributions are taxed as ordinary income as she takes them, so their buying power will be reduced by both inflation and taxes. Add into that equation the fact that the RMDs are front-loaded (larger distributions early, smaller distributions later), but the increase in Jo's cost of living may well be back-loaded, as advancing age takes a toll on her health and vigor. Whether Jo's IRS ends up with a balance of $600,000 at age 70½ or a fraction of it, along about the time she reaches octogenarian status, her balance will be reduced by almost half. That's why Jo will use every reasonable opportunity over the years to transfer her funds from the traditional IRA to the Roth, where she can get the maximize stretch out of her account.

Given all these factors, here's how Jo and her financial advisor, Bill, have prioritized her asset depletion after she retires. You'll notice that she will reserve the assets in her Roth IRA for last, because they offer her and her heirs the greatest opportunity to continue to grow compounded and untaxed for virtually forever.

Table 39. JO'S ASSET DEPLETION PLAN

	INCOME SOURCE	TAX TREATMENT
First	Non-IRA	Taxed as ordinary income and capital gains
Second	Traditional IRA	Taxed as ordinary income
Last	Roth IRA	Tax-free

Non-Cash Distributions

If, some time over the past decades, Jo bought a retirement home or some other physical asset for use during retirement, she'll want to take it as a distribution at some point. To do so, all she has to do is to work with her IRA administrator to transfer title from the IRA to Jo. The value of the asset will be recorded as a distribution and count toward her RMD if it was held in a traditional IRA.

If transferring the whole property all in one year creates an unreasonable tax burden, Jo has another option available to her. She can change the title to *tenancy in common* and break up the transfer over several years. Her administrator will report the value of the portion transferred to the IRS. If the value of the transfer by itself meets her RMD, she won't have to take any further distributions for that year.

Breaking the Rules: A Costly Mistake

Now that Jo knows how she wants to spend her money, or more accurately, which accounts she wants to tap first, it's time to look at the repercussions for doing it wrong. Whether Jo needs the distributions from her traditional IRA or not, on the first day of April the year after she turns 70½, she needs to have taken one. Failure to do so will cost her a penalty of 50 percent of the excess accumulation. Let's refer back to Table 37 to compute the penalty if Jo is enjoying an around-the-world cruise that spring and forgets that she has an RMD due.

> **Excess accumulation:** The portion of a required minimum distribution (RMD) that is left in the traditional IRA account, instead of being withdrawn. A 50 percent penalty applies to excess accumulations.

ACCOUNTING TIP: Do not trust your IRA administrator or even your accountant to remind you that your RMD is due.

- Know what you must withdraw and when.
- Request the distribution early enough to receive it by the due date (December 31 of the year it is due).
- Follow up to make sure it has been received.

Jo's RMD worksheet says that her first RMD is $21,818. If Jo completely forgets that this is the big year—the one in which she must begin taking a minimum distribution—her penalty will total $10,909. That's right, 50 percent of the excess accumulation (the amount she was supposed to withdraw from her traditional IRA for her own benefit) goes out of her account and right into the coffers of the IRS. If she miscalculates and takes only $20,000, she will be penalized $409, or half of the $818 RMD shortfall. Needless to say, Jo will be exceedingly careful to take at least the required amount and perhaps even round upward to build in a margin for safety.

Another safety precaution Jo will take to avoid potentially staggering penalties is tending to the task herself. Perhaps her IRA administrator, accountant, and financial manager will all have added scheduling her RMD to their calendars, and maybe she'll receive three different telephone calls reminding her. Still, the ultimate responsibility for requesting the RMD and seeing to it that it arrives before the deadline lies with her, and she is the one who will pay the penalty if the reminder falls through the cracks.

Jo certainly could begin taking distributions as soon as she can do so without triggering penalties, but once she turns 70½, Jo *must* begin taking at least the RMD. At her own discretion, she can choose to take more at any time, but she must take at least the minimum required distribution every year from that year forward until she either depletes the account or it passes into her estate at her death.

CHAPTER SIXTEEN

Estate Planning

We pay for the mistakes of our ancestors, and it seems only fair that they should leave us the money to pay with.

–DONALD MARQUIS

Retire rich: that's the goal Jo set early on in this process. Rich means different things to different people. Throughout this book, we've bandied about some pretty hefty numbers to demonstrate Jo's financial options and how she went about making her decisions. Perhaps seven- and eight-digit numbers define your perception of wealth. Perhaps they seem impossible and improbable. Coming up with the exact numbers is not the point. The point is getting through this life with the maximum comfort  and security you can arrange and ending up with at least a little left over when you're finished. Of course, we hope you'll have a lot left over, so that you can make the lives of your heirs more comfortable and secure too.

It's the reason you chose the self-directed IRA and have chosen to manage it in a way to take advantage of the stretch benefit. If you are successful in that endeavor, you'll have one more responsibility—shepherding your wealth to your chosen beneficiaries. Of course, you won't be around to personally manage the job, so you'll have to set everything up on this end before you go.

Some people foolishly trust that the court system and their loved ones will do the job for them. Rest assured, they will. But whether the results will be to anyone's best benefit is another matter. So, once again, the responsibility rests with you. Let's begin with a quick review of why you want to do everything you can to keep your IRA intact for as long as possible.

Stretching an IRA

The earlier Jo starts saving and the longer her assets remain in the IRA, the bigger the account can grow. It follows then that anything that reduces the balance impairs future earnings. On the other hand, if each year the account's net income exceeds Jo's withdrawals, her savings can outlast her lifetime requirements. And, of course, the greater the difference between the net income and her net withdrawals, the longer it will last. This is the cornerstone of the stretch IRA.

That's the primary reason Jo moved as much as she could into a Roth IRA which, unlike the traditional IRA, does not have a mandatory distribution attached to it. She intends to use her non-IRA savings first, followed by her traditional IRA account. Above all, she wants to preserve the Roth IRA, her compound growth workhorse, until she needs it in her later years — and hopefully for her heirs.

Passing on the Stretch IRA Benefit

There are two ways to inherit an IRA. The person whose name is written on the IRA's beneficiary form is called a *named beneficiary*. Named beneficiaries have the most options, and a named beneficiary who is also the spouse has the most options of all. The named beneficiary also has the advantage of inheriting the IRA directly without the delay and expense of it having to pass through probate.

An IRA without a named beneficiary, on the other hand, has two potential destinies. Sometimes the language in the trustee agreement will stipulate a default beneficiary, perhaps a spouse, for example. In that case, again, probate can generally be avoided. If, on the other hand, the default beneficiary language is lacking in the trustee agreement or does not apply to the circumstances of the deceased, the IRA will generally pass into probate. In that case, which heir inherits the IRA will be determined by the account holder's will (or state law, if the deceased also failed to sign a will), and the rule of unintended consequences will be triggered.

In all likelihood the original account holder didn't intend to make the IRS a key beneficiary of the account. Yet, by neglecting to name a beneficiary to the account (not the will), that is exactly what happens. Special distribution rules apply to an IRA that passes into an estate. Even though the IRA will ultimately pass to an heir, the damage will have already been done.

By the time the heirs receive control of the IRA, which can be years after the account holder's death, they may have a very narrow window of opportunity to withdraw the funds without triggering the 50 percent penalty for excess accumulations.

You probably don't need to be reminded one more time about the tax consequences of taking large distributions over a short period of time. It's not a pretty picture, and the authors are willing to bet that very few people have such an outcome in mind when they envision passing their hard-earned money on to their loved ones.

Before this book discusses how and when beneficiaries can take distributions, let's take a quick look at the rules about naming beneficiaries. To keep the terminology straight, use the term *estate beneficiary* to designate the unfortunate heir who inherits the obligation to pay extra taxes and cut future earnings short. Let's call the heir who inherits the opportunity to stretch IRA the *named beneficiary*.

Who Can Be a Beneficiary?

Jo can pass her IRAs to anyone she chooses. The beneficiary can be her spouse, one or all of her children, any friend or relative, or a trust for their benefit. It can even be a charity.

As you've learned, Jo's decision will determine how quickly the funds must be withdrawn from the account and how much of it will be lost to taxes. And any opportunity to continue the stretch can be jeopardized if Jo fails to name a beneficiary. That's why Jo named a beneficiary as soon as she opened her IRA accounts and revisits her decision on an annual basis. Beneficiaries' ages, circumstances and relationships change. Sometimes they die.

If Jo marries, she will probably want to name her spouse as her IRA beneficiary. If she lives in a community property state, she may not have a choice. Sometimes the law requires it.

Perhaps before she married, she had her fiancé listed as a co-beneficiary with her cousin Shirley. She may still want to preserve a portion of her estate for Shirley, but a spouse who is not named as a sole beneficiary on an IRA loses some important privileges. If her state allows it and if Jo has sufficient IRA assets, she might choose to name Shirley as the beneficiary of one of her other IRAs or she can leave different assets to her cousin. The point is that choosing a beneficiary is not a one-shot decision. It needs to be revisited from time to time, and for sure, every time there is a major change in Jo's life.

Naming a Beneficiary

What if Jo's circumstances don't fit into a neat little box at the bottom of a boilerplate form? You've probably had that happen to you too. You receive a form in the mail that instructs you to fill in the blanks, sign it, and mail it back. You look at the space provided and toss it aside in frustration,

rather than trying to fit a square peg in a round hole. Fortunately, when the issue is a beneficiary designation, you usually will have the option of having a lawyer draw up a beneficiary designation that fits your circumstances.

That's what Jo will do. Her administrator may have requirements that must be included, but that shouldn't be a problem for a qualified attorney. If the administrator isn't open to the idea, Jo will find one who is. This is an important issue—every bit as important as the other factors Jo considered when she chose an administrator. In the end, the most she can do to help her heirs is to choose them well and name them as beneficiaries to the IRAs. After that, it will be up to her heirs to make the most of the opportunity Jo leaves them. There may points for which compromise is an option. Naming a beneficiary is not one of them.

Naming a Contingent Beneficiary

Another step that IRA account holders often overlook is naming a *contingent beneficiary*, a person who will be second in line to inherit the IRA if the named beneficiary can't inherit it (for instance in the event that the beneficiary dies before the owner) or declines the inheritance. This is always important, but can be especially useful to ensure that the IRA passes directly to (not through probate) to the account holder's children if her spouse (who is a named beneficiary) dies first.

Inherited IRA Distributions

Let's dismiss the simplest—and usually most foolish—disposition for an IRA, whether you're the original account holder, a named beneficiary, or an estate beneficiary. The IRS won't mind a bit if you cash out the account, pay the taxes, and walk away with whatever is left. If you're a beneficiary, you won't even be charged a 10 percent early withdrawal penalty if you drain the account the very day you gain possession. You, on the other hand, will probably live to regret the decision.

If you find yourself the beneficiary of an IRA, the authors strongly recommend that you consult one of numerous books available that examines your options in detail. It is a complex subject that far exceeds the space to address it. For the purposes of our discussion, however, we can cover the points that an IRA account holder will want to consider when selecting a beneficiary.

> **LEGAL TIP:** An inherited IRA will forever be an inherited IRA (except in the case of a spousal rollover, which we will look at in a moment). This is an important, if subtle, point. When and if the account is drained, it ceases to exist. Until then, it will be titled and treated as a beneficiary account.

Beneficiaries can be divided into two broad groups. Named beneficiaries have the honor and advantage of being considered individuals, in IRS lingo. An individual can be a spouse or non-spouse. Everyone and everything else, estates and charities, for example, are considered to be "not an individual." By extension, the distribution rules for an heir who inherits an IRA from the estate are defined by that association. Let's look at them by classification.

Table 40. DISTRIBUTION OPTIONS FOR SPOUSE AS A NAMED BENEFICIARY

Option 1:	
The spouse can treat the IRA as his or her own (this is known as a rollover).	
With this option, the balance in the inherited IRA is rolled over to an account owned by the surviving spouse. Once the rollover is complete, it is as if the account had always belonged to the surviving spouse, and the same rules for early withdrawal and required minimum distributions apply, as they would to any other like IRA.	
10% early withdrawal penalty?	Yes
Required minimum distribution?	Yes (Traditional IRA only)
Required beginning date	April 1 or the year after turning 70½
Distribution period	The beneficiary spouse's life expectancy (Table I)
50% penalty for excess accumulations (failing to take RMD)	Yes (Traditional IRA only)
Option 2:	
The spouse can choose to remain a beneficiary to the account.	
Early withdrawal penalties do not apply to inherited accounts, so a surviving spouse who needs access to the funds right away may opt to retain all or a portion of the funds in the inherited account.	
10% early withdrawal penalty?	No
Required minimum distribution?	Yes (Traditional IRA only)
Required beginning date	*The later of:* The year in which the deceased spouse would have turned 70½ **Or** The year following the death of the account holder
Distribution period	The beneficiary spouse's life expectancy (Table I)
50% penalty for excess accumulations (failing to take RMD)	Yes

Table 41. DISTRIBUTION OPTIONS FOR NONSPOUSE AS A NAMED BENEFICIARY

10% early withdrawal penalty	No
Required minimum distribution?	Yes (Traditional IRA only)
Required beginning date	The year following the account holder's death
Distribution period	The beneficiary's life expectancy (Table I)
50% penalty for excess accumulations (failing to take RMD)	Yes

Table 42. DISTRIBUTION OPTIONS FOR MULTIPLE NAMED BENEFICIARIES

10% early withdrawal penalty	No
Required minimum distribution?	Yes (Traditional IRA only)
Required beginning date	The year following the account holder's death
Distribution period	The life expectancy (using Table I) of the oldest beneficiary, *unless the account holder specified the percent ownership for each beneficiary. If this designation is made, the beneficiaries can split the inherited account into separate accordingly.**
*For example, Jo, Ted, and Shirley are all named beneficiaries on an IRA. The account holder specifies that Jo and Ted are to inherit 20 percent each. Shirley is to inherit 60 percent. Upon the death of the account holder, the three named beneficiaries can split the account into their respective portions and retain the stretch option. *Without the percent designation, however, the distribution for each of the shares would have been based on Jo's age (since she is the oldest). Alternatively, they could have cashed out the account and divided it equally.*	
50 percent penalty for excess accumulations (failing to take RMD)	Yes

Table 43. DISTRIBUTION OPTIONS FOR ESTATE BENEFICIARY

No Designated Beneficiary Account Holder Dies Before Reaching Age of 70½	
10% early withdrawal penalty	No
Required minimum distribution?	Yes
Required beginning date	Five years after the account holder's death
Distribution period	None - Full distribution required
50 percent penalty for excess accumulations (failing to take RMD)	Yes
No Designated Beneficiary Account Holder Dies On or After Reaching Age of 70 ½	
10% early withdrawal penalty	No
Required minimum distribution?	Yes
Required beginning date	The year following the account holder's death
Distribution period	Life expectancy for account holder as of his or her birthday in the year of death (Table I, Single Life Expectancy)
50 percent penalty for excess accumulations (failing to take RMD)	Yes

Protecting the Stretch Option

IRA beneficiaries can continue to stretch for as long as the distribution period for their specific situations or until they shoot themselves in the foot. The surest way to do that is to take a distribution in a manner not permitted under the stretch rules. (That's why we keep harping on the need to consult with an expert—preferably an attorney who understands IRAs inside and out.)

The surest (but not the only) way to take an inappropriate distribution is to incorrectly change the name on a beneficiary account. Let us repeat that, phrasing it a bit differently. If a beneficiary retitles the account in his or her name, the IRS will interpret it as a total distribution. The 'ka-ching, ka-ching, ka-ching' you hear is the cash register over at the Treasury Department. To keep from inadvertently creating financial disaster out of the good will of the benefactor, the beneficiary needs to make sure that the account is retitled, but in the correct manner.

For example, if Jo's father names her the beneficiary of one of his IRAs, when he dies, Jo will have the IRA retitled like this:

David Moneymaker IRA (deceased 7/1/09), FBO Joanne Moneymaker (Social Security Number xxx-xxxx-xxx)

Or in other words it must contain:

- Name of original account holder
- Date of death
- FBO [*For the Benefit Of*] beneficiary's name
- Beneficiary's Social Security number)

Any other title will be considered an irreversible and complete distribution. The only exception to this rule is for the spouse. A spouse who is a named beneficiary may choose the rollover option, in which case the account will be retitled in his or her own name.

It would be hard to overemphasize the importance of consulting a professional for any aspect of estate planning. Because of the complex nature of inherited IRA distribution rules, this is especially true for IRAs. This brief overview cannot hope to cover all of the nuances of the law. That's where good attorneys are worth their weight in gold.

Estate Taxes And Probate

Commonly referred to as the *death tax*, the estate tax kicks in when the value of an estate going through the probate process exceeds a certain threshold. Why do we care about the estate tax in a discussion of IRAs? Because an IRA with a designated beneficiary gets to sidestep probate, but not estate taxes. And sooner or later, they will have to be paid (typically, by the estate) if the estate is large enough. In addition to Uncle Sam's portion, many states also have an estate tax. Often, it is a percentage of what you owe Uncle Sam for the federal estate taxes.

"Probate" is the name of the process whereby a decedent (a person who has died) has the terms of his/her Last Will and Testament enforced by the courts to make sure the wishes as expressed in the Will are followed in distributing the estate to the beneficiaries. "Probatable estate" refers to the assets actually passing through the probate process. If you have previously named beneficiaries on things like your IRAs, your bank accounts, on real estate you own, life insurance policies, etc., these things pass to your beneficiaries automatically on proof of your death. They do NOT go through probate. The only things that go through probate are the things that you did not name beneficiaries on; then your Will takes control and governs their distribution.

LEGAL TIP: You can avoid probate entirely if, at the time you die, all of your assets have previously had named beneficiaries applied to them.

As between spouses, you can pass unlimited amounts of assets to each other estate tax-free. However, when the property is going to children, relatives, friends, etc., that's a different story. Estate taxes may be owed to Uncle Sam.

As said a moment ago, only probateable assets go through the probate process. Part of the probate is the preparation of an Inventory. This document lists all the various assets going through the probate process. A copy of this is often sent to the IRS. If the IRS sees that the probated estate exceeds the exclusion amount, an Estate Tax return will be required and may result in estate taxes being levied.

When an estate does trigger estate taxes, the tax is not charged against the entire estate. Instead, it only applies to the portion of the estate above the threshold.

$$\frac{\begin{array}{c} \text{Total value of the estate} \\ \text{- Exclusion} \end{array}}{= \text{Taxable portion of the estate}}$$

$$\frac{\times \text{Tax rate}}{= \text{Estate tax}}$$

Table 44. ESTATE TAX EXCLUSION TABLE

TAX YEAR	EXCLUSION	MAXIMUM ESTATE AND GIFT TAX RATE
2012	$ 5,120,000	35%
2013	$ 5,250,000	40%
2014	$ 5,340,000	40%
2015 and beyond	$ 5,340,000*	40%*
*If no changes are made during the 2015 Congressional session.		

NOTE: This chart is for general reference purposes only. There are numerous exceptions and qualifications, such as combining lifetime gifts with estate gifts, etc. It is imperative that you understand your personal situation may alter these numbers; seek the assistance of a qualified accountant and estate tax lawyer to properly understand your own personal circumstances.

If the estate lacks sufficient cash to pay the estate tax, assets have to be liquidated to come up with the cash. Sometimes those assets turn out to be IRAs, and all those decades of careful planning end up being wasted.

A good financial planner can help avoid those kinds of problems. One approach is to establish a life insurance trust, in which the trust holds one or more life insurance policies that will be used to pay the estate taxes, burial expenses, and probate costs. Anything left over when all of the expenses are paid can be distributed according to the terms of the trust.

A life insurance trust is an irrevocable instrument, meaning that once established, there's no going back. So, once again, a qualified financial planner and an attorney should be consulted to identify the best solution for you.

Conclusion

According to the most recent figures, about 99 percent of all IRA owners limit their account investments to traditional financial instruments like stocks, bonds, and mutual funds. My own anecdotal experience suggests that most IRA owners don't know they have another choice.

Since their inception in 1978, IRAs have been the purview of the banking industry, brokerage firms, and insurance companies. Certainly your banker and broker aren't likely to introduce you the alternatives either. Why would they? You're their cash cow.

This is not meant to disparage brokers and bankers and other financial institutions. It is meant to point out that no one has the degree of vested interest in your financial success that you alone have. The nature of business is to look out for number one, with the hope that its customers and clients can prosper as a by-product.

If you have ever owned your own business, you understand the competing objectives between you and your clients or customers. You also understand that taking responsibility for your own future is the only solution.

Over the course of the preceding chapters, we've tagged along as Jo Moneymaker examined strategies for achieving the goal of retiring rich. We started out by acknowledging that stocks, bonds, and mutual funds have a place in her portfolio, but that she is the best judge as to how they should be weighted against her other investments. Her visit to financial planner Bill Cash opened her eyes to new possibilities. Together, they developed a plan for an extreme makeover of her retirement plan.

Before we wrap things up, let's take a quick look at where she stands with that plan after all these months of planning and execution.

BILL'S EXTREME MAKEOVER PLAN	JO'S SCORE
Step 1: Build Wealth	
Capitalize on compound growth	
• Start early.	10
• Save the max.	10
• Roll over 401(k) to an IRA whenever possible.	10
• Redistribute assets between assets as needed.	Planned
• Stretch distributions over the longest period possible.	Planned
Choose the right investments	
• Stocks, bonds, financial instruments	10
• Real estate	10
• Real estate-backed notes	Planned
• Business ownership	Planned
• Precious metals	10
Manage risk	
• Planning	10
• Due diligence	10
• Structure	10
Step 2: Keep What's Yours	
Reduce taxes	

BILL'S EXTREME MAKEOVER PLAN	JO'S SCORE
• Pay taxes up front for high-yield investments (Roth IRA)	10
• Defer taxes for low-yield investments (traditional IRA)	10
Use 401(k) rollover to best advantage	
• Boost IRA balance	10
• Capture stretch opportunities on more of your savings	10
Avoid extra taxes and penalties	
• Avoid early withdrawal penalties	Planned
• Take required distributions on time	Planned
• Use a Roth IRA to avoid required distributions (a technique called a *stretch*)	Planned

Clearly, she's not finished, but she's done everything right so far. Some steps won't need to be dealt with for years, so she's made careful note of what she needs to do when the time comes.

Like you, Jo may not choose to invest in all of the vehicles we've explored. Some require more research and active management than she'll have time to give them. Others require more risk than she may be comfortable with, when the opportunities present themselves. But, she did learn a few new ideas. we hope that you did as well.

Like my friend Jo, you'll find the investments you choose are the bricks and mortar out of which you will construct your financial house. A house is never any stronger than the foundation on which it is built, however. The self-directed IRA can be the rock-solid cornerstone for that foundation, because it puts you in control of your own future.

Taking control means accepting additional responsibility. Gaining and using knowledge is one of them. The authors have tried to present the information in this book in a way that makes you curious to learn more and eager put it to work. This book also covered the basics about the differences between the various IRA plans, the importance of contributing the maximum possible as early as possible, the absolute value of withdrawing the funds as slowly as possible, and how to pass on what's left to your heirs. Still, there is so much more to the subject than we could even hope to cover in a volume you would be able to lift without mechanical assistance. We hope you will refer to the list of resources in the back of this book and continue to expand your knowledge.

Taking control means taking responsibility for applying that knowledge with commitment and discipline. We talked a lot about due diligence, altering an investment's structure and using careful planning and analysis tools to manage risk. Yet, discipline may well be the single most important tool for managing risk, because it is what makes you careful and consistent.

Saving requires sacrifice. Discipline is what makes you pass up the Hawaii trip to make this year's IRA contribution. Growing money requires hard work—as hard as hefting real bricks to build your real house. As with those real bricks, using the right tools can make all the difference in the world. Time is one of the most important tools, because it is the key to compound growth, and compound growth, as we've seen time and time again, does the heavy lifting. Thus, we complete the circle.

The principles you've learned about are relatively basic, even if the application of them may not always be. Our wish for you is that you save well, invest wisely, use carefully, and prosper always.

Additional Resources

Business Brokers

INTERNATIONAL BUSINESS BROKERS ASSOCIATION ® (IBBA)

3525 Piedmont Road NE, Building 5, Suite 300
Atlanta, GA 30305
888-686-IBBA (4222)
www.ibba.org

Regional business broker associations can be located by searching for business broker associations for your state on the Internet.

Business Appraisers

Appraisers Association of America, Inc.

212 W. 35th Street, 11th Floor South
New York, NY 10001
212-889-5404
http://www.appraisersassoc.org

Institute of Business Appraisers
5217 S. State Street, Suite 400
Salt Lake City, UT 84107
800-299-4130
http://www.go-iba.org

Certified Financial Planners

Certified Financial Planner Board of Standards, Inc.
1425 K Street NW, Suite 800
Washington, DC 20005
800-487-1497
http://www.cfp.net

Financial Planning Association
Denver Office
Suite 600, 7535 E. Hampden Ave.
Denver, CO 80231
800-322-4237
http://www.fpanet.org/

The National Association of Personal
Financial Advisors (NAPFA)
3250 North Arlington Heights Road, Suite 109
Arlington Heights, IL 60004
847-483-5400
info@napfa.org

Society of Financial Service Professionals
19 Campus Boulevard, Suite 100
Newtown Square, PA 19073-3239
610-526-2500
http://www.financialpro.org/

Home Inspections

American Society of Home Inspectors,® Inc.
932 Lee Street, Suite 101
Des Plaines, IL 60016
847-759-2820
http://www.ashi.org

National Institute of Building Inspectors
2 N. Main Street, #203
Medford, NJ 08055
http://www.nibi.com/

IRA Information

Internal Revenue Service (IRS)
800-TAX-FORM (800-829-3676)
http://www.irs.gov

IRS Publication 590A and 590B (for 2015)
Individual Retirement Arrangements (IRAs)
http://www.irs.gov/publications

IRA Trustees, Administrators, and Custodians

The following are samples: This is not a recommendation of one company over another; you should do your own research before selecting a trustee, administrator or custodian.

Guidant Financial Group, Inc.
Corporate Headquarters
1120 112th Ave. NE, Suite 410
Bellevue, WA 98004
888-472-4455
info@guidantfinancial.com

PENSCO Trust Company
866-818-4472
http://www.pensco.com/

Entrust USA
5430 LBJ Freeway, Suite 1250
Dallas, Texas 75240
972-728-0447
http://www.iraplus.com/

Equity International,
Two North Riverside Plaza, Suite 1500
Chicago, IL 60606
312-675-7400
info@equityinternational.com

Mortgage Brokers

National Association of Mortgage Brokers
2701 W. 15th Street, Suite 536
Plano, TX 75075
http://www.namb.org/namb/Default.asp

Real Estate Brokers

Commercial Brokers Association
12131 113 Ave. NE, Suite 100
Kirkland, WA 98034
425-820-3348 or 800-275-2522
cba@commercialmls.com

National Association of Realtors
430 N. Michigan Ave.,
Chicago, IL 60611
800-874-6500
http://www.realtor.com

IRS Life Expectancy Tables (current for 2014 returns)

Joint Life and Last Survivor Expectancy

For Use by Owners Whose Spouses Are More Than 10 Years Younger and are the Sole Beneficiaries of Their IRAs

AGES	20	21	22	23	24	25	26	27	28	29
20	70.1	69.6	69.1	68.7	68.3	67.9	67.5	67.2	66.9	66.6
21	69.6	69.1	68.6	68.2	67.7	67.3	66.9	66.6	66.2	65.9
22	69.1	68.6	68.1	67.6	67.2	66.7	66.3	65.9	65.6	65.2
23	68.7	68.2	67.6	67.1	66.6	66.2	65.7	65.3	64.9	64.6
24	68.3	67.7	67.2	66.6	66.1	65.6	65.2	64.7	64.3	63.9
25	67.9	67.3	66.7	66.2	65.6	65.1	64.6	64.2	63.7	63.3
26	67.5	66.9	66.3	65.7	65.2	64.6	64.1	63.6	63.2	62.8
27	67.2	66.6	65.9	65.3	64.7	64.2	63.6	63.1	62.7	62.2
28	66.9	66.2	65.6	64.9	64.3	63.7	63.2	62.7	62.1	61.7
29	66.6	65.9	65.2	64.6	63.9	63.3	62.8	62.2	61.7	61.2
30	66.3	65.6	64.9	64.2	63.6	62.9	62.3	61.8	61.2	60.7
31	66.1	65.3	64.6	63.9	63.2	62.6	62.0	61.4	60.8	60.2
32	65.8	65.1	64.3	63.6	62.9	62.2	61.6	61.0	60.4	59.8
33	65.6	64.8	64.1	63.3	62.6	61.9	61.3	60.6	60.0	59.4
34	65.4	64.6	63.8	63.1	62.3	61.6	60.9	60.3	59.6	59.0
35	65.2	64.4	63.6	62.8	62.1	61.4	60.6	59.9	59.3	58.6
36	65.0	64.2	63.4	62.6	61.9	61.1	60.4	59.6	59.0	58.3
37	64.9	64.0	63.2	62.4	61.6	60.9	60.1	59.4	58.7	58.0
38	64.7	63.9	63.0	62.2	61.4	60.6	59.9	59.1	58.4	57.7

AGES	20	21	22	23	24	25	26	27	28	29
39	64.6	63.7	62.9	62.1	61.2	60.4	59.6	58.9	58.1	57.4
40	64.4	63.6	62.7	61.9	61.1	60.2	59.4	58.7	57.9	57.1
41	64.3	63.5	62.6	61.7	60.9	60.1	59.3	58.5	57.7	56.9
42	64.2	63.3	62.5	61.6	60.8	59.9	59.1	58.3	57.5	56.7
43	64.1	63.2	62.4	61.5	60.6	59.8	58.9	58.1	57.3	56.5
44	64.0	63.1	62.2	61.4	60.5	59.6	58.8	57.9	57.1	56.3
45	64.0	63.0	62.2	61.3	60.4	59.5	58.6	57.8	56.9	56.1
46	63.9	63.0	62.1	61.2	60.3	59.4	58.5	57.7	56.8	56.0
47	63.8	62.9	62.0	61.1	60.2	59.3	58.4	57.5	56.7	55.8
48	63.7	62.8	61.9	61.0	60.1	59.2	58.3	57.4	56.5	55.7
49	63.7	62.8	61.8	60.9	60.0	59.1	58.2	57.3	56.4	55.6
50	63.6	62.7	61.8	60.8	59.9	59.0	58.1	57.2	56.3	55.4
51	63.6	62.6	61.7	60.8	59.9	58.9	58.0	57.1	56.2	55.3
52	63.5	62.6	61.7	60.7	59.8	58.9	58.0	57.1	56.1	55.2
53	63.5	62.5	61.6	60.7	59.7	58.8	57.9	57.0	56.1	55.2
54	63.5	62.5	61.6	60.6	59.7	58.8	57.8	56.9	56.0	55.1
55	63.4	62.5	61.5	60.6	59.6	58.7	57.8	56.8	55.9	55.0
56	63.4	62.4	61.5	60.5	59.6	58.7	57.7	56.8	55.9	54.9
57	63.4	62.4	61.5	60.5	59.6	58.6	57.7	56.7	55.8	54.9
58	63.3	62.4	61.4	60.5	59.5	58.6	57.6	56.7	55.8	54.8
59	63.3	62.3	61.4	60.4	59.5	58.5	57.6	56.7	55.7	54.8
60	63.3	62.3	61.4	60.4	59.5	58.5	57.6	56.6	55.7	54.7
61	63.3	62.3	61.3	60.4	59.4	58.5	57.5	56.6	55.6	54.7
62	63.2	62.3	61.3	60.4	59.4	58.4	57.5	56.5	55.6	54.7
63	63.2	62.3	61.3	60.3	59.4	58.4	57.5	56.5	55.6	54.6
64	63.2	62.2	61.3	60.3	59.4	58.4	57.4	56.5	55.5	54.6
65	63.2	62.2	61.3	60.3	59.3	58.4	57.4	56.5	55.5	54.6
66	63.2	62.2	61.2	60.3	59.3	58.4	57.4	56.4	55.5	54.5
67	63.2	62.2	61.2	60.3	59.3	58.3	57.4	56.4	55.5	54.5
68	63.1	62.2	61.2	60.2	59.3	58.3	57.4	56.4	55.4	54.5
69	63.1	62.2	61.2	60.2	59.3	58.3	57.3	56.4	55.4	54.5
70	63.1	62.2	61.2	60.2	59.3	58.3	57.3	56.4	55.4	54.4
71	63.1	62.1	61.2	60.2	59.2	58.3	57.3	56.4	55.4	54.4
72	63.1	62.1	61.2	60.2	59.2	58.3	57.3	56.3	55.4	54.4

AGES	20	21	22	23	24	25	26	27	28	29
73	63.1	62.1	61.2	60.2	59.2	58.3	57.3	56.3	55.4	54.4
74	63.1	62.1	61.2	60.2	59.2	58.2	57.3	56.3	55.4	54.4
75	63.1	62.1	61.1	60.2	59.2	58.2	57.3	56.3	55.3	54.4
76	63.1	62.1	61.1	60.2	59.2	58.2	57.3	56.3	55.3	54.4
77	63.1	62.1	61.1	60.2	59.2	58.2	57.3	56.3	55.3	54.4
78	63.1	62.1	61.1	60.2	59.2	58.2	57.3	56.3	55.3	54.4
79	63.1	62.1	61.1	60.2	59.2	58.2	57.2	56.3	55.3	54.3
80	63.1	62.1	61.1	60.1	59.2	58.2	57.2	56.3	55.3	54.3
81	63.1	62.1	61.1	60.1	59.2	58.2	57.2	56.3	55.3	54.3
82	63.1	62.1	61.1	60.1	59.2	58.2	57.2	56.3	55.3	54.3
83	63.1	62.1	61.1	60.1	59.2	58.2	57.2	56.3	55.3	54.3
84	63.0	62.1	61.1	60.1	59.2	58.2	57.2	56.3	55.3	54.3
85	63.0	62.1	61.1	60.1	59.2	58.2	57.2	56.3	55.3	54.3
86	63.0	62.1	61.1	60.1	59.2	58.2	57.2	56.2	55.3	54.3
87	63.0	62.1	61.1	60.1	59.2	58.2	57.2	56.2	55.3	54.3
88	63.0	62.1	61.1	60.1	59.2	58.2	57.2	56.2	55.3	54.3
89	63.0	62.1	61.1	60.1	59.1	58.2	57.2	56.2	55.3	54.3
90	63.0	62.1	61.1	60.1	59.1	58.2	57.2	56.2	55.3	54.3
91	63.0	62.1	61.1	60.1	59.1	58.2	57.2	56.2	55.3	54.3
92	63.0	62.1	61.1	60.1	59.1	58.2	57.2	56.2	55.3	54.3
93	63.0	62.1	61.1	60.1	59.1	58.2	57.2	56.2	55.3	54.3
94	63.0	62.1	61.1	60.1	59.1	58.2	57.2	56.2	55.3	54.3
95	63.0	62.1	61.1	60.1	59.1	58.2	57.2	56.2	55.3	54.3
96	63.0	62.1	61.1	60.1	59.1	58.2	57.2	56.2	55.3	54.3
97	63.0	62.1	61.1	60.1	59.1	58.2	57.2	56.2	55.3	54.3
98	63.0	62.1	61.1	60.1	59.1	58.2	57.2	56.2	55.3	54.3
99	63.0	62.1	61.1	60.1	59.1	58.2	57.2	56.2	55.3	54.3
100	63.0	62.1	61.1	60.1	59.1	58.2	57.2	56.2	55.3	54.3
101	63.0	62.1	61.1	60.1	59.1	58.2	57.2	56.2	55.3	54.3
102	63.0	62.1	61.1	60.1	59.1	58.2	57.2	56.2	55.3	54.3
103	63.0	62.1	61.1	60.1	59.1	58.2	57.2	56.2	55.3	54.3
104	63.0	62.1	61.1	60.1	59.1	58.2	57.2	56.2	55.3	54.3
105	63.0	62.1	61.1	60.1	59.1	58.2	57.2	56.2	55.3	54.3
106	63.0	62.1	61.1	60.1	59.1	58.2	57.2	56.2	55.3	54.3

AGES	20	21	22	23	24	25	26	27	28	29
107	63.0	62.1	61.1	60.1	59.1	58.2	57.2	56.2	55.3	54.3
108	63.0	62.1	61.1	60.1	59.1	58.2	57.2	56.2	55.3	54.3
109	63.0	62.1	61.1	60.1	59.1	58.2	57.2	56.2	55.3	54.3
110	63.0	62.1	61.1	60.1	59.1	58.2	57.2	56.2	55.3	54.3
111	63.0	62.1	61.1	60.1	59.1	58.2	57.2	56.2	55.3	54.3
112	63.0	62.1	61.1	60.1	59.1	58.2	57.2	56.2	55.3	54.3
113	63.0	62.1	61.1	60.1	59.1	58.2	57.2	56.2	55.3	54.3
114	63.0	62.1	61.1	60.1	59.1	58.2	57.2	56.2	55.3	54.3
115	63.0	62.1	61.1	60.1	59.1	58.2	57.2	56.2	55.3	54.3

AGES	30	31	32	33	34	35	36	37	38	39
30	60.2	59.7	59.2	58.8	58.4	58.0	57.6	57.3	57.0	56.7
31	59.7	59.2	58.7	58.2	57.8	57.4	57.0	56.6	56.3	56.0
32	59.2	58.7	58.2	57.7	57.2	56.8	56.4	56.0	55.6	55.3
33	58.8	58.2	57.7	57.2	56.7	56.2	55.8	55.4	55.0	54.7
34	58.4	57.8	57.2	56.7	56.2	55.7	55.3	54.8	54.4	54.0
35	58.0	57.4	56.8	56.2	55.7	55.2	54.7	54.3	53.8	53.4
36	57.6	57.0	56.4	55.8	55.3	54.7	54.2	53.7	53.3	52.8
37	57.3	56.6	56.0	55.4	54.8	54.3	53.7	53.2	52.7	52.3
38	57.0	56.3	55.6	55.0	54.4	53.8	53.3	52.7	52.2	51.7
39	56.7	56.0	55.3	54.7	54.0	53.4	52.8	52.3	51.7	51.2
40	56.4	55.7	55.0	54.3	53.7	53.0	52.4	51.8	51.3	50.8
41	56.1	55.4	54.7	54.0	53.3	52.7	52.0	51.4	50.9	50.3
42	55.9	55.2	54.4	53.7	53.0	52.3	51.7	51.1	50.4	49.9
43	55.7	54.9	54.2	53.4	52.7	52.0	51.3	50.7	50.1	49.5
44	55.5	54.7	53.9	53.2	52.4	51.7	51.0	50.4	49.7	49.1
45	55.3	54.5	53.7	52.9	52.2	51.5	50.7	50.0	49.4	48.7
46	55.1	54.3	53.5	52.7	52.0	51.2	50.5	49.8	49.1	48.4
47	55.0	54.1	53.3	52.5	51.7	51.0	50.2	49.5	48.8	48.1
48	54.8	54.0	53.2	52.3	51.5	50.8	50.0	49.2	48.5	47.8
49	54.7	53.8	53.0	52.2	51.4	50.6	49.8	49.0	48.2	47.5
50	54.6	53.7	52.9	52.0	51.2	50.4	49.6	48.8	48.0	47.3
51	54.5	53.6	52.7	51.9	51.0	50.2	49.4	48.6	47.8	47.0

AGES	30	31	32	33	34	35	36	37	38	39
52	54.4	53.5	52.6	51.7	50.9	50.0	49.2	48.4	47.6	46.8
53	54.3	53.4	52.5	51.6	50.8	49.9	49.1	48.2	47.4	46.6
54	54.2	53.3	52.4	51.5	50.6	49.8	48.9	48.1	47.2	46.4
55	54.1	53.2	52.3	51.4	50.5	49.7	48.8	47.9	47.1	46.3
56	54.0	53.1	52.2	51.3	50.4	49.5	48.7	47.8	47.0	46.1
57	54.0	53.0	52.1	51.2	50.3	49.4	48.6	47.7	46.8	46.0
58	53.9	53.0	52.1	51.2	50.3	49.4	48.5	47.6	46.7	45.8
59	53.8	52.9	52.0	51.1	50.2	49.3	48.4	47.5	46.6	45.7
60	53.8	52.9	51.9	51.0	50.1	49.2	48.3	47.4	46.5	45.6
61	53.8	52.8	51.9	51.0	50.0	49.1	48.2	47.3	46.4	45.5
62	53.7	52.8	51.8	50.9	50.0	49.1	48.1	47.2	46.3	45.4
63	53.7	52.7	51.8	50.9	49.9	49.0	48.1	47.2	46.3	45.3
64	53.6	52.7	51.8	50.8	49.9	48.9	48.0	47.1	46.2	45.3
65	53.6	52.7	51.7	50.8	49.8	48.9	48.0	47.0	46.1	45.2
66	53.6	52.6	51.7	50.7	49.8	48.9	47.9	47.0	46.1	45.1
67	53.6	52.6	51.7	50.7	49.8	48.8	47.9	46.9	46.0	45.1
68	53.5	52.6	51.6	50.7	49.7	48.8	47.8	46.9	46.0	45.0
69	53.5	52.6	51.6	50.6	49.7	48.7	47.8	46.9	45.9	45.0
70	53.5	52.5	51.6	50.6	49.7	48.7	47.8	46.8	45.9	44.9
71	53.5	52.5	51.6	50.6	49.6	48.7	47.7	46.8	45.9	44.9
72	53.5	52.5	51.5	50.6	49.6	48.7	47.7	46.8	45.8	44.9
73	53.4	52.5	51.5	50.6	49.6	48.6	47.7	46.7	45.8	44.8
74	53.4	52.5	51.5	50.5	49.6	48.6	47.7	46.7	45.8	44.8
75	53.4	52.5	51.5	50.5	49.6	48.6	47.7	46.7	45.7	44.8
76	53.4	52.4	51.5	50.5	49.6	48.6	47.6	46.7	45.7	44.8
77	53.4	52.4	51.5	50.5	49.5	48.6	47.6	46.7	45.7	44.8
78	53.4	52.4	51.5	50.5	49.5	48.6	47.6	46.6	45.7	44.7
79	53.4	52.4	51.5	50.5	49.5	48.6	47.6	46.6	45.7	44.7
80	53.4	52.4	51.4	50.5	49.5	48.5	47.6	46.6	45.7	44.7
81	53.4	52.4	51.4	50.5	49.5	48.5	47.6	46.6	45.7	44.7
82	53.4	52.4	51.4	50.5	49.5	48.5	47.6	46.6	45.6	44.7
83	53.4	52.4	51.4	50.5	49.5	48.5	47.6	46.6	45.6	44.7
84	53.4	52.4	51.4	50.5	49.5	48.5	47.6	46.6	45.6	44.7
85	53.3	52.4	51.4	50.4	49.5	48.5	47.5	46.6	45.6	44.7

AGES	30	31	32	33	34	35	36	37	38	39
86	53.3	52.4	51.4	50.4	49.5	48.5	47.5	46.6	45.6	44.6
87	53.3	52.4	51.4	50.4	49.5	48.5	47.5	46.6	45.6	44.6
88	53.3	52.4	51.4	50.4	49.5	48.5	47.5	46.6	45.6	44.6
89	53.3	52.4	51.4	50.4	49.5	48.5	47.5	46.6	45.6	44.6
90	53.3	52.4	51.4	50.4	49.5	48.5	47.5	46.6	45.6	44.6
91	53.3	52.4	51.4	50.4	49.5	48.5	47.5	46.6	45.6	44.6
92	53.3	52.4	51.4	50.4	49.5	48.5	47.5	46.6	45.6	44.6
93	53.3	52.4	51.4	50.4	49.5	48.5	47.5	46.6	45.6	44.6
94	53.3	52.4	51.4	50.4	49.5	48.5	47.5	46.6	45.6	44.6
95	53.3	52.4	51.4	50.4	49.5	48.5	47.5	46.5	45.6	44.6
96	53.3	52.4	51.4	50.4	49.5	48.5	47.5	46.5	45.6	44.6
97	53.3	52.4	51.4	50.4	49.5	48.5	47.5	46.5	45.6	44.6
98	53.3	52.4	51.4	50.4	49.5	48.5	47.5	46.5	45.6	44.6
99	53.3	52.4	51.4	50.4	49.5	48.5	47.5	46.5	45.6	44.6
100	53.3	52.4	51.4	50.4	49.5	48.5	47.5	46.5	45.6	44.6
101	53.3	52.4	51.4	50.4	49.5	48.5	47.5	46.5	45.6	44.6
102	53.3	52.4	51.4	50.4	49.5	48.5	47.5	46.5	45.6	44.6
103	53.3	52.4	51.4	50.4	49.5	48.5	47.5	46.5	45.6	44.6
104	53.3	52.4	51.4	50.4	49.5	48.5	47.5	46.5	45.6	44.6
105	53.3	52.4	51.4	50.4	49.4	48.5	47.5	46.5	45.6	44.6
106	53.3	52.4	51.4	50.4	49.4	48.5	47.5	46.5	45.6	44.6
107	53.3	52.4	51.4	50.4	49.4	48.5	47.5	46.5	45.6	44.6
108	53.3	52.4	51.4	50.4	49.4	48.5	47.5	46.5	45.6	44.6
109	53.3	52.4	51.4	50.4	49.4	48.5	47.5	46.5	45.6	44.6
110	53.3	52.4	51.4	50.4	49.4	48.5	47.5	46.5	45.6	44.6
111	53.3	52.4	51.4	50.4	49.4	48.5	47.5	46.5	45.6	44.6
112	53.3	52.4	51.4	50.4	49.4	48.5	47.5	46.5	45.6	44.6
113	53.3	52.4	51.4	50.4	49.4	48.5	47.5	46.5	45.6	44.6
114	53.3	52.4	51.4	50.4	49.4	48.5	47.5	46.5	45.6	44.6
115	53.3	52.4	51.4	50.4	49.4	48.5	47.5	46.5	45.6	44.6

AGES	40	41	42	43	44	45	46	47	48	49
40	50.2	49.8	49.3	48.9	48.5	48.1	47.7	47.4	47.1	46.8
41	49.8	49.3	48.8	48.3	47.9	47.5	47.1	46.7	46.4	46.1

AGES	40	41	42	43	44	45	46	47	48	49
42	49.3	48.8	48.3	47.8	47.3	46.9	46.5	46.1	45.8	45.4
43	48.9	48.3	47.8	47.3	46.8	46.3	45.9	45.5	45.1	44.8
44	48.5	47.9	47.3	46.8	46.3	45.8	45.4	44.9	44.5	44.2
45	48.1	47.5	46.9	46.3	45.8	45.3	44.8	44.4	44	43.6
46	47.7	47.1	46.5	45.9	45.4	44.8	44.3	43.9	43.4	43
47	47.4	46.7	46.1	45.5	44.9	44.4	43.9	43.4	42.9	42.4
48	47.1	46.4	45.8	45.1	44.5	44.0	43.4	42.9	42.4	41.9
49	46.8	46.1	45.4	44.8	44.2	43.6	43.0	42.4	41.9	41.4
50	46.5	45.8	45.1	44.4	43.8	43.2	42.6	42.0	41.5	40.9
51	46.3	45.5	44.8	44.1	43.5	42.8	42.2	41.6	41.0	40.5
52	46.0	45.3	44.6	43.8	43.2	42.5	41.8	41.2	40.6	40.1
53	45.8	45.1	44.3	43.6	42.9	42.2	41.5	40.9	40.3	39.7
54	45.6	44.8	44.1	43.3	42.6	41.9	41.2	40.5	39.9	39.3
55	45.5	44.7	43.9	43.1	42.4	41.6	40.9	40.2	39.6	38.9
56	45.3	44.5	43.7	42.9	42.1	41.4	40.7	40.0	39.3	38.6
57	45.1	44.3	43.5	42.7	41.9	41.2	40.4	39.7	39.0	38.3
58	45.0	44.2	43.3	42.5	41.7	40.9	40.2	39.4	38.7	38.0
59	44.9	44.0	43.2	42.4	41.5	40.7	40.0	39.2	38.5	37.8
60	44.7	43.9	43.0	42.2	41.4	40.6	39.8	39.0	38.2	37.5
61	44.6	43.8	42.9	42.1	41.2	40.4	39.6	38.8	38.0	37.3
62	44.5	43.7	42.8	41.9	41.1	40.3	39.4	38.6	37.8	37.1
63	44.5	43.6	42.7	41.8	41.0	40.1	39.3	38.5	37.7	36.9
64	44.4	43.5	42.6	41.7	40.8	40.0	39.2	38.3	37.5	36.7
65	44.3	43.4	42.5	41.6	40.7	39.9	39.0	38.2	37.4	36.6
66	44.2	43.3	42.4	41.5	40.6	39.8	38.9	38.1	37.2	36.4
67	44.2	43.3	42.3	41.4	40.6	39.7	38.8	38.0	37.1	36.3
68	44.1	43.2	42.3	41.4	40.5	39.6	38.7	37.9	37.0	36.2
69	44.1	43.1	42.2	41.3	40.4	39.5	38.6	37.8	36.9	36.0
70	44.0	43.1	42.2	41.3	40.3	39.4	38.6	37.7	36.8	35.9
71	44.0	43.0	42.1	41.2	40.3	39.4	38.5	37.6	36.7	35.9
72	43.9	43.0	42.1	41.1	40.2	39.3	38.4	37.5	36.6	35.8
73	43.9	43.0	42.0	41.1	40.2	39.3	38.4	37.5	36.6	35.7
74	43.9	42.9	42.0	41.1	40.1	39.2	38.3	37.4	36.5	35.6
75	43.8	42.9	42.0	41.0	40.1	39.2	38.3	37.4	36.5	35.6

AGES	40	41	42	43	44	45	46	47	48	49
76	43.8	42.9	41.9	41.0	40.1	39.1	38.2	37.3	36.4	35.5
77	43.8	42.9	41.9	41.0	40.0	39.1	38.2	37.3	36.4	35.5
78	43.8	42.8	41.9	40.9	40.0	39.1	38.2	37.2	36.3	35.4
79	43.8	42.8	41.9	40.9	40.0	39.1	38.1	37.2	36.3	35.4
80	43.7	42.8	41.8	40.9	40.0	39.0	38.1	37.2	36.3	35.4
81	43.7	42.8	41.8	40.9	39.9	39.0	38.1	37.2	36.2	35.3
82	43.7	42.8	41.8	40.9	39.9	39.0	38.1	37.1	36.2	35.3
83	43.7	42.8	41.8	40.9	39.9	39.0	38.0	37.1	36.2	35.3
84	43.7	42.7	41.8	40.8	39.9	39.0	38.0	37.1	36.2	35.3
85	43.7	42.7	41.8	40.8	39.9	38.9	38.0	37.1	36.2	35.2
86	43.7	42.7	41.8	40.8	39.9	38.9	38.0	37.1	36.1	35.2
87	43.7	42.7	41.8	40.8	39.9	38.9	38.0	37.0	36.1	35.2
88	43.7	42.7	41.8	40.8	39.9	38.9	38.0	37.0	36.1	35.2
89	43.7	42.7	41.7	40.8	39.8	38.9	38.0	37.0	36.1	35.2
90	43.7	42.7	41.7	40.8	39.8	38.9	38.0	37.0	36.1	35.2
91	43.7	42.7	41.7	40.8	39.8	38.9	37.9	37.0	36.1	35.2
92	43.7	42.7	41.7	40.8	39.8	38.9	37.9	37.0	36.1	35.1
93	43.7	42.7	41.7	40.8	39.8	38.9	37.9	37.0	36.1	35.1
94	43.7	42.7	41.7	40.8	39.8	38.9	37.9	37.0	36.1	35.1
95	43.6	42.7	41.7	40.8	39.8	38.9	37.9	37.0	36.1	35.1
96	43.6	42.7	41.7	40.8	39.8	38.9	37.9	37.0	36.1	35.1
97	43.6	42.7	41.7	40.8	39.8	38.9	37.9	37.0	36.1	35.1
98	43.6	42.7	41.7	40.8	39.8	38.9	37.9	37.0	36.0	35.1
99	43.6	42.7	41.7	40.8	39.8	38.9	37.9	37.0	36.0	35.1
100	43.6	42.7	41.7	40.8	39.8	38.9	37.9	37.0	36.0	35.1
101	43.6	42.7	41.7	40.8	39.8	38.9	37.9	37.0	36.0	35.1
102	43.6	42.7	41.7	40.8	39.8	38.9	37.9	37.0	36.0	35.1
103	43.6	42.7	41.7	40.8	39.8	38.9	37.9	37.0	36.0	35.1
104	43.6	42.7	41.7	40.8	39.8	38.8	37.9	37.0	36.0	35.1
105	43.6	42.7	41.7	40.8	39.8	38.8	37.9	37.0	36.0	35.1
106	43.6	42.7	41.7	40.8	39.8	38.8	37.9	37.0	36.0	35.1
107	43.6	42.7	41.7	40.8	39.8	38.8	37.9	37.0	36.0	35.1
108	43.6	42.7	41.7	40.8	39.8	38.8	37.9	37.0	36.0	35.1
109	43.6	42.7	41.7	40.7	39.8	38.8	37.9	37.0	36.0	35.1

AGES	40	41	42	43	44	45	46	47	48	49
110	43.6	42.7	41.7	40.7	39.8	38.8	37.9	37.0	36.0	35.1
111	43.6	42.7	41.7	40.7	39.8	38.8	37.9	37.0	36.0	35.1
112	43.6	42.7	41.7	40.7	39.8	38.8	37.9	37.0	36.0	35.1
113	43.6	42.7	41.7	40.7	39.8	38.8	37.9	37.0	36.0	35.1
114	43.6	42.7	41.7	40.7	39.8	38.8	37.9	37.0	36.0	35.1
115	43.6	42.7	41.7	40.7	39.8	38.8	37.9	37.0	36.0	35.1

AGES	50.0	51.0	52.0	53.0	54.0	55.0	56.0	57.0	58.0	59.0
50	40.4	40.0	39.5	39.1	38.7	38.3	38.0	37.6	37.3	37.1
51	40.0	39.5	39.0	38.5	38.1	37.7	37.4	37.0	36.7	36.4
52	39.5	39.0	38.5	38.0	37.6	37.2	36.8	36.4	36.0	35.7
53	39.1	38.5	38.0	37.5	37.1	36.6	36.2	35.8	35.4	35.1
54	38.7	38.1	37.6	37.1	36.6	36.1	35.7	35.2	34.8	34.5
55	38.3	37.7	37.2	36.6	36.1	35.6	35.1	34.7	34.3	33.9
56	38.0	37.4	36.8	36.2	35.7	35.1	34.7	34.2	33.7	33.3
57	37.6	37.0	36.4	35.8	35.2	34.7	34.2	33.7	33.2	32.8
58	37.3	36.7	36.0	35.4	34.8	34.3	33.7	33.2	32.8	32.3
59	37.1	36.4	35.7	35.1	34.5	33.9	33.3	32.8	32.3	31.8
60	36.8	36.1	35.4	34.8	34.1	33.5	32.9	32.4	31.9	31.3
61	36.6	35.8	35.1	34.5	33.8	33.2	32.6	32.0	31.4	30.9
62	36.3	35.6	34.9	34.2	33.5	32.9	32.2	31.6	31.1	30.5
63	36.1	35.4	34.6	33.9	33.2	32.6	31.9	31.3	30.7	30.1
64	35.9	35.2	34.4	33.7	33.0	32.3	31.6	31.0	30.4	29.8
65	35.8	35.0	34.2	33.5	32.7	32.0	31.4	30.7	30.0	29.4
66	35.6	34.8	34.0	33.3	32.5	31.8	31.1	30.4	29.8	29.1
67	35.5	34.7	33.9	33.1	32.3	31.6	30.9	30.2	29.5	28.8
68	35.3	34.5	33.7	32.9	32.1	31.4	30.7	29.9	29.2	28.6
69	35.2	34.4	33.6	32.8	32.0	31.2	30.5	29.7	29.0	28.3
70	35.1	34.3	33.4	32.6	31.8	31.1	30.3	29.5	28.8	28.1
71	35.0	34.2	33.3	32.5	31.7	30.9	30.1	29.4	28.6	27.9
72	34.9	34.1	33.2	32.4	31.6	30.8	30.0	29.2	28.4	27.7
73	34.8	34.0	33.1	32.3	31.5	30.6	29.8	29.1	28.3	27.5
74	34.8	33.9	33.0	32.2	31.4	30.5	29.7	28.9	28.1	27.4
75	34.7	33.8	33.0	32.1	31.3	30.4	29.6	28.8	28.0	27.2

AGES	50.0	51.0	52.0	53.0	54.0	55.0	56.0	57.0	58.0	59.0
76	34.6	33.8	32.9	32.0	31.2	30.3	29.5	28.7	27.9	27.1
77	34.6	33.7	32.8	32.0	31.1	30.3	29.4	28.6	27.8	27.0
78	34.5	33.6	32.8	31.9	31.0	30.2	29.3	28.5	27.7	26.9
79	34.5	33.6	32.7	31.8	31.0	30.1	29.3	28.4	27.6	26.8
80	34.5	33.6	32.7	31.8	30.9	30.1	29.2	28.4	27.5	26.7
81	34.4	33.5	32.6	31.8	30.9	30.0	29.2	28.3	27.5	26.6
82	34.4	33.5	32.6	31.7	30.8	30.0	29.1	28.3	27.4	26.6
83	34.4	33.5	32.6	31.7	30.8	29.9	29.1	28.2	27.4	26.5
84	34.3	33.4	32.5	31.7	30.8	29.9	29.0	28.2	27.3	26.5
85	34.3	33.4	32.5	31.6	30.7	29.9	29.0	28.1	27.3	26.4
86	34.3	33.4	32.5	31.6	30.7	29.8	29.0	28.1	27.2	26.4
87	34.3	33.4	32.5	31.6	30.7	29.8	28.9	28.1	27.2	26.4
88	34.3	33.4	32.5	31.6	30.7	29.8	28.9	28.0	27.2	26.3
89	34.3	33.3	32.4	31.5	30.7	29.8	28.9	28.0	27.2	26.3
90	34.2	33.3	32.4	31.5	30.6	29.8	28.9	28.0	27.1	26.3
91	34.2	33.3	32.4	31.5	30.6	29.7	28.9	28.0	27.1	26.3
92	34.2	33.3	32.4	31.5	30.6	29.7	28.8	28.0	27.1	26.2
93	34.2	33.3	32.4	31.5	30.6	29.7	28.8	28.0	27.1	26.2
94	34.2	33.3	32.4	31.5	30.6	29.7	28.8	27.9	27.1	26.2
95	34.2	33.3	32.4	31.5	30.6	29.7	28.8	27.9	27.1	26.2
96	34.2	33.3	32.4	31.5	30.6	29.7	28.8	27.9	27.0	26.2
97	34.2	33.3	32.4	31.5	30.6	29.7	28.8	27.9	27	26.2
98	34.2	33.3	32.4	31.5	30.6	29.7	28.8	27.9	27	26.2
99	34.2	33.3	32.4	31.5	30.6	29.7	28.8	27.9	27	26.2
100	34.2	33.3	32.4	31.5	30.6	29.7	28.8	27.9	27	26.1
101	34.2	33.3	32.4	31.5	30.6	29.7	28.8	27.9	27	26.1
102	34.2	33.3	32.4	31.4	30.5	29.7	28.8	27.9	27	26.1
103	34.2	33.3	32.4	31.4	30.5	29.7	28.8	27.9	27	26.1
104	34.2	33.3	32.4	31.4	30.5	29.6	28.8	27.9	27	26.1
105	34.2	33.3	32.3	31.4	30.5	29.6	28.8	27.9	27	26.1
106	34.2	33.3	32.3	31.4	30.5	29.6	28.8	27.9	27	26.1
107	34.2	33.3	32.3	31.4	30.5	29.6	28.8	27.9	27	26.1
108	34.2	33.3	32.3	31.4	30.5	29.6	28.8	27.9	27	26.1
109	34.2	33.3	32.3	31.4	30.5	29.6	28.7	27.9	27	26.1

AGES	50.0	51.0	52.0	53.0	54.0	55.0	56.0	57.0	58.0	59.0
110	34.2	33.3	32.3	31.4	30.5	29.6	28.7	27.9	27	26.1
111	34.2	33.3	32.3	31.4	30.5	29.6	28.7	27.9	27	26.1
112	34.2	33.3	32.3	31.4	30.5	29.6	28.7	27.9	27	26.1
113	34.2	33.3	32.3	31.4	30.5	29.6	28.7	27.9	27	26.1
114	34.2	33.3	32.3	31.4	30.5	29.6	28.7	27.9	27	26.1
115	34.2	33.3	32.3	31.4	30.5	29.6	28.7	27.9	27	26.1

AGES	60	61	62	63	64	65	66	67	68	69
60	30.9	30.4	30.0	29.6	29.2	28.8	28.5	28.2	27.9	27.6
61	30.4	29.9	29.5	29.0	28.6	28.3	27.9	27.6	27.3	27.0
62	30.0	29.5	29.0	28.5	28.1	27.7	27.3	27.0	26.7	26.4
63	29.6	29.0	28.5	28.1	27.6	27.2	26.8	26.4	26.1	25.7
64	29.2	28.6	28.1	27.6	27.1	26.7	26.3	25.9	25.5	25.2
65	28.8	28.3	27.7	27.2	26.7	26.2	25.8	25.4	25.0	24.6
66	28.5	27.9	27.3	26.8	26.3	25.8	25.3	24.9	24.5	24.1
67	28.2	27.6	27.0	26.4	25.9	25.4	24.9	24.4	24.0	23.6
68	27.9	27.3	26.7	26.1	25.5	25.0	24.5	24.0	23.5	23.1
69	27.6	27.0	26.4	25.7	25.2	24.6	24.1	23.6	23.1	22.6
70	27.4	26.7	26.1	25.4	24.8	24.3	23.7	23.2	22.7	22.2
71	27.2	26.5	25.8	25.2	24.5	23.9	23.4	22.8	22.3	21.8
72	27.0	26.3	25.6	24.9	24.3	23.7	23.1	22.5	22.0	21.4
73	26.8	26.1	25.4	24.7	24.0	23.4	22.8	22.2	21.6	21.1
74	26.6	25.9	25.2	24.5	23.8	23.1	22.5	21.9	21.3	20.8
75	26.5	25.7	25.0	24.3	23.6	22.9	22.3	21.6	21.0	20.5
76	26.3	25.6	24.8	24.1	23.4	22.7	22.0	21.4	20.8	20.2
77	26.2	25.4	24.7	23.9	23.2	22.5	21.8	21.2	20.6	19.9
78	26.1	25.3	24.6	23.8	23.1	22.4	21.7	21.0	20.3	19.7
79	26.0	25.2	24.4	23.7	22.9	22.2	21.5	20.8	20.1	19.5
80	25.9	25.1	24.3	23.6	22.8	22.1	21.3	20.6	20.0	19.3
81	25.8	25.0	24.2	23.4	22.7	21.9	21.2	20.5	19.8	19.1
82	25.8	24.9	24.1	23.4	22.6	21.8	21.1	20.4	19.7	19.0
83	25.7	24.9	24.1	23.3	22.5	21.7	21.0	20.2	19.5	18.8
84	25.6	24.8	24.0	23.2	22.4	21.6	20.9	20.1	19.4	18.7
85	25.6	24.8	23.9	23.1	22.3	21.6	20.8	20.1	19.3	18.6

AGES	60	61	62	63	64	65	66	67	68	69
86	25.5	24.7	23.9	23.1	22.3	21.5	20.7	20.0	19.2	18.5
87	25.5	24.7	23.8	23.0	22.2	21.4	20.7	19.9	19.2	18.4
88	25.5	24.6	23.8	23.0	22.2	21.4	20.6	19.8	19.1	18.3
89	25.4	24.6	23.8	22.9	22.1	21.3	20.5	19.8	19.0	18.3
90	25.4	24.6	23.7	22.9	22.1	21.3	20.5	19.7	19.0	18.2
91	25.4	24.5	23.7	22.9	22.1	21.3	20.5	19.7	18.9	18.2
92	25.4	24.5	23.7	22.9	22.0	21.2	20.4	19.6	18.9	18.1
93	25.4	24.5	23.7	22.8	22.0	21.2	20.4	19.6	18.8	18.1
94	25.3	24.5	23.6	22.8	22.0	21.2	20.4	19.6	18.8	18.0
95	25.3	24.5	23.6	22.8	22.0	21.1	20.3	19.6	18.8	18.0
96	25.3	24.5	23.6	22.8	21.9	21.1	20.3	19.5	18.8	18.0
97	25.3	24.5	23.6	22.8	21.9	21.1	20.3	19.5	18.7	18.0
98	25.3	24.4	23.6	22.8	21.9	21.1	20.3	19.5	18.7	17.9
99	25.3	24.4	23.6	22.7	21.9	21.1	20.3	19.5	18.7	17.9
100	25.3	24.4	23.6	22.7	21.9	21.1	20.3	19.5	18.7	17.9
101	25.3	24.4	23.6	22.7	21.9	21.1	20.2	19.4	18.7	17.9
102	25.3	24.4	23.6	22.7	21.9	21.1	20.2	19.4	18.6	17.9
103	25.3	24.4	23.6	22.7	21.9	21.0	20.2	19.4	18.6	17.9
104	25.3	24.4	23.5	22.7	21.9	21.0	20.2	19.4	18.6	17.8
105	25.3	24.4	23.5	22.7	21.9	21.0	20.2	19.4	18.6	17.8
106	25.3	24.4	23.5	22.7	21.9	21.0	20.2	19.4	18.6	17.8
107	25.2	24.4	23.5	22.7	21.8	21.0	20.2	19.4	18.6	17.8
108	25.2	24.4	23.5	22.7	21.8	21.0	20.2	19.4	18.6	17.8
109	25.2	24.4	23.5	22.7	21.8	21.0	20.2	19.4	18.6	17.8
110	25.2	24.4	23.5	22.7	21.8	21.0	20.2	19.4	18.6	17.8
111	25.2	24.4	23.5	22.7	21.8	21.0	20.2	19.4	18.6	17.8
112	25.2	24.4	23.5	22.7	21.8	21.0	20.2	19.4	18.6	17.8
113	25.2	24.4	23.5	22.7	21.8	21.0	20.2	19.4	18.6	17.8
114	25.2	24.4	23.5	22.7	21.8	21.0	20.2	19.4	18.6	17.8
115	25.2	24.4	23.5	22.7	21.8	21.0	20.2	19.4	18.6	17.8

AGES	70	71	72	73	74	75	76	77	78	79
70	21.8	21.3	20.9	20.6	20.2	19.9	19.6	19.4	19.1	18.9
71	21.3	20.9	20.5	20.1	19.7	19.4	19.1	18.8	18.5	18.3

AGES	70	71	72	73	74	75	76	77	78	79
72	20.9	20.5	20.0	19.6	19.3	18.9	18.6	18.3	18.0	17.7
73	20.6	20.1	19.6	19.2	18.8	18.4	18.1	17.8	17.5	17.2
74	20.2	19.7	19.3	18.8	18.4	18.0	17.6	17.3	17.0	16.7
75	19.9	19.4	18.9	18.4	18.0	17.6	17.2	16.8	16.5	16.2
76	19.6	19.1	18.6	18.1	17.6	17.2	16.8	16.4	16.0	15.7
77	19.4	18.8	18.3	17.8	17.3	16.8	16.4	16.0	15.6	15.3
78	19.1	18.5	18.0	17.5	17.0	16.5	16.0	15.6	15.2	14.9
79	18.9	18.3	17.7	17.2	16.7	16.2	15.7	15.3	14.9	14.5
80	18.7	18.1	17.5	16.9	16.4	15.9	15.4	15.0	14.5	14.1
81	18.5	17.9	17.3	16.7	16.2	15.6	15.1	14.7	14.2	13.8
82	18.3	17.7	17.1	16.5	15.9	15.4	14.9	14.4	13.9	13.5
83	18.2	17.5	16.9	16.3	15.7	15.2	14.7	14.2	13.7	13.2
84	18.0	17.4	16.7	16.1	15.5	15.0	14.4	13.9	13.4	13.0
85	17.9	17.3	16.6	16.0	15.4	14.8	14.3	13.7	13.2	12.8
86	17.8	17.1	16.5	15.8	15.2	14.6	14.1	13.5	13.0	12.5
87	17.7	17.0	16.4	15.7	15.1	14.5	13.9	13.4	12.9	12.4
88	17.6	16.9	16.3	15.6	15.0	14.4	13.8	13.2	12.7	12.2
89	17.6	16.9	16.2	15.5	14.9	14.3	13.7	13.1	12.6	12.0
90	17.5	16.8	16.1	15.4	14.8	14.2	13.6	13.0	12.4	11.9
91	17.4	16.7	16.0	15.4	14.7	14.1	13.5	12.9	12.3	11.8
92	17.4	16.7	16.0	15.3	14.6	14.0	13.4	12.8	12.2	11.7
93	17.3	16.6	15.9	15.2	14.6	13.9	13.3	12.7	12.1	11.6
94	17.3	16.6	15.9	15.2	14.5	13.9	13.2	12.6	12.0	11.5
95	17.3	16.5	15.8	15.1	14.5	13.8	13.2	12.6	12.0	11.4
96	17.2	16.5	15.8	15.1	14.4	13.8	13.1	12.5	11.9	11.3
97	17.2	16.5	15.8	15.1	14.4	13.7	13.1	12.5	11.9	11.3
98	17.2	16.4	15.7	15.0	14.3	13.7	13.0	12.4	11.8	11.2
99	17.2	16.4	15.7	15.0	14.3	13.6	13.0	12.4	11.8	11.2
100	17.1	16.4	15.7	15.0	14.3	13.6	12.9	12.3	11.7	11.1
101	17.1	16.4	15.6	14.9	14.2	13.6	12.9	12.3	11.7	11.1
102	17.1	16.4	15.6	14.9	14.2	13.5	12.9	12.2	11.6	11.0
103	17.1	16.3	15.6	14.9	14.2	13.5	12.9	12.2	11.6	11.0
104	17.1	16.3	15.6	14.9	14.2	13.5	12.8	12.2	11.6	11.0
105	17.1	16.3	15.6	14.9	14.2	13.5	12.8	12.2	11.5	10.9

AGES	70	71	72	73	74	75	76	77	78	79
106	17.1	16.3	15.6	14.8	14.1	13.5	12.8	12.2	11.5	10.9
107	17.0	16.3	15.6	14.8	14.1	13.4	12.8	12.1	11.5	10.9
108	17.0	16.3	15.5	14.8	14.1	13.4	12.8	12.1	11.5	10.9
109	17.0	16.3	15.5	14.8	14.1	13.4	12.8	12.1	11.5	10.9
110	17	16.3	15.5	14.8	14.1	13.4	12.7	12.1	11.5	10.9
111	17	16.3	15.5	14.8	14.1	13.4	12.7	12.1	11.5	10.8
112	17	16.3	15.5	14.8	14.1	13.4	12.7	12.1	11.5	10.8
113	17	16.3	15.5	14.8	14.1	13.4	12.7	12.1	11.4	10.8
114	17	16.3	15.5	14.8	14.1	13.4	12.7	12.1	11.4	10.8
115	17	16.3	15.5	14.8	14.1	13.4	12.7	12.1	11.4	10.8

AGES	80	81	82	83	84	85	86	87	88	89
80	13.8	13.4	13.1	12.8	12.6	12.3	12.1	11.9	11.7	11.5
81	13.4	13.1	12.7	12.4	12.2	11.9	11.7	11.4	11.3	11.1
82	13.1	12.7	12.4	12.1	11.8	11.5	11.3	11	10.8	10.6
83	12.8	12.4	12.1	11.7	11.4	11.1	10.9	10.6	10.4	10.2
84	12.6	12.2	11.8	11.4	11.1	10.8	10.5	10.3	10.1	9.9
85	12.3	11.9	11.5	11.1	10.8	10.5	10.2	9.9	9.7	9.5
86	12.1	11.7	11.3	10.9	10.5	10.2	9.9	9.6	9.4	9.2
87	11.9	11.4	11.0	10.6	10.3	9.9	9.6	9.4	9.1	8.9
88	11.7	11.3	10.8	10.4	10.1	9.7	9.4	9.1	8.8	8.6
89	11.5	11.1	10.6	10.2	9.9	9.5	9.2	8.9	8.6	8.3
90	11.4	10.9	10.5	10.1	9.7	9.3	9.0	8.6	8.3	8.1
91	11.3	10.8	10.3	9.9	9.5	9.1	8.8	8.4	8.1	7.9
92	11.2	10.7	10.2	9.8	9.3	9.0	8.6	8.3	8.0	7.7
93	11.1	10.6	10.1	9.6	9.2	8.8	8.5	8.1	7.8	7.5
94	11.0	10.5	10.0	9.5	9.1	8.7	8.3	8.0	7.6	7.3
95	10.9	10.4	9.9	9.4	9.0	8.6	8.2	7.8	7.5	7.2
96	10.8	10.3	9.8	9.3	8.9	8.5	8.1	7.7	7.4	7.1
97	10.7	10.2	9.7	9.2	8.8	8.4	8.0	7.6	7.3	6.9
98	10.7	10.1	9.6	9.2	8.7	8.3	7.9	7.5	7.1	6.8
99	10.6	10.1	9.6	9.1	8.6	8.2	7.8	7.4	7.0	6.7
100	10.6	10.0	9.5	9.0	8.5	8.1	7.7	7.3	6.9	6.6

AGES	80	81	82	83	84	85	86	87	88	89
101	10.5	10.0	9.4	9.0	8.5	8.0	7.6	7.2	6.9	6.5
102	10.5	9.9	9.4	8.9	8.4	8.0	7.5	7.1	6.8	6.4
103	10.4	9.9	9.4	8.8	8.4	7.9	7.5	7.1	6.7	6.3
104	10.4	9.8	9.3	8.8	8.3	7.9	7.4	7.0	6.6	6.3
105	10.4	9.8	9.3	8.8	8.3	7.8	7.4	7.0	6.6	6.2
106	10.3	9.8	9.2	8.7	8.2	7.8	7.3	6.9	6.5	6.2
107	10.3	9.8	9.2	8.7	8.2	7.7	7.3	6.9	6.5	6.1
108	10.3	9.7	9.2	8.7	8.2	7.7	7.3	6.8	6.4	6.1
109	10.3	9.7	9.2	8.7	8.2	7.7	7.2	6.8	6.4	6.0
110	10.3	9.7	9.2	8.6	8.1	7.7	7.2	6.8	6.4	6.0
111	10.3	9.7	9.1	8.6	8.1	7.6	7.2	6.8	6.3	6.0
112	10.2	9.7	9.1	8.6	8.1	7.6	7.2	6.7	6.3	5.9
113	10.2	9.7	9.1	8.6	8.1	7.6	7.2	6.7	6.3	5.9
114	10.2	9.7	9.1	8.6	8.1	7.6	7.1	6.7	6.3	5.9
115	10.2	9.7	9.1	8.6	8.1	7.6	7.1	6.7	6.3	5.9

AGES	90	91	92	93	94	95	96	97	98	99
90	7.8	7.6	7.4	7.2	7.1	6.9	6.8	6.6	6.5	6.4
91	7.6	7.4	7.2	7.0	6.8	6.7	6.5	6.4	6.3	6.1
92	7.4	7.2	7.0	6.8	6.6	6.4	6.3	6.1	6.0	5.9
93	7.2	7.0	6.8	6.6	6.4	6.2	6.1	5.9	5.8	5.6
94	7.1	6.8	6.6	6.4	6.2	6.0	5.9	5.7	5.6	5.4
95	6.9	6.7	6.4	6.2	6.0	5.8	5.7	5.5	5.4	5.2
96	6.8	6.5	6.3	6.1	5.9	5.7	5.5	5.3	5.2	5.0
97	6.6	6.4	6.1	5.9	5.7	5.5	5.3	5.2	5.0	4.9
98	6.5	6.3	6.0	5.8	5.6	5.4	5.2	5.0	4.8	4.7
99	6.4	6.1	5.9	5.6	5.4	5.2	5.0	4.9	4.7	4.5
100	6.3	6.0	5.8	5.5	5.3	5.1	4.9	4.7	4.5	4.4
101	6.2	5.9	5.6	5.4	5.2	5.0	4.8	4.6	4.4	4.2
102	6.1	5.8	5.5	5.3	5.1	4.8	4.6	4.4	4.3	4.1
103	6.0	5.7	5.4	5.2	5.0	4.7	4.5	4.3	4.1	4.0
104	5.9	5.6	5.4	5.1	4.9	4.6	4.4	4.2	4.0	3.8
105	5.9	5.6	5.3	5.0	4.8	4.5	4.3	4.1	3.9	3.7
106	5.8	5.5	5.2	4.9	4.7	4.5	4.2	4.0	3.8	3.6

AGES	90	91	92	93	94	95	96	97	98	99
107	5.8	5.4	5.1	4.9	4.6	4.4	4.2	3.9	3.7	3.5
108	5.7	5.4	5.1	4.8	4.6	4.3	4.1	3.9	3.7	3.5
109	5.7	5.3	5.0	4.8	4.5	4.3	4.0	3.8	3.6	3.4
110	5.6	5.3	5.0	4.7	4.5	4.2	4.0	3.8	3.5	3.3
111	5.6	5.3	5.0	4.7	4.4	4.2	3.9	3.7	3.5	3.3
112	5.6	5.3	4.9	4.7	4.4	4.1	3.9	3.7	3.5	3.2
113	5.6	5.2	4.9	4.6	4.4	4.1	3.9	3.6	3.4	3.2
114	5.6	5.2	4.9	4.6	4.3	4.1	3.9	3.6	3.4	3.2
115	5.5	5.2	4.9	4.6	4.3	4.1	3.8	3.6	3.4	3.1

AGES	100	101	102	103	104	105	106	107	108	109
100	4.2	4.1	3.9	3.8	3.7	3.5	3.4	3.3	3.3	3.2
101	4.1	3.9	3.7	3.6	3.5	3.4	3.2	3.1	3.1	3.0
102	3.9	3.7	3.6	3.4	3.3	3.2	3.1	3.0	2.9	2.8
103	3.8	3.6	3.4	3.3	3.2	3.0	2.9	2.8	2.7	2.6
104	3.7	3.5	3.3	3.2	3.0	2.9	2.7	2.6	2.5	2.4
105	3.5	3.4	3.2	3.0	2.9	2.7	2.6	2.5	2.4	2.3
106	3.4	3.2	3.1	2.9	2.7	2.6	2.4	2.3	2.2	2.1
107	3.3	3.1	3.0	2.8	2.6	2.5	2.3	2.2	2.1	2.0
108	3.3	3.1	2.9	2.7	2.5	2.4	2.2	2.1	1.9	1.8
109	3.2	3.0	2.8	2.6	2.4	2.3	2.1	2.0	1.8	1.7
110	3.1	2.9	2.7	2.5	2.3	2.2	2.0	1.9	1.7	1.6
111	3.1	2.9	2.7	2.5	2.3	2.1	1.9	1.8	1.6	1.5
112	3.0	2.8	2.6	2.4	2.2	2.0	1.9	1.7	1.5	1.4
113	3.0	2.8	2.6	2.4	2.2	2.0	1.8	1.6	1.5	1.3
114	3.0	2.7	2.5	2.3	2.1	1.9	1.8	1.6	1.4	1.3
115	2.9	2.7	2.5	2.3	2.1	1.9	1.7	1.5	1.4	1.2

Uniform Lifetime Table (current for 2014 returns)

For Use by
- Unmarried Owners,
- Married Owners Whose Spouses Are Not More Than 10 Years Younger, and
- Married Owners Whose Spouses Are Not the Sole Beneficiaries of their IRAs

AGE	DISTRIBUTION PERIOD	AGE	DISTRIBUTION PERIOD
70	27.4	93	9.6
71	26.5	94	9.1
72	25.6	95	8.6
73	24.7	96	8.1
74	23.8	97	7.6
75	22.9	98	7.1
76	22.0	99	6.7
77	21.2	100	6.3
78	20.3	101	5.9
79	19.5	102	5.5
80	18.7	103	5.2
81	17.9	104	4.9
82	17.1	105	4.5

AGE	DISTRIBUTION PERIOD	AGE	DISTRIBUTION PERIOD
83	16.3	106	4.2
84	15.5	107	3.9
85	14.8	108	3.7
86	14.1	109	3.4
87	13.4	110	3.1
88	12.7	111	2.9
89	12.0	112	2.6
90	11.4	113	2.4
91	10.8	114	2.1
92	10.2	115 and over	1.9

Glossary

Adjusted gross income (AGI): The amount of your income that determines when and if IRA contributions can be deducted. It is calculated by taking your AGI from Form 1040A or Form 1040 and adding back certain items such as foreign earned income, housing deductions, or both; student-loan interest, tuition, and fees; excluded qualified savings bond interest; and excluded employer-provided adoption benefits.

Balloon payment: A lump-sum payment due at the end of a loan. Balloon payments are usually structured as part of a short-term loan, sometimes referred to as a bullet loan. A bullet note can be written either of two ways. The most common requires periodic payments throughout the term of the loan, followed by the final balloon payment. Alternatively, the payments can be deferred to the end of the term, at which time the borrower pays the balloon payment, covering both interest and principal.

Blanket mortgage: One mortgage that uses two or more properties to secure a real estate-backed note. If the borrower fails to pay back the loan according to the terms of the note, the lender has recourse against all of the property securing the loan.

Capital gain: The net profit realized from the sale of a capital asset (stocks or real estate, for example). Taxes on capital gains are paid at a different rate from regular income, depending on how long the asset was owned.

Cash-on-cash return: A calculation often used for analyzing return on real estate investments. It is computed by dividing net income by the total cash invested (cash on cash ROI = net income ÷ cash invested).

Collateral: Property used as security against a loan.

Excess accumulation: The portion of a required minimum distribution (RMD) that is left in the traditional IRA account instead of being withdrawn. A 50 percent penalty applies to excess accumulations.

Excluded individuals: Parties with whom your IRA is specifically prohibited from transacting business.

Excluded transactions: IRA investments and business transactions specifically prohibited by the IRS.

Fiduciary: A person or institution with a special relationship of financial trust or responsibility to others.

Foreclosure: A legal procedure taken for the purpose of terminating a property owner's rights, usually due to default on a note or tax obligation.

Junior note: Any note that is secured after the senior note. There can be any number of junior notes, but only one senior note. In the event the borrower defaults on the loan, the holder of a junior note can file a claim for payment, but the claim will be paid only after the senior note is satisfied.

Modified adjusted gross income (MAGI): MAGI is calculated by adding back in certain deductions, such as foreign income, student loans, and IRA that were subtracted to establish the adjusted gross income. MAGI is used to determine eligibility for IRA deductions and Roth IRA participation.

Primary market: When you sign a note directly with your lender, the transaction is said to take place on the primary market.

Real estate investment trust (REIT): A business enterprise established for the sole purpose of buying, managing, and selling real estate holdings.

Required beginning date: The year in which required minimum distributions must begin, typically 70½, although it can vary in the case of an inherited IRA.

Rollover IRA: A traditional or Roth IRA that holds assets that originated from an employer-sponsored retirement plan.

Secondary market: When one lender sells a note to another lender, the transaction is said to take place on the secondary market.

Senior note: A secured debt that will be paid first in the event of a foreclosure.

Short sale: A real estate transaction where the sales price falls short of the outstanding balance on the mortgage.

Special-needs beneficiary: Any individual who needs additional time to complete his or her education or requires ongoing special care due to a physical, mental, or emotional condition.

Spot price: The current market price for a commodity such as precious metals, petroleum, or agricultural products.

Tax-advantaged account: A savings account, such as a 401(k) or IRA, which receives favorable tax treatment by the IRS. The IRS requires that rollovers from an employer plan go directly into another employer plan or into a traditional IRA. From a traditional IRA they can later be converted to a Roth IRA. By keeping these funds separate from your other IRA assets, you reserve the option of later rolling them into another employer-sponsored plan. But once they are co-mingled with your other IRAs, you lose that flexibility.

Bibliography and Web Sources

TITLE	AUTHOR	PUBLISHER
IRA Wealth	Patrick W. Rice with Jennifer Dirks	Square One Finance Guide
The Retirement Savings Time Bomb	Ed Slott	Penguin Books
Parlay Your IRA Into A Family Fortune	Ed Slott	Viking
The New IRAs	Neil Downing	Dearborn Trade Publishing

CMI Gold & Silver	http://cmi-gold-silver.com/gold-silver-ira.html
Creative Wit	http://creativewit.com/yogi_berra.html
Wikipedia	http://en.wikipedia.org/
CNN	http://money.cnn.com/2005/08/11/pf/updegrave_0509/
Freeadvice.com	http://real-estate-law.freeadvice.com/mortgage_payment.htm
Allstate Insurance	http://www.allstate.com/Finance/EstatePlanning/Trusts/pagerender.asp?page=IrrevocableLifeInsuranceTrusts.htm
AmeriGold	http://www.amerigold.com/precious_metals_ira/
Answerbag	http://www.answerbag.com/q_view.php/5511
American Society of Home Inspectors	http://www.ashi.org/about/contact.asp
Bankrate.com	http://www.bankrate.com/brm/news/sav/20010213a.asp

Bartleby Quotations	http://www.bartleby.com
Biggerpockets.com	http://www.biggerpockets.com/bank-reo.html
Bullion Direct	http://www.bulliondirect.com/IRA/overview.do
U.S. Census Department	http://www.census.gov/prod/ec02/ec0253i08t.pdf
Certified Mint Inc.	http://www.certifiedmint.com/ira_investments.htm
Certified Financial Planners Board of Standards	http://www.cfp.net/
Checkbook IRA	http://www.checkbookira.com/
Commercial Brokers Association	http://www.commercialmls.com/
CRE Online	http://www.creonline.com/articles/art-240.html
Denver Discount Lending	http://www.denverdm.com/Mortgage%20Terminology.htm
Employee Benefit Research Institute	http://www.ebri.org/publications/facts/index.cfm?fa=1200fact
ExpertPlan, Inc.	http://www.expertplan.com/faq401k/general.jsp#1
Fannie Mae	http://www.fanniemae.com
Fed Bureau of Investigation	http://www.fbi.gov
Society of Financial Service Professionals	http://www.financialpro.org/
Motley Fool	http://www.fool.com/school/mutualfunds/performance/record.htm
Federal Trade Commission	http://www.ftc.gov/bcp/conline/pubs/homes/mortgserv.htm
Heart Quotes Centers	http://www.heartquotes.net/Training.html
Investopedia	http://www.investopedia.com
Investorwords.com	http://www.investorwords.com/4901/tax_lien.html
IRA Expert.net	http://www.iraexpert.net/
Entrust USA	http://www.theentrustgroup.com
Internal Revenue Service	http://www.irs.gov/
Mortgage-Investments.com	http://www.mortgage-investments.com/

Fair Isaac Corporation	http://www.myfico.com/Downloads/Files/myFICO_UYFS_Booklet.pdf
Asset Exchange Strategies LLC	http://www.myrealestateira.com
Nat'l Assoc of Mortgage Brokers	http://www.namb.org/namb/Default.asp
Nat'l Committee of Preserve Social Security	http://www.ncpssm.org/news/archive/ssprimer/
Nat'l Institute of Building Inspectors	http://www.nibi.com/
Note Investors.com	http://www.noteinvestors.com/bonanza.htm
Note Servicing Corporation	http://www.noteservicing.com/Pricing.htm
Northwest Territorial Mint	http://www.nwtmintbullion.com/articles_faq.php
Ocwen Financial Corp	http://www.ocwen.com/reo/reofindbystate.cfm
Palmer, Allen & McTaggart LLP	http://www.pamlaw.com
Pensco	http://www.pensco.com/
Planningtips.com	http://www.planningtips.com/cgi-bin/roth.pl
Quotations Page	http://www.quotationspage.com/
Realtor.com	http://www.realtor.com/Basics/Sell/Closing/Finance.asp?poe=realtor
Realtor.org	http://www.realtor.org
USDA-RD/FSA Properties	http://www.resales.usda.gov
Rogue Investor	http://www.rogueinvestor.com
RothIra.com	http://www.rothira.com
Securities & Exchange Commission	http://www.sec.gov/investor/pubs/promise.htm
Equity Institutional	http://www.equityinstitutional.com
Stop Foreclosure.com	http://www.stopforeclosure.com/Arizona_Foreclosure_Law.htm

Summit Daily News	http://www.summitdaily.com/article/20050601/REALESTATE/1060 10026&SearchID=73226648749628
Sunvest Int'l	http://www.sunvestinc.com/regulations.htm
The Other Place Quotations	http://www.theotherpages.org/topic-i3.html
Real Estate Library	http://www.therealestatelibrary.com/sherriff.html
U.S. Treasury Dept	http://www.treasury.gov
Equity Trust	http://www.trustetc.com/self-directed-ira/ira-faq.html
USA Gold	http://www.usagold.com
Wexford Capital Management	http://www.wexfordcoin.com/PreciousMetalsIRA.htm
Wisdom Quotes	http://www.wisdomquotes.com
Capital Investment Advisors	http://www.yourwealth.com

(Footnotes)

See Appendix C, IRS Publication 590, *How Much Can You Deduct?* for more information pertaining to tax deductions.

Rolodex is a Registered Trademark of Berol Corporation.

FICO is a Registered Trademark of FairIsaac Corporation.

Index